Lessons of the Inca Shamans

Piercing the Veil

Deborah Bryon

Pine Winds Press

An imprint of Idyll Arbor, Inc.
39129 264th Ave SE, Enumclaw, WA 98022
www.PineWindsPress.com

Pine Winds Press Editor: Thomas M. Blaschko

Photographs and paintings: Deborah Bryon and Perry Edwards

ISBN 9780937663264 print version
ISBN 9780937663271 e-book version

To the Q'ero shamans,

the urpicheeyas,

"sweet doves of my heart."

Contents

Foreword

When I first met Deborah, now over ten years ago, she was beginning her training as a Jungian analyst. As one of her training analysts, I remember her being very inquisitive and full of questions. She had a deep passion for learning that she frequently struggled to contain in classroom settings.

I watched Deborah traverse between the worlds of shamanism and Jungian analysis, grappling with finding ways of weaving her personal experience into a cohesive tapestry, integrating all three. As the years passed, when Deborah and I would encounter each other in the halls at analytic conferences, we often had brief conversations about shamanism. As time progressed, it became clear that we shared a great love and respect for shamanic traditions, and this common ground developed into a bond that exists between us.

Lessons from the Inca Shamans: Piercing the Veil is a fascinating, first-hand account of Deborah Bryon's personal journey down the path of shamanism, into the realm of nonordinary reality. Deborah describes in detail her own dismemberment experience into nonordinary reality and the reentry process involved in her return. As is the case with any sacred, spiritual practice, shamanism requires commitment as a way of living, a way of being in the world, and way of being in relationship with nature, ourselves, and others.

It is a serious, ethical practice that demands integrity and continual self-examination. Following a shamanic path is *not* a fun and interesting hobby. Shamanism involves facing both the light and the dark aspects of reality. Similar to Jungian analysis, whatever is hidden in our psyches that we do not want to look at is usually the first to emerge when we enter the world of the unconscious. Jungian analysts talk about this as working with the shadow, while shamans call this a dismemberment process that takes place before an initiatory rite of passage.

Many previous books on the topic have presented the "love and light" version and have omitted the shadow side of the story. Deborah's careful, well-written narrative of her initiatory process into shamanism is honest and courageous. In staying as close to the actual experience as possible she offers an uncensored account of both the pain and the ecstasy of the experience. This book bridges the gap between modern civilization and the natural world and provides a way of supporting the wisdom in ancient teaching.

— *Linda Leonard, Jungian analyst*
Author of The Wounded Woman
and On the Way to the Wedding

Introduction

It is a process of adaptation, of merging two diametrical conversations. When one can produce the dialogue it becomes the doorway.

— Dona Alahandrina, *altomesayoq*, conversation 2011

In our last meeting together during my most recent visit to Peru, the Q'ero shaman Don Sebastian said to those of us who had received *Mosoq Karpay* and *Hatun Karpay* initiation rites,[1] "We have been chosen by the mountain spirit for a path of service and must take the ancestral knowledge we have been given back to our communities."

Andean shamans, such as Don Sebastian, have had the prophetic vision that time on our planet is speeding up and that great change in the nature of our world is beginning to occur. Although we are on the verge of planetary destruction, we are also living at a time of great opportunity for change, which is brought about by existing in a point in history when things are shifting rapidly and are in a state of flux. For this reason, Andean

---

[1] In Andean shamanism, *Hatun Karpay* translates as "Great Initiation." It is the fourth level of initiation, which comes with the understanding that "God is everywhere" (p. 11). *Mosoq Karpay* is the fifth level of sacred work, which emphasizes life shifts from physical to energetic expression. (J.P. Wilcox, *Masters of the Living Energy*, 1999, p. 72.)

shamans are, for the first time, passing down their lineage to Westerners such as myself. They are giving us the wisdom of their ancestors' teachings. The shamans believe that the next group of medicine people will come from the West.

The old sacred lineages are dying. The Andean shamans believe that the next generation of shamans must be able to bridge both the shamanic realm and the modern world. There once were twelve sacred lineages of Inca shamans living in the Andes Mountains. Today only four lineages remain. The four ancestral lineages in existence are from the regions of Surimana, Vilcabamba, Lake Titicaca, and the Q'ero nation. The teachings that I have received are a combination of the cosmology of these four. The *altomesayoqs* that I worked with, who are the most powerful group of Andes medicine people working directly with the *Apu* mountain spirits, are from Vilcabamba, and their *mesas* (medicine bundle of sacred stones) belong to the Vilcabamba lineage. Most of the *pampamesayoqs* (shamans who are healers and stewards of the land) that I encountered are from the Q'ero nation and Lake Titicaca.

Because the Q'ero shamans have performed the majority of the sacred shamanic initiation rites I have been given, I will reference them as the source of the body of knowledge. In actuality, the teaching that I have received is a hybrid from all four lineages.

I am grateful that I have been fortunate to be a recipient of the Q'ero teachings. I have been blessed to work with the Q'ero shamans who have imparted their knowledge to me and other Western *mesa* carriers. This knowledge has come through the transmission of the *Hatun Karpay* and *Mosoq Karpay* initiation rites. In exchange, those of us given these sacred rites have promised to bring this information to others in the West, to help heal our communities, the planet, and ourselves. By receiving sacred rites of passage from the medicine people, which were downloaded into us by the great mountain spirits, we agreed to take the awareness we received to our Western cultures for healing.

I am writing to fulfill Don Sebastian's words by trying to create a bridge between the experience of shamanism and Western culture. My hope is that imparting the knowledge I have received will contribute to keeping the native tradition alive. Ultimately, my motivation for writing comes from the commitment I made to all of the Q'ero shamans who generously shared their knowledge and to the spirits I met on those mountains. They have welcomed me into their lineage, and the lineage of their sacred mountains. In exchange, I promised I would take what I have learned back to my community in the West.

While writing the introduction I came across an entry that I made in my journals in July 2007 after a conversation I had with the *altomesayoq*, Adolpho, during my first visit to Peru. Adolpho said to me, "You will be writing a book about the spirit world that must combine the theory you are learning with practice. The love of the mountain will be felt, and that love will make the information sacred." He saw, years before I did, what would happen.

The spiritual wisdom of the past is rapidly becoming lost in our quickly changing culture. In the following pages, I will stay true to my own voice and as close as possible to my own experience. Because I am a member of Western culture with an academic background, a part of me, even now, feels the need to substantiate what I am writing by quoting other well-published sources. Yet in an attempt to maintain the integrity of my work, I focus primarily on what I have learned based upon what I have actually felt and seen, on my own and through my experience with the shamans. For the most part, references are included as footnotes, and are not incorporated into the body of the writing.

Some of what I write may sound like magical thinking or appear as metaphor. However, it is the best I can do in translating experiences of the Belly and the Heart that cannot be contained by any written language devised by the Mind. I will describe what has happened in the course of my apprenticeship as best I can from my current understanding of the experience. I say current understanding because I have observed that my perception of what has taken place seems to change as my frame of reference deepens in shamanic work.

I recently came across the book, *Dark Night, Early Dawn: Steps to a Deep Ecology of Mind,* written by Christopher Bache. In the introduction of the book, Bache states that he believes it is necessary to speak and write from personal experience in order to anchor events occurring in nonordinary reality and create a framework that the reader will be able to relate to and understand. Through my own process of writing, I have come to a similar conclusion. When I began this writing project in 2008, I was afraid that much of what I had to say might seem too fantastic and that I would be perceived as being too out there by colleagues and members of the analytic community. Months — and several initiations later — the veil between my perception of ordinary and nonordinary reality has continued to grow thinner — to the point of becoming transparent at times.

The following pages are my autobiographical story, arranged chronologically with a few shifts in time sequencing as needed. Because my understanding of what has occurred has evolved with time, I will attempt to differentiate what was then and what is now. My words are a work in progress, and my experience is an evolving process. My intention is to stay as true as possible to the wisdom of the teachings I have received from the dear shamans with whom I have studied— although I recognize that taking in and writing down words that are being translated from the Quechua language in an altered state does leave some room for error. I expect that my story will continue to change and grow as it has in the past, as my vision increases and my experience deepens.

I want to express my gratitude toward the kind and loving shamans who have helped me learn to open up my heart and see. They have patiently held my hand as I trip down mountains, attempting to regain my balance. They have walked next to me at a steady pace — much slower than their usual speed — as I huff and puff my way up the mountain in my pilgrimage to the *Apus*, the great collective mountain spirits. The way of the Q'ero shamans is a way of the Heart. I hope that I can do justice to the clarity, wisdom, and feeling behind their words.

Pacha 1. The Beginning

A pacha *is an allocation of time and space. That's the* pacha *in which events, themes, directions, everything has a momentum, is going someplace. Anything that has not been, that has not come into* ayni, *or has not been fulfilled will always be trying to find a* pacha *to fulfill itself.*

— Don Alarijo, *pampamesayoq*, conversation 2010

In recent years, people have asked me how I started down the path toward becoming a shaman. This seemingly simple question has proven challenging to answer. Sometimes remembering the exact moment a decision is made, changing the direction of our life, changing who we are, is difficult to pinpoint. This is because we do not recognize that we have reached this point in our life until much later.

Often we are not conscious of the significance of a choice we are making until years have passed and we look back with new eyes on major life events we have experienced, as I am doing now. Yet, even though I was unaware at the time, sorting through these memories I am able track some decisive moments that inevitably led to the sequence of events that permanently changed the course of my life forever.

The Q'ero shamans in Peru, who are the descendents of the Incas, call these types of intersections between space and time *pachas*. A *pacha* is an Inca map of consciousness that refers to the structure that contains the *kausay*, or life force in every person's life. There are significant events occurring at specific times and places that help shape personal fate and destiny. These pivotal points on one's life journey are considered to possess greater amounts of *kausay*.

When my first journeys into shamanic experience began, I had no idea what a *pacha* was or that meaningful junctures between time and space even existed. Even so, there were two moments or *pachas* that I can now identify where I made the choice to learn from the Q'ero shamans.

1. The Innocuous Envelope

So, you have to walk in the world like a big p'aqo, *a* hatun p'aqo. *So it's not that you are going to walk in the world with a big banner on your foreheads.* "Soosi koo yowun" *in Quechua is a metaphor. It means it's not that you have a title.* Soosi koo yowun *is not something that you traditionally wear as an outfit. It's a way of being.*

— Don Andre, *pampamesayoq*, conversation 2011

The first *pacha* occurred when I opened and read the contents of an innocuous envelope that arrived in the mail early in the afternoon on a warm summer day in July 2005. I was sitting alone in my psychotherapy office, between seeing clients, casually sorting through the mail I had just retrieved from the mailbox. Relaxing in my comfortable armchair and enjoying the rays of the sun streaming through the window, I had fallen into the contemplative practice of sorting mail. I had dropped into a easy rhythm of quickly glancing at the return addresses and logos printed on the articles of mail, keeping the few pieces I recognized and tossing the majority that I had determined was "junk" mail into the trashcan nearby.

Then, I came across a thick, white envelope with a handwritten address and no return label. My curiosity was sparked. It was intriguing that the material had no commercial letterhead. Not knowing whom it was from, I decided to open it instead of pitching it into the trash along with most of the other mail that had appeared less interesting.

I opened the envelope and discovered that inside was a simple handwritten invitation to attend a weekend retreat to learn about Peruvian shamanism. The invitation included a short description of shamanism and the "three worlds." I was immediately drawn to the spirit that I sensed lay behind the words that were written on the page, and appreciated that there was no advertising or company logo at the top. The workshop was being held in a couple of weeks in a location reasonably close to our home.

I have always loved to travel. At the time this letter arrived, I had never been to Peru, although it was on my list of places to visit before I die. I had been to India, Nepal, and Tibet in recent years and in the back of my mind had considered that at some point in life, I would like to visit South America. The notice stated that there was an opportunity to travel to Peru to work with Q'ero shamans after receiving necessary preliminary training.

Although I did not consciously admit it to myself at the time, a deeper part of me knew I was going as soon as I opened the envelope and read the contents. Unknown to my conscious mind, another part of my psyche was making a decision that would permanently change my life and alter the way I perceive the world.

That evening, after returning home from my office, I casually mentioned the letter to my husband. A couple of days went by. Then, about a week later, after giving the material a chance to seep into my conscious psyche, I announced to my husband that I would like to attend the weekend workshop on Peruvian shamanism — and asked him to come with me. Consistent with his open-minded nature, he agreed to accompany me. Enthusiastically I signed us both up for an upcoming weekend workshop. This encounter was the first *pacha*, my opening introduction into Peruvian shamanism.

2. Before the Beginning

The earth opened up, I went through it and came out in a place in the open air with green grass and blue sky.

— Deborah Bryon, dream 1986

Before moving any further with my story, let me provide some background about the state of our lives when our introduction into shamanism began. In the fall of 2005, I had recently completed a doctorate in counseling psychology and was expanding my private practice. I had been accepted into the Inter-Regional Society of Jungian Analysts to begin training to become a Jungian analyst. Ironically, when looking back, I realized I began Jungian analytic training two weeks before attending the first workshop on Peruvian shamanism.

At the time this was taking place, my husband and I were happily married and building our home together. Perry is an amazing builder. At the time the letter arrived, he was in the midst of the creative design process of constructing our dream home. I was basking in the afterglow of passing my state boards and becoming a licensed psychologist. Both my sons were settled and seemed to be doing well, and I was enjoying tending to my garden and painting in all my newly acquired spare time. Analytic training was not overly taxing at this point, and life was good.

At the time, part of me was aware of my yearning to connect with something deeper (a shaman might refer to this as wanting connections with the spirit world). Yet, I felt somewhat ambivalent about what I actually considered real. I believed in nonordinary reality, in principle, having had mystical experiences most of my life. However, for the last couple of years, I had been immersed in a PhD program at University of Denver (DU) in counseling psychology. DU is a conservative graduate school and Jungian Depth Psychology — or even transpersonal psychology — is not part of the standard curriculum. Focusing on nonordinary reality while interning in a psychiatric hospital to learn to diagnose and evaluate adults with psychosis would have been too incongruent for me to hold psychologically. As a result, my encounters with the other realm were shelved during my years of graduate training. My nonordinary part was aware that my mentors for my ordinary reality training might have considered these kinds of encounters delusional.

Fortunately for me, Perry had always been respectful of my outside interests. Throughout our fifteen-year relationship and marriage, my good-natured husband had supported my decisions to become a psychologist and to apply for analytic training — as well as pretty much anything else I wanted to do along the lines of career development and self-discovery. At the time, Perry probably would have said that he had never given much thought to his own spiritual beliefs — except perhaps to be a "good" person and to be respectful of nature. This was a time before all of his memories came back.

During this time, I remember having a number of dreams about Perry leaving me. I often woke up feeling afraid and abandoned. I was confused as to why I kept having the dreams. My Jungian analyst at the time had asked me if Perry's leaving was an actual fear of mine. I told her "no." At the time, relying on Jungian dream interpretation, I thought my dreams symbolically represented a fear of being deserted by an inner animus, a masculine figure but not necessarily Perry. I did not think that the dream was actually linked to anything going on in the "real" world. I tried not to give the dreams too much thought, and continued enjoying life.

At this point in my life, I had very little awareness of shamanism. Unlike many other people I have heard about, it was not something I had "always been drawn to." Frankly, I had thought Westerners who followed the teachings of indigenous people rather than that of their own culture seemed a bit contrived. To me it seemed hokey and out of context — like the Hare Krishna converts I had observed hanging around the Los Angeles airport during the 1970s passing out flyers and pamphlets.

Two decades earlier, in 1983, my first direct introduction to metaphysics and nonordinary reality was with a group called the Tibetan Foundation. This was during a period in my life when I was caught up with my identity as a vice president in a brokerage firm. At the time, although I resisted admitting it to myself, I hated my career as a stockbroker but was afraid to give up the social status and financial security of a position that I had worked so hard to achieve.

Toward the later years of my career as a stockbroker, I dealt with my ambivalence by psychologically splitting between metaphysics and my day job. I managed bond portfolios during the week, while during my free time I began working with someone who used hypnosis techniques to facilitate remembering past lives. Over time, I became acquainted with energy work, which eventually led to my teaching experiential weekend workshops on channeling and etheric healing.

Although I was not consciously interested in shamanism during the period of my life when I was a stockbroker and teaching at the Tibetan Foundation, somehow shamanism still managed to seep into my awareness during dreamtime. I had a dream with imagery that was so vivid it remains with me today.

> *A male Hopi elder was writing symbols in the earth with a stick. The earth opened up, I went through it and came out in a place in the open air with green grass and blue sky. The atmosphere had an electric quality, with intense colors. I saw a male Kachina figure that appeared to be about eight feet tall. He told me that we must begin to attend to the earth or there would be serious consequences.*

When I had the dream, environmental concerns were not at the forefront of my awareness. Perhaps the dream was compensatory — showing me the other side of the equation, different from my experience in the world of the stockbroker. Years later, working with the dream in my Jungian analysis, I understood the Kachina figure to be a symbol for the Self, telling me it was time to attend to the neglected feminine aspect of my own psyche, which was represented in the dream by Mother Earth. Jung (1989) stated that the psyche of modern man has lost the archetypal connection to primordial images or the numinous connection to the "Great Mother" and "Father Sky," and that this enormous loss is often compensated for in dream symbology. As I reflect upon the dream today, I am more aware of the imbalance that exists in the collective psyche of our culture.

Looking back, I realize the dream about the Hopi shaman was also my psyche's attempt to balance the split between my professional career and my longing for spiritual connection. Although on some level, I was aware that the energetic experience was real — I could feel it in my body — I was never able to come to terms with what it really meant. At the time, I did not feel particularly drawn to caring for the land, and definitely was not wowed by mystical Kachina figures. I had seen too many Kachina figures and dream catchers in tacky gift shops. Overall, the metaphysical culture had begun to seem too flakey and theatrical to me.

I was hesitant to risk my career *persona* by outing my weekend activities to my colleagues from the financial markets. I had begun to feel split between the two worlds and eventually the incongruence between them became too difficult for me to maintain. A week before my second son was born I was finally able to shift out of my role of bank vice-president. I became a mother for the second time and my life changed. This marked my exit out of the career I had grown to hate but had previously been unable to leave.

My persona out in the world was beginning to change. In the 1980s, I designed, developed, and sold a resort wear business. While in the resort wear business, I met and married my husband Perry, who at the time was a friendly competitor. After Perry and I eventually merged our companies, we sold the business. Perry applied his creative talent toward designing a hugely profitable T-shirt program for the Walt Disney Corporation and spent his free time designing and building our home. During the next decade, as my children were growing and in school, I pursued training as an artist. This was something I had always wanted to do and I finally gave myself permission to do it.

After completing an art degree in drawing, I decided to return to graduate school to complete a doctorate program in counseling psychology. At about the same time, I began Jungian analysis and continued to grapple with my spirituality and life's purpose. Metaphysics had seemed too ungrounded and out there for me, and yet I was again feeling a longing to reconnect with my spirituality as a greater focus in my life. I was looking for a way to combine my interest in the psyche with something in the day world.

3. First Shamanic Experience

You must speak the language of the land. The mountains are seeing us, hearing us, and have been healing us for many years.
— Don Sebastian, *pampamesayoq*, conversation 2010

My study of Peruvian shamanism began on October 6, 2005, the date of my first journal entry. It was the first day of the introductory workshop. On a warm fall weekend, my husband Perry and I drove to a small retreat center in Evergreen, Colorado, located about 45 minutes from our home in Denver. A neatly groomed, stocky Peruvian man with intense dark brown eyes and a pleasant smile politely greeted us at the door. He introduced himself as Jose Luis Herrera and cordially invited us in. In a slightly formal and reserved manner, he respectfully shook my hand when we met that first day. Since then, I have come to appreciate Jose Luis's wonderful bear hugs, his standard greeting for anyone who knows him reasonably well.

Minutes later, after walking into the room, Perry and I found ourselves sitting on a comfortable couch, facing a window with a view of trees and mountains. The door was open, with a light breeze occasionally blowing through the room. The smell of fall and pine needles was in the air. There were six or seven other people, who apparently also had an interest in shamanism, already seated and waiting for the class to begin. A couple of them were talking about their professions and personal goals they were working on. They seemed pleasant and willing to engage in easy conversation. After the weekend, Perry and I never saw any of them again.

As we waited for the class to begin, I curiously glanced at Jose Luis out of the corner of my eye, attempting to study him inconspicuously. Although over the years I have come to know Jose Luis as a "trickster" with an infectious sense of humor, on the day I met him he seemed serious and quiet. I tried to discern if there was anything remarkable about him. Like the rest of us, he was casually dressed in a shirt and blue jeans. I decided that, at least on the surface, nothing about him stood out as being particularly unusual.

October 6, 2005

The class began lecture style, starting with a description of Peruvian cosmology. The entire first day we listened to an overview of the belief structure of Q'ero shamans. Jose Luis had been a civil engineer before, as he later put it, he "was claimed by the mountains." I found him to be an articulate speaker, who was easy to listen to. Jose Luis's well-organized presentation appealed to my analytic mind, yet at the same time I found myself struggling to reconcile my view of reality with what he was saying. It seemed a bit out there.

I did not quite know what to make of it when he said that "a snake, a jaguar, and a condor" were the guiding principles of the three major energy centers in the body, which corresponded to states of perception, and the middle, lower, and upper worlds. Although the content of what he was saying stretched my perception of reality a bit, his words held together well and I intuitively sensed that what he was saying was right. I felt the deeper truth in what Jose Luis was saying, but at the time, my Western mind had no way to organize his new information into my existing cognitive framework. Jose Luis gave no indication that he was speaking in metaphor — which given my background in Jungian psychology would have been much easier for me to digest. He acted as if he actually believed that what he was describing literally existed. During the first break, another student quietly got up and left, with the explanation, "This isn't for me." I noticed that a couple of the other students seemed somewhat rattled and anxious to get away.

During my career as a stockbroker, even though my life had always looked reasonably conventional, I had been involved in channeling and etheric healing. At one point, I had even taught weekend classes in both of these areas through a local organization, but had walked away from the group when it began to feel too ungrounded. One of the things I had learned from experiences that were difficult to explain in ordinary reality was to put uncomfortable ideas or events on the shelf when they did not make rational sense. I found this coping skill of compartmentalization extremely helpful in adopting an open and receptive beginner's mind. It made it easier for me to tolerate experiences that were incongruent with my existing belief structure. I continue to suggest this "mental mindset" technique to psychotherapy clients I work with as a way of helping them deal with anxiety.

At the time I attended the introductory class in Peruvian shamanism in 2005, I was still accustomed to sitting through long lectures — and usually enjoyed them. It's part of surviving psychology training. As the hours passed that first day, I found myself mentally occupied in an internal process of grappling with the new concepts Jose Luis was presenting. I was busy attempting to assimilate the material into a cognitive format that I could more easily digest.

Although I was absorbed with thinking about the material being presented, my husband Perry was not. Perry did not enjoy classroom learning. He had became bored with college and left after the first semester. Perry preferred learning on his own and was self-taught. He obtained his education from being out in the world, taking a more "hands on" approach. I had hoped that he might be benefiting from the class.

Although most of the other people in the room probably did not notice, it was clear to me as the day wore on that he was not enjoying himself. Concerned, I glanced over at Perry periodically throughout the day and saw that he was alternating between being agitated, bored, and sleepy. Perry informed me that night at dinner that he did not want to return to the class the next day to listen to another eight-hour lecture. He reminded me that he did not enjoy sitting and hearing someone explain theory all day, and would rather be outside doing something. Somehow, I persuaded him to return with me the following day. He agreed — but made it clear that he was only doing this to be with me — not to listen to another long, boring lecture.

Years later, Perry informed me that — although he was not fully conscious of it at the time — he had the foreboding sense that day that he was on the verge of being exposed to something that would be extremely uncomfortable for him. In retrospect, the analyst in me would have interpreted Perry's "zoned out" behavior as a defense against underlying anxiety toward an "unthought known."[2] Neither one of us had any inkling of the magnitude of what we would encounter in the weeks that followed.

---

[2] C. Bollas, *The Shadow of the Object: Psychoanalysis of the Unthought Known*, 1987.

Pacha 2. Coming Apart

Here we come to see and recognize each other, to remember ourselves in each other. The land has brought us together.
— Don Andre, *pampamesayoq*, conversation 2011

In the film *The Matrix*, the main character, Neo, who has been searching all of his life for something greater, is given the opportunity to learn — and live with — the truth about the illusion of reality he has been living. He is asked whether he wants to take the blue pill to forget and return to the illusion or the red pill and face knowing the painful truth of his existence. Being the hero, Neo, of course, chooses the red pill. As the story in the film progresses and the odds against Neo appear almost insurmountable, the antagonist asks Neo if he wished he had taken the blue pill instead.

Neo's predicament is the same quandary many of us face when we begin working with deeper aspects of our psyche and start to separate from identifying with the collective mass culture, or consensual reality. This identification with consensual reality is often associated with a strong identification with how we are perceived by others in the world. The obvious question becomes, so why do it? In a culture that promotes self-care to the point of narcissism, we are taught to fight long and hard to build successful identities out in the world. Why would we then choose to give up what we fought so hard to achieve? Many people that walk through the doors into my psychotherapy office are asking themselves this same question.

This compelling need to connect with something greater is the call from the numinous to reconnect with the energetic collective.

Surrendering to the call is threatening. Swallowing the red pill and following a path seeking greater spiritual connection can be painful because it dismantles who we think we are and becomes even more difficult when it challenges the constitution of our egos, the center of our consciousness.[3] In the movie *Star Wars*, as the renegade pilot Han Solo takes his spaceship into warp speed, the structure of the ship, like the structure of the ego, is challenged and rattles under the strain. The ship, like the ego, is not directing the mission, but it needs to remain intact to pierce the veil into the energetic realm of light speed.

A supervisor in analytic training told me that one of his supervisors who had known Jung had told him that what made Jung, "Jung" was not his incredible insights, rather it was his hearty constitution and his receptive attitude toward the unconscious. His willingness to "listen with an open mind" beyond the comfort of what was familiar led him into his own descent and into the depths of a dismemberment, as Jung wrote, "into a strange world ruled by forces unconcerned with man."[4]

A story about the encounter abstract expressionist artist Phillip Guston had with a fellow artist is another illustration of this phenomenon. Guston was painting figures at a time most of his peers were painting a record of their experience. The fellow artist commented on the disturbing images in Guston's paintings. In response, Guston said he felt the same way about the images emerging in his art — but had no choice because he was "painting what he must paint" — the images that were inside of him that were forcing their way into expression.

If we choose to live our lives fully, we really do not have a choice about whether or not we follow "the path." Once we hear

---

[3] Jung said, "The experience of the Self is always a defeat for the ego." *Mysterium Conjunctions, CW 14*, par 788.

[4] Jung, "Psychological Commentary on the Tibetan Book of the Great Liberation," in *Psychology and the East*, p 106, par 765.

the call to enter into the veil, something bigger than us becomes the irresistible driving force, and taking the red pill is the only option. We may have the illusion that following a spiritual track is something we decide, but in the end we do not choose it — it chooses us. The path, like ingesting the red pill, is not pursued because it is fun or enjoyable; it is taken because the alternative path away from it is deadening and intolerable.

4. Finding the Past, Facing the Future

How big is your heart? How big is your all-encompassing love? How deep can you go? How can you surrender? The amount of love, the depth of your availability, and the power that you bring forth through your love is what makes the transaction happen.

— Don Sebastian, *pampamesayoq*, conversation 2011

The second day of the introductory workshop (October 7, 2005) involved learning energy healing techniques with the luminous body. Jose Luis gave us an experiential exercise to do that involved using the stones we had each brought with us, which were the beginnings of our *mesas*, or medicine bundles. Because of my experience with etheric healing through the Tibetan Foundation, none of this seemed that unfamiliar to me — but working with *mesa* stones was new.

We downloaded our three different *kuyas* (stones) with the negative patterns (*hucha*) we wanted to let go of, blowing our intentions into each stone with our breath. In Quechua, this process of exhaling with intention to send prayers or medicine is called *phikhuy*. Prayers are always said aloud to give force to the words used in calling the spirits. After performing the act of *phikhuy* on each of the three stones, the members of the group broke into sets of two and three and took turns working energetically on each other with the stones.

While experimenting on Perry with the healing techniques Jose Luis had shown us, I was surprised that I intuitively sensed something emanating from his throat in the energetic realm that seemed to be pulling back energetically. When I placed one of his stones over this area of his body, he started coughing. In a short time, Perry's coughing became more intense, and he began to gag. It appeared that Perry had no control over what seemed to be coming out of his throat. Perry's coughing turned into raspy gasps and he started choking. Alarmed, I removed the stone from his throat. Perry collapsed back into the pillow he was lying on and seemed stunned. He wanted to know what we had seen.

The skeptic in me proceeded to dismiss the experience while the receptive aspect of my nature — that had brought me to the workshop in the first place — was curious, concerned, and puzzled. I did not know what I thought — beyond wanting Perry to be okay. The weekend ended and during the next week I did not give much thought to what had happened to Perry during the exercise. Although I was intrigued by Jose Luis and what I had learned in the workshop, I decided to put it on the shelf for the time being.

Then, unexpectedly, about a week and a half later, I had two big dreams. The dreams proved to be life changing for me, although I was unaware of this at the time the dreams took place. In these dreams, the second *pacha* occurred, marking my passage into shamanism.

For me, these dreams were the beginning of what Jungians and shamans sometimes refer to as an initiatory dismemberment process.[5] The next two italicized passage below are the actual

-----

[5] In Jungian psychology, dismemberment refers to the ego's process of separation from the experience of something greater associated with

dreams, followed by my personal narrative of what unfolded for Perry and me in the day world a week later.

October 18, 2005
The first dream was as follows:

I was in the earth and saw the shaman. I saw a white snake and a black snake. I was not afraid of the image of the white snake because I had worked with it before. The shaman invited me to study with him but told me that this would require me working with the black snake. I told him that I was repulsed and afraid of black snakes. He laughed and said, "I knew you would say that." I then told him that I would agree to work with the black snake if that was what was required. After I answered him, I awoke from dreaming in the dream.

A couple of weeks later I had the second dream:

November 3, 2005

I dreamt the shaman saw me and knew I was coming back to work with him and I saw him acknowledging that he saw me and I saw him.

November 5, 2005
The night after I dreamt about the Shaman again, I experienced a burning sensation accompanied with a *lot* of energy. I could taste the energy. Although at times it felt *empowering* I cannot say it was comfortable...it was somewhat *disorienting*. In

---

collective experience. This may occur in the initial stages of separation from a symbiotic, uroboric state, through the process of forming a separate identity often associated with a hero's journey or rite of passage. It may also occur through entering a process of descent and separating from being identified with the persona associated with the collective culture.

my own analytic process, I had already begun working with the energy as movement toward a deeper symbolic relationship with the dream imagery of the snake.

November 6, 2005

I attended a weekend analytic training class, still feeling like I was on fire. I spoke in the class and realized people were having difficulty tracking my intuitive leaps. I decided to be quiet and started drawing snakes on my notepad in an attempt to contain the energy and the impulse to describe aloud what was happening to me.

While I was in the middle of a drawing, I looked over to the left of the page — an inch from where my pen was — and noticed a tiny worm that was actually moving. I was stunned. I was in Denver, in freezing cold weather, and had not bought any produce to eat...so I was not sure where the worm came from...especially since it had not been on the page minutes before! It had a small greenish-white body and a black head...The fire that I had felt pulsing continued and I felt pretty disoriented...my world was spinning.

I went home after the class and told Perry about my experience of seeing the worm. Perry asked me if it had a small greenish-white body with a black head...I said yes...waiting for a logical explanation. I asked him if he had seen worms like that. He told me that he had never seen them in Colorado, but that they were his favorite kind of worms. Then he told me that earlier that day he had bought a conch shell for me to hold, to help me with the spinning. I curled my hand around inside it and noticed that for some reason it helped. My husband was also going through his own shift into the realm of nonordinary reality, and these places were becoming more familiar to him, and more uncomfortably real to me.

Working with the black snake marked the beginning of an initiation process for me, and descent into darker, more primal areas of my psyche than I had ever explored in the past. At the time I had the dream, the black snake was the most frightening and undesirable shadow symbol I could imagine. In my own analysis, I worked with this dream. Symbolically, I understood the dream inside a dream to mean that the material was coming from a very deep layer of my unconscious psyche. The shaman was interpreted as representing a symbol for the Self, and his invitation to work with the snake was an invitation to engage with my shadow and the parts of my psyche less acceptable to my ego.

Although looking back, on one level I still believe this subjective symbolic interpretation holds true, on another level the dream was foretelling what was to follow. A series of corresponding life events occurred, which greatly affected both me and the members of my immediate family. Shortly after I had the dream, my youngest son's developing drug addiction became apparent, and we faced the frightening challenge of his recovery. Then, while verbally defending his younger brother, my older son was beaten up and had his nose broken, requiring him to undergo hours of surgery — and new developments in my personal life continued to unfold.

November 15, 2005

About a week after my dream encounter with the black snake, I awoke to find my husband in a highly excited state. During the night, Perry had entered a lucid dream and remembered severe physical abuse he had experienced — and forgotten — as a child. He told me he loved me, and that he had spent the entire night reliving past events from a time when he was about five or six years old. Perry's speech was becoming increasingly speedy and his thoughts seemed tangential to me — which at the time did not strike me as being that out of the ordinary. Perry has always had a tendency to passionately express himself when making a new discovery. Although I was a bit perplexed, I was still waking up and was not (yet) overly alarmed.

Sitting up in bed, Perry rapidly began to recount the series of events that had happened to him as a young boy. He said he remembered running through the house hugging his favorite blanket that he often carried with him. His father, who was sitting on the couch watching television, reached out and stopped Perry during one of his laps through the living room. He told Perry that it was time that he gave his blanket up because he was "too old to be carrying a sissy blanket." Perry had stubbornly refused, telling his father that he still wanted his blanket.

Perry said he now remembered that suddenly his father had jumped up, grabbed him, and whisked him up to the attic. Once in the attic, Perry's father threw him against an unfinished wall in a rage. After kicking Perry in the mouth, ribs, and chest, his father left him alone in the attic overnight, bleeding and bruised. Perry remembered being terrified at the time, thinking that his father was going to kill him. He said, that night he learned a new way of being quiet just so he could survive. He did not remember moving until morning. At daybreak, a sparrow chirped outside and Perry knew he had made it through that night of hell.

The next morning, his father left for a weeklong business trip. Perry's mother retrieved him from the attic and put him to bed. Perry remembered his mother telling him that he would not be able to go to school for a couple of days because of the cuts and bruises on his face and his body. Perry said that his mother then shook her finger at him, telling him that he could not tell anyone about what had happened. During the following days he spent in bed, Perry heard his older sister repeatedly asking their mother where he was. Perry's mother told his sister that she could not "see Perry, because Perry was sick."

That morning, sitting in our bed, Perry remembered that he had feared for his life through most of his early childhood. The only place he felt safe as a child was alone in the woods. Perry recalled that he continually buried little objects in the forest, asking "Mother Nature" for help to save his life from a father who continued to attack him randomly with severe beatings.

When Perry first told me his memory, I was stunned and did not know what to make of it. The memory seemed so incongruent with the man I knew to be Perry. I had lived with Perry for over fifteen years, and worked with people with trauma histories as a profession. How could an event of this magnitude have happened to Perry with neither of us knowing about it after all this time?

Perry had always seemed to me to have an unusually high pain threshold. In infrequent moments, looking back, I realized I had occasionally felt the subtle and fleeting presence of something buried behind a wall in his psyche. Perry had always been warm and responsive to me, so I had never given it much thought — until now. Although I did not know it at the time, the reemergence of these childhood memories was to have a drastic and disastrous effect on both our lives over the course of the next several years.

Several months later, my father had a stroke and died. After these events occurred, involving the significant males in my life, my brother-in-law uneasily joked with me that nothing bad would happen to him because he was not related to me or in my immediate family. Luckily, he was correct.

Perry did not slow down over the next couple of weeks. He kept speeding up as more memories began to break through, flooding his conscious awareness. The onslaught of the waves of memories grew even worse. On December 30, 2005, Perry remembered another incident that had happened when he was even younger. This event led to his family being forced to move, after Perry's preschool counselor questioned his condition. Perry recalled a time, while his mother had been away from the house running errands, that his father suddenly became upset and angry — this time ostensibly because Perry had been given "too many toys for Christmas" a week or so earlier. His father, in a raging outburst, stomped and crushed Perry's new collection of toys — many of which were plastic. After all the toys lay in pieces on the floor, his father had jabbed the shards of broken plastic underneath the skin of Perry's forearms.

As this unpleasant chain of memory events continued into January, the reality that this was much bigger than a bad dream began to sink in. Perry said as a young boy he had only felt safe when he was "outdoors running a trap line." He recalled more of his memories of making a trade with Mother Nature — if she helped him survive his father's fury and stay alive, he would do something important for humankind.

When Perry told me this, I did not know what to think. I suspected that he was delusional and was again at a loss about what to do. In desperation, I scheduled an appointment for Perry with my analyst, Jeffery Raff, whom I trusted and respected. Jeff has a deep understanding of the psyche and experience in nonordinary reality, and I hoped he could help. Previously, Perry had been working with another therapist who was also confused by what was happening to Perry — and did not know what to do. I was desperate, and Perry (and I) needed help understanding what was happening.

Although his physical body was there, my husband essentially had disappeared, and a young boy — who talked incessantly at a speed that was difficult to follow — had taken his place. The protective psychic veil between Perry's ego and the archetypal energies of the unconscious (between ordinary and nonordinary reality) had been ripped away.

Although what I am describing may sound like a full-blown manic episode, and most likely it was by Western medicine standards (Perry met diagnostic criteria according to the DSM IV), I sensed that this was not all of it. Jeff reassured me that some of the ideas Perry was bringing back were brilliant, although unbelievable. I was reminded of the fine line between genius and insanity. When I pleaded with Perry to try to come back, he told me that he could not because he had to bring back all he could from the realm he was in.

Years later, as I look back on this incredibly painful period of my life, I realize what happened to my husband and our relationship in our dismemberment process was devastating. I have witnessed similar psychological events occurring with clients and friends who have embarked upon similar shamanic paths. For me, agreeing to work with the snake was the initial catalyst in this process of shamanic initiation and psychological dismemberment. Three years later, in July 2008, after the shaman and the snakes first appeared in my dreams, I would experience being eaten by a giant anaconda during a sacred *ayahuasca* ceremony in the Amazon jungle. (Please see page 153.)

Snake Symbolism

References to snakes and serpents as universal symbols of transformation are found in myths throughout the world. As a student of Jung, I have found references in his writings to snakes, which have also enriched my understanding of this powerful image. Jung believed that images of serpents in caves are common with baptisms or beginnings. The cave or Underworld represents a layer of the unconscious where there is no discrimination; male and female are no longer distinguishable. Snakes exist in the primordial realm of creation.

Originating in Greek mythology, the staff with the serpent represents healing, wisdom, and prophecy. In Asia, Kundalini is the snake fire that burns and cleanses the chakras in the body. In conversations, Nathan Schwartz-Salant described these kinds of snake symbols as Dionysian, involving the lower *anthropos*, chakras or energy centers in the subtle body and etheric field.

Books have already been written on the mystical symbolism of snakes by experts that know much more about the topic than I do. What continues to be most meaningful to me about the snake — beyond providing me entry into my own shadow and dismemberment process — has been my deepening connection to Peruvian cosmology. In Peruvian shamanism, the great snake Amaru rules the Underworld (Uhu Pacha). It is the womb of the Great Mother, Pachamama, and the place of manifestation. This is the primordial realm where a complete "union of opposites" exists. The symbol of the snake began to take on a life of its own for me as I continued to work with it, and is now much more than a description written on a page. As my journey into shamanism continued, my relationship with the snake deepened. "She" has become a protector in my inner world. I have called on her when I have felt in need.

In April 2006, more and more traumatic memories kept emerging into Perry's consciousness — and in reaction Perry kept speeding up, talking nonstop, and becoming tangential. Looking back now, I realize that Perry was diagnosably in a full-blown manic episode. At the time, I suppose I was in denial. I kept waiting for him to return to his former self, the man I had loved and lived with for fifteen years. Perry started talking to me — and anyone who would listen — about the fantastic inventions he was seeing and would create. His thoughts sped up even faster, becoming more and more surreal and incredible — and I grew more and more frightened. In my own analysis, it was suggested that I consider that Perry may never return to his former self, and that we were both following our own paths of individuation.

During this period, in August 2006 I had a dream, symbolic of a place I would actually visit with Perry a couple of years later on a trip to Mesa Verde.

August 12, 2006
I had the following dream:

> *Perry and I were out hiking and came up to a chain link fence, which was a boundary to Rajasthan or Afghanistan — a foreign place I had never been but was curious about. I encouraged Perry to duck with me underneath the fence to explore what was on the other side. We walked up a hill and spotted an old white farmhouse that reminded me of Dorothy's house in* The Wizard of Oz. *We entered the house, walked through the kitchen, and started going down the stairs to the basement. Perry went down ahead of me and disappeared. Suddenly the stairs started coming apart and sharp metal sword-like objects started coming out of the floor and the ceiling. I grabbed the top stair, pulled myself back up into the kitchen, and called for Perry to come back. Finally, he came back, but he had shrunk, and was two years old. He pulled something out of his pocket and told me that it was blotter acid and that he had taken six hits. I did not want to scare him, although I was frightened, and picked him up carrying him outside on my hip. We walked outside onto a wooden porch with rocking chairs. It was raining and the colors seemed electric, they were so vibrant. A bright golden crop of corn that looked like wheat in the dream was growing. A woman with bright golden curly hair greeted me and asked me to sit and watch the corn grow with her.*

In September 2006, the onslaught of painful memories began to ease for Perry. The last batch of memories that came back to Perry was of participating in a study at Cleveland Clinic. He remembered being part of an experiment, known as "Operation Artichoke," as a child, and having wires hooked up to his head as an electric current passed through his body. At the time, Perry was told he had been chosen to be part of a military study. (Apparently, his father had remained connected with the military in some capacity after serving in an intelligence unit of the Coast Guard).

Perry continuously wrote pages and pages about new inventions he was seeing and imagining. One invention was an "energy cone" that could change the way we obtained energy. Another invention was a "grow tube" that was a self-sustaining plant water source to aid world hunger. Perry has studied physics (and is very bright) — and most of the time, due to lack of knowledge and my own high anxiety level, I had a hard time relating to what he was talking about.[6]

In March 2007, Perry started journeying on a daily basis. Journeying, a term coined by the anthropologist Michael Harner, is a form of active imagination, a shamanic way finding things in the imaginal world. On one of our trips to the desert, Perry was led by his inner guides to dig in a specific location and uncovered some unfamiliar green stones. He put some of the stones in his backpack and took a journey on the spot where he had found the stones. In the journey, he saw a curly haired, bearded man wearing rose-colored glasses. After returning home for our trip, while Perry was unloading the truck, he saw the man he had seen in his vision ride by at high speed on his bicycle. Perry had seconds to react before the man vanished around the corner. Perry was surprised to see the man's face appearing out of nowhere. At the time, Perry happened to be holding one of the stones he had

---

[6] Months later, Perry began to seem slightly more comprehensible and easier to follow. Either I was growing more accustomed to the new Perry, or he was acclimating to his new energy source — or both.

dug up and placed in his backpack. He asked the stone what he should do, and received a clear message back that he should chase the man down. Perry jumped in his truck and raced after the man in order to catch him before he disappeared.

When Perry caught up with the man, he did not exactly know what he should do so he did the first thing that he could think of. He rolled down the window and yelled out to the man, "Hey is your name Ed?"

The man stopped and so did Perry. The man replied, "No, but you are the second person this week who asked me if my name was Ed. My name is Larry. Why did you ask me that?"

While Perry was explaining to Larry that he did not exactly know why, Larry casually glanced over and looked at the stones that were lying next to Perry on the front seat of his truck, the stones that he had brought back from our recent trip to the desert.

Larry asked Perry about where he had found the stones and Perry told him. Larry was able to identify each of the stones Perry had found by their scientific names. He informed Perry that he was the chair of the archeology department at the University of Denver. Perry then handed him the green stone he had been holding in his hand, and asked Larry if he could identify that stone. Larry was silent for a minute and then said, "I wish I could find something like this. What species is this? This is a dinosaur, not a rock."

Perry became friends with Larry and saw him periodically when Larry rode by on his bicycle while Perry was working in the yard. Larry encouraged Perry to contact a well-known paleontologist, which Perry agreed to follow up on later.

These kinds of unusual events began to occur on a somewhat regular basis. Perry became busier and, after the first burst associated with these discoveries, rarely followed them to fruition. Some other new idea or discovery would emerge in the moment, catching Perry's attention. Distracted, he would leave what he had previously been focusing on, promising to return to it later.

In August 2007, Perry moved back and forth through the veil, into semi-lucid, visionary states. He had been working on a major house-building project that was now way over budget and more expansive than what we had both previously imaged. The house that had been started with the plan of it becoming our future home became another outlet for Perry's creative expression. He created a glass block, domed ceiling above an internally supported sweeping cement staircase that stretched over a swimming pool with waterfalls made out of foam materials using methods never done before. Perry's genius intrigued other builders. A scout looking for places to shoot upcoming motion pictures stopped by and inquired whether his production company could shoot a film in the house after it was completed. We continued living in the house in the midst of the major building project.

Saying that I was feeling run over by Perry's expansive extroversion is a major understatement. While all of this was going on, I feebly kept hoping for the best, and tried to find solace in my own analysis. I was learning more about the practices of the Q'ero Shamans. Finally, I reached the end of my tolerance for living in chaos and construction and found an older home nearby for us to live in.

5. Becoming a Shaman

We're at the threshold of huge change, and witnessing unusual weather, environmental change, family makeup, etc. Things are shifting massively. Celestial alignment is now changing as result of this inkari — return of light, of the Inca

— Asunta,

daughter of the late *altomesayoq* Don Manuel Q'uispe, 2011

The second *pacha* had changed me. In many ways my life was coming apart, but the basics for putting myself back together were also being made available to me. From the time of the workshop until I went to Peru in June 2007, I worked with Jose Luis, attending weekend classes to prepare for the trip.

There were about 12 people in the group — or *ayllu* — usually held in a Rhode Island Zen center with no chairs or beds. We met every three or four months. Beyond that there were additional casual conversations within the group and between members of the group and Jose Luis — but not sessions.

There was much to learn before we met the spirits of the mountains and tried to take our places healing the spirit of the earth, Pachamama. The first task was learning what it meant to be a shaman.

Shamanism is a spiritual method with functional application. I have frequently heard shamans ask, "Can you grow corn with it?"

meaning if a shamanic experience cannot be used to help the planet, our communities, and our selves, it has no redeeming value. As I describe fundamental components in the practice of shamanism, I will also offer examples and suggestions that you may use to begin experiencing and working with shamanism on your own.

The practice of shamanism honors the relationship between all living things. All living things on the planet connect energetically and originate from the earth, or Pachamama. This connection with Pachamama is the source of the shaman's power. In this writing, I will refer to this universal power source, originating from Pachamama in an energetic state, as the "energetic collective." I am using this term because "sourcing" from Pachamama occurs at an energetic level through connecting with the collective unity of all living things.

A shaman's ability to work with the life force energy of the energetic collective determines his or her degree of power. Power refers to the ability to source — or access, channel, and hold — the life force, or *kausay*, of the energetic collective. Shamanism is different from the practice of sorcery that Carlos Castaneda described in his books in which he reports his experience learning from the Yaqui Indians, Don Juan and Don Genero. This is because in shamanism, power is used for the benefit of the "highest good," not for personal gain. In shamanism, power is never used to control someone against his or her will. Power is used in acts of service, only after consent has been given by whomever we are trying to help. In this writing, I will use the word power to refer to the shaman's capacity to contain and channel the life force of Pachamama.

In shamanism, the four major components in the relationship between all living things are (1) humans, (2) the earth, (3) shamans, and (4) the shaman's medicine bundle or *mesa*. To describe the rest of what happened to me as a result of my second *pacha*, let me share with you what the Q'ero whom I have worked with have taught me about each of these elements and their role in shamanism.

6. Humans

The mythic element gives you one thousand and one ways to understand it. One thousand and one ways to express it — and all of them are valid.

— Dona Alahandrina, *altomesayoq*, conversation 2010

The Q'ero shamans believe humans and all other living things have a luminous body, or energetic field, surrounding them. The energy held in the luminous body is the creative force existing in the universe. This energetic expression separately defines and holds all aspects of the psyche, and the totality of psychic energy. It is the blueprint — the underlying mechanism in the way we perceive the world and find meaning in our experiences. The luminous body is the urn that contains the collective experience of one's ancestors and the imprint that will be passed on to the generations of children to come. It is composed of lived and unlived individual and collective experiences. For the shaman, the luminous body is the vessel that contains their power.

In humans, the luminous body can be seen as an energetic web of light consisting of three chakras or important energy centers located in the Belly, the Heart, and the Mind.[7] As we become more

---

[7] In this writing, to distinguish between physical and spiritual I will capitalize the words Belly, Heart, and Mind when I am referring to the

familiar with the shamanic realm, our ability to sense a vibrational frequency through feeling a pulse or seeing the surrounding energy field of the luminous body grows stronger. Some people see the particles of luminous energy as light. Others feel it more as a touch. In any case practice improves our ability to sense the fields. Over time, what we may have initially accepted on faith becomes real and tangible in our experience of a shared reality.

Exercise 1: Becoming acquainted with the luminous body

Close your eyes. Imagine being wrapped in a glowing and pulsating bubble of iridescent light made up of thin threads and fibers that surround you. The density of these strands has some slight variation, with the greatest concentration being in your belly. Next, imagine some of the filaments of light energy that make up your *luminous body* reaching out into the world, touching the ground, while others attach to whatever else is around you. These threads are part of the energetic field that connects you to everything surrounding you. Fully focus your attention on what you are perceiving and feeling, noticing any subtle changes occurring in your body. This is how perception on the energetic level is experienced. Working with this imagery repeatedly over time will strengthen your ability to experience the world differently, as an energetic expression of life.

When we are feeling healthy and alive, the light of our surrounding bubble expands and grows stronger and brighter. In areas of our body where we may have had an injury or some

---

energy centers. I will use the uncapitalized words belly and heart when I am writing about the physical locations of the lower abdomen and heart, respectively. I will use the word mind when I am describing mental processing or referring to our perception of self based in ordinary reality.

ailment, there may be fewer threads and the light may be dimmer. If we are scared or afraid, our light body contracts and becomes smaller. When physically rested, the luminous body becomes more vibrant. We have the ability to influence the state of our luminous body and the energetic field around us by the way we envision it.

As we grow accustomed to perceiving at the energetic level, we develop the ability to sense our energetic link to everything living around us by experiencing it through our energetic field. Interacting with nonordinary reality occurs in this heightened state of awareness. As we become more accustomed to experiencing the world through our luminous body, we become aware of being connected by seeing or feeling the connection at the same time we are observing the world through our ordinary senses. This kind of perceptual state that bridges ordinary and nonordinary reality allows us to experience both states simultaneously.

The Belly, the Heart, and the Mind are the three energy centers that the Q'ero shamans work with. Each of these three energy centers has specific and unique functions. The Belly is the center of creativity and fluidity, the Heart is the center of love and connectivity, and the center for vision and wisdom is located in the Mind. All of these centers expand out from their focus points to form the luminous body. Understanding how these parts function and interact is required for understanding how we interact with other humans, fellow shamans, and the spirits of our world.

The Belly

The Belly, the energy center associated with the mythic snake Amaru, contains the blueprint of creation.[8] Shamans teach that if

---

[8] The Q'ero shamans refer to the center I call the Belly as *yachai*.

our egos are negotiable, experiencing through the Belly enables us to enter an essential state of fluidity, also known as a state of no separation, where anything is possible. In this center, everything exists in a primary state of volatility. An energetic exchange between spirit and matter is realizable — and inception and physical manifestation occur. The energetic state of variability associated with the Belly corresponds to the Taoist experience of "being in the flow," in balance with the energetic world around us. Like the snake, which moves through direct physical contact with the earth, the physical mechanics of doing happen by connecting with the environment through the Belly.

There is a famous story about a rainmaker, which illustrates this practice of actively interacting with the world through the Belly:

> *A rainmaker is asked to visit a village that is suffering from famine caused by a serious drought, where the crops and livestock are dying, to help restore the balance with nature. When the rainmaker arrives in the village, he goes off and isolates himself in a tent. The villagers are confused about why he has disappeared. When the rainmaker later comes out of the tent, it starts to rain and the villagers are pleased. The rainmaker tells the villagers that he had to restore the balance in himself and in his body first, which then restored balance to the rest of the world and brought rain to the village.*

Being in relation with the earth by sensing through the Belly is the means for us to link to the source, or energetic collective, the shamanic definition of power. When we are in the state of perception associated with Amaru, everything is immediate, black and white, and all or none — focused on instinctual survival by engaging through the autonomic nervous system.

In the spirit of Amaru, I have heard shamans exclaim, "There are no plan Bs! A shaman commits fully to his or her life by living in the present moment, with no contingency plans!" Experiencing through the perceptual realm of Amaru is particularly useful in assessing situations requiring a gut reaction, or an immediate fight or flight response.

When we are experiencing energetic connection through the Belly, we may feel it in degrees — from a light tingling sensation and sense of expansion, to an intense rush of vibrating energy pulsing through our limbs. This is not dependent on a drug-induced state. During shamanic initiations, there is an intense download of energy being transferred into the luminous body, and contractions and/or temporary paralysis in the outer extremities of the physical body may occur. There is often a rippling effect, experienced somatically as a strong charge or surging electric current. On occasion, I have found it hard to remain standing and have felt my knees give out while an energy transmission is taking place. Although physical movement may become difficult during these states, these experiences are often accompanied by invigorating vitality, along with the acute sense of being alive and highly energized. Vision may also become more acute and vivid, especially while in nature, where it becomes possible to see the energy emanating from the luminous field of every living thing around us.

Exercise 2: Shifting into Body Awareness through the Belly

One of the ways that you can expand your energy body is through your Belly. First, find a comfortable place, lying down or leaning back into a relaxed sitting position. Close your eyes and gradually shift your attention to your Belly. It may help to place something, such as a piece of clothing or a pillow, over your eyes to block out ordinary reality. Take several long, slow, deep breaths, focusing on the exhale — relaxing and breathing directly and fully from your Belly. Notice the way your Belly expands and contracts as you breathe. You may begin to feel your awareness shifting, so that you begin to experience yourself from the vantage point of your Belly.

As you settle into this state, you will probably observe that the thoughts running through your mind are slowing down as your focus shifts toward what you are feeling physically. Emotionally you may begin to feel the tension you have been carrying falling away as you move into a more peaceful and centered frame of mind. From this place of Belly relaxation, use your intention to sense the vibrant energizing light body surrounding you. Feel yourself becoming energized as your energetic field grows larger, moving into an expanded state. Observe the light becoming brighter and more brilliant. Spend a few moments in this state, feeling the light moving through your cells as you continue to breathe in the light.

Feel yourself beginning to harmonize with the nonordinary energy vibration that is becoming anchored in your body. Take some time to acclimate to these sensations, becoming familiar with how this experience feels. This will make it easier to remember and connect to in the future. When you are ready, slowly bring yourself back to your outer awareness and open your eyes. You may be aware of feeling more rested and alert. This is one way to visualize and work with your luminous body. Practicing this exercise may help open the door for perceiving nonordinary reality. This visual imagery technique is one I often suggest to clients to aid in stress reduction.

The Heart

Although energetic connection in the Belly and the Heart centers may occur simultaneously and be experienced as equally intense, we usually register the sensations in each of the two centers differently.[9] Connecting with a collective energy source using the Heart frequently comes as numinous energetic bursts. Shamans often refer to these kinds of experiences as states of ecstasy. A common experience associated with having an open Heart is the instinctual sense — transcending words and experience — of belonging or feeling we are home. The phrase "feeling as though one's heart is bursting open" is an accurate description of what connecting through the Heart center may feel like.

During my first trip to Peru, when I entered the energetic fields of the shamans for the first time, I felt my Heart stretching and opening — even before any words were spoken. I noticed that my Heart was actually aching as I felt the fullness of being in the shamans' presence. I had an overwhelming sense of finally coming home that brought me to tears. I noticed myself crying regularly over the course of my initial journey. The process of expanding the Heart center frequently involves shedding tears.

The Heart is the hub of energetic connectivity, the vehicle of relatedness, and the center of non-doing. Q'ero shamans say that the Heart is where we experience *munay* energetically. *Munay* is the universal feeling-state of love connecting us to the earth and life on our planet, and as being in a blissful state of union. As an expression of universal relatedness, the capacity to love unconditionally, beyond personal experience and limitation, takes place in the Heart as an expression of Pachamama. This is different from personal love, which focuses on another person, often with the need for reciprocation attached. As an expression of the energetic relationship with spirit, in this form of loving there is no need to get something back. Everything is automatically linked and available.

---

[9] The Q'ero shamans refer to the Heart center as *sonqo*.

In Peruvian shamanism the Heart center is the domain of Chocachinchi, the mythic jaguar. The jaguar lives in the present moment, and through existing in an open and receptive state of immediacy, is able to take in the world as it is happening through all of the senses. As Chocachinchi, who senses and feels everything intensely as it adeptly moves through the jungle, we experience the fullness and fulfillment of our lives through our Heart center.

The Mind

As the energy center associated with the mythic being of the condor, Apucheen, the Mind holds the capacity for spiritual wisdom and global vision. The Mind also functions as the bridge between perceptual states associated with objective ordinary and nonordinary reality — both inside and outside the framework of sequential time and space. In ordinary reality, the conscious mind is the center of analytic thought and the mechanism necessary for constructing a schemata, or cognitive map, to process and organize information from the external world.

As the condor that flies above, the Mind perceives from a bird's eye view, giving us a vantage point from which we can see the big picture and avoid becoming bogged down in minutiae and superfluous detail. Dreamers and visionaries use their Minds in realms of nonordinary reality, with the awareness of existing outside of time and space.[10] In deep visionary experiences, one is actually creating the experience as one is having it — creation, transformation, and observation occur simultaneously. Through the process of dreaming while asleep or purposefully imagining with intention while awake, the Mind can create and design templates of form, through crafting vision.

---

[10] Q'ero shamans call the organizing principle of wisdom *yuya.*

7. Mythic Beings: Amaru, Chocachinchi, and Apucheen

May your walk be embraced with the Mind and Heart. Make that your everyday walk. This journey is a journey of your soul — master of power and master of deficiencies.

Apu Huascaran,
Ceremony with Dona Alahandrina's *mesa*, 2011

Many cultures have the concept of energy centers like the Belly, the Heart, and the Mind. As the Q'ero explain it, though, these are much more than just human constructs. In addition to being part of the human energy body, each center is connected to and associated with a mythic being.

The three energy mythic beings are Amaru the powerful snake, Chocachinchi the commanding jaguar, and Apucheen the great condor. They correspond to the shamanic realms of the lower, middle, and upper worlds. The Q'ero shamans connect to Amaru through the Belly, Chocachinchi through the Heart, and Apucheen through the Mind.

Each of these three mythic beings has specific qualities and properties, known as guiding principles, which relate to how the energy in each of these centers is experienced — as well as to specific states of perception in ordinary and nonordinary reality. In addition to being the guiding principles of the energy centers in

49

the body, these mythic beings often manifest as emanations of the spirit world as we intentionally open up to the experience.

When I was first introduced to Inca cosmology, the notion that mythic beings were material forms of a cultural collective spirit — and actually existed — seemed foreign and irrational to me. I remember telling myself that these figures, as used in the Q'ero culture, symbolized archetypal experience.

Although this may be partially true, as I have continued along the experiential path of shamanism, Amaru, Chocachinchi, and Apucheen have become real to me, as manifestations in their actual mythic forms. They have become my companions and my mentors during my encounters in nonordinary reality. They have each individually appeared to me during different periods in dream and vision states, and have helped guide me in their own ways. Over time, I have developed relationships with each of them in the inner world, as well as with the *Apus,* the great collective mountain spirits in both the inner and outer worlds. I have also become acquainted with the *Santa Tierras,* the feminine spirit of the land.

Amaru, Chocachinchi, and Apucheen have emerged in waking and dream states, depending upon my current focus in the inner world. As I described earlier, within weeks after my introduction to Q'ero shamanism, I began working with a snake that first appeared to me in a dream — and forced me to face aspects of my personal shadow.

After encountering Amaru, before going to the Amazon in July 2007, a jaguar being began emerging in my vision states. During my time in the jungle, I experienced my body being held by a powerful black jaguar that was all around me, surrounding and protecting me during a rather intense, unexpected *ayahuasca* ceremony. Although I did not speak to the jaguar using verbal language, I felt a strong emotional connection with the jaguar's presence deep inside of me. I was comforted by his warmth and protection. I felt completely safe. I was aware that his great claws would keep away anything that might harm me. He shielded me from the energetic debris flying all around me as others near me were encountering dark aspects of their own personal shadows. I burrowed myself deeply into the soft fur of his massive chest and was not afraid. I later learned that the jaguar was Chocachinchi, the animal spirit of the Amazon jungle.

After this *ayahuasca* ceremony, there was no doubt in my mind that Chocachinchi was real. In my private psychotherapy practice, as I am helping clients working through deep layers of emotional trauma in the "psychic underworld," with their permission I often call on Chocachinchi for assistance. I have brought his presence into the session by describing how to feel his protection. Subsequently, Chocachinchi has often shown up in their dreams and his being there has comforted them.

Through my activities in nonordinary reality, I eventually came to know a manifestation of Apucheen. In May 2007, the figure of a Birdman arrived during in a waking vision, and started speaking to me through my Mind. A couple of weeks later, I was walking through a market with one of the shamans in Peru. Suddenly, the shaman stopped me. Pointing to a painting of a Birdman being displayed by one of the local vendors, he said, using a combination of motion-gestures and Spanish words, "There is the figure that appears in your visions."

Over the course of the last five years, I have been most closely connected to the inner figure I now refer to as Birdman. The Birdman is an integral part of my travels into the shamanic realms — and has become my ally, guide, and mentor. He has a life and purpose of his own apart from mine, and together we are partners. The Birdman is direct in his style of communication — he confronts me if I reach a psychological blind spot and does not soften his words in a way that would help me to avoid seeing the sometimes-painful truth. Birdman takes me into the realms of nonordinary reality, often serving as an intermediary when I journey into the mountain collective of the spirit world. In exchange, I provide the Birdman with the opportunity to experience manifestation in a physical form. We are inseparably linked.

As my work in shamanism continued, I came to recognize that these inner mythic animal figures — the snake, the jaguar, and the Birdman that I encountered in dream and vision states, were the same mythological beings found in the cosmology of Peruvian shamanism — Amaru the snake, Chocachinchi the jaguar, and Apucheen the great condor. I was somewhat perplexed and wondered if perhaps I had plugged into a collective shamanic experience that was influencing my dreams and visions. Years later, I understand Amaru, Chocachinchi, and Apucheen to be an aspect of the objective manifestation of the energetic collective experienced by the Q'ero shamans.

These mythic beings can actually be experienced in physical reality, and are most easily accessed through connecting with them through their corresponding energy centers in the body.

8. Pachamama:
the Shaman's Power Source

P'aqos of the West need medicine of the heart and old technologies to be spoken again. The first set of keys, through initiation rites, was given last year — bringing memory of a new time, creating a new story, a new tradition. The p'aqos *from the West will propel [our teachings] and the ancient technology of ritual will be spoken again.*

— *Apu* Huascaran,
ceremony with Dona Alahandrina's *mesa*, 2011

The mythic beings are aspects of the land, but in Q'ero shamanism, everything in life begins, exists, and ends through direct dialogue and communion with Pachamama, the collective of the land itself. The land is not only a symbol of the Great Mother; the land *is* the Great Mother. The land exists both inside and outside of time and space, as matter and spirit.

Everything is understood as part of natural order. To complete the cycle of life, what is born and taken from the land returns to the land so that it can be born again. Similar to the Force in *Star Wars*, the land is the collective subtle body existing between all living things, the energetic realm from which a shaman derives power. Q'ero shamans source from Pachamama because, unlike people, Pachamama remains constant and is always there.

A reciprocal relationship and dialogue develop between the shaman and the land, serving as a functional spiritual gateway between ordinary and nonordinary reality. The Q'ero shamans refer to the relationship existing between all living things as Kausay Pacha.

Shamans connect with the collective of the land — or energetic collective — using the energy centers in their luminous body, the conduit into experiencing on a much greater, collective scale. By connecting with the land through the luminous body, the land becomes the medium the shaman uses to shift from personal experience to accessing the universal state of the collective. In Peruvian shamanism, the collective of the land is similar to the collective unconscious in the psyche but is much greater. It is the depository of all experience.

As Adolpho, an *altomesayoq*, explained it, shamans experience the actual presence of the collective of the land through "membership," (affiliation) with sacred mountains. The concept of affiliation with a mountain is similar to the function of bodhisattvas in eastern religions and to Christ as the intermediary to God in the Christian religion. The sacred mountains are an active expression or collective composite of Pachamama, the great Earth Mother, and the collective spirit existing between the person and the energetic collective.

The collective spirits of the sacred mountains in Peru are referred to as *"Apus"* or "the winged beings." Besides entering into direct dialogue with the *Apus,* another aspect of the *altomesayoq's* job description involves opening *ceke* lines (ley lines), to promote global healing. *Ceke* lines are energy meridians that form an energetic grid. They encompass the earth in a way similar to the luminous body in humans. The *ceke* lines are the energy channels flowing through the earth that keep the earth alive.

These *ceke* lines intersect at *wakas,* or specific geographic locations that are power spots, which are infused with energy.

Activating *ceke* lines allows for a greater flow of energy through the earth and greater capacity for communion with the collective. Physically standing inside a *waka* usually heightens a person's perception, making it easier to enter into expanded states of awareness.

In Peru today, the *wakas* are still marked by stone and rock formations created by the Incas. Sourcing from these spots enables the *p'aqo*, or person practicing ancient Andean tradition, to draw in the energy from the earth to promote well-being. Although most of the mountains are considered sources of light energy, one mountain outside of Cusco is inhabited by sorcerers and is understood to hold the dark shadow aspect of the collective.

There are many *wakas* located near Machu Picchu, as well as in the sacred mountains of the *Apus* surrounding the Sacred Valley outside of Cusco. Shamans often make pilgrimages to the sacred mountains to strengthen their relationships with Pachamama and the mountain spirits and to undergo initiations. In my own travels with the Q'ero shamans, I have visited the sacred mountains of Waquay Wilka and Ausangate on separate occasions for initiation rites.

There are other types of sacred places existing in the land of Peru where the veil is more transparent.

Pakarinas, feminine mythic places found in caves or bodies of water, are places of origin where life emerges.

Wankas are fertility spots, often identified as rocks in open fields. In *wankas*, it is believed that the ancestors have broken through the veil. These are places where the land can become impregnated so that lineage continues and the crops will grow.

Saywas and *sukankas* are considered luminous markers that are connected to the celestial bodies. All of these are part of Pachamama.

9. The Shamans:
Serving the Experience

We see walls through our own walls. In order to participate, we need to bring down our own inner walls. You can't see from only one lens of perception; there is more to it. Undo the walls that hold your own inner understanding, only then can you see you are free. The challenge is to think beyond what you perceive. Liberate yourself — celebrate life.

— *Apu* Señor Chauipicaro
ceremony with Juanito's *mesa*, 2011

Don Sebastian, a wise *pampamesayoq* shaman I met in the Andes Mountains of Peru, stressed many times the role shamans play in connection with Pachamama and the other spirits. The shaman's experience working in nonordinary reality is rooted in an ancient tradition, historically accepted, and respected within the community. What the shaman brings back from the other side is viewed as an act of service that facilitates the well-being of all of the members of the community.

Don Sebastian said the role of the shaman is to serve numinous experience. When Don Sebastian described what he meant by "numinous experience," he actually used the Quechua word *kausay*. The organizing principles for Q'ero shamans' lives centers around tending to *kausay*, or fertility in nature. Serving in shamanism requires putting *kausay* before individual need.

Kausay is the energy of creation, often experienced in the body as a vibration, or in the heart as a feeling of universal love towards everyone and everything. *Kausay* may be seen as an intense light, or experienced as clarity, or a sense of all-knowing wisdom. *Kausay* is often experienced in altered states of ecstasy. In serving the experience of *kausay*, the shaman attends to the energetic collective, the essential level at which everything is connected in a state of fluidity.

Shamans become masters of invisibility by working in harmony with *kausay*, in accordance with Pachamama. Through being in *ayni* (right relationship) with the living world of Pachamama, shamans are able to track who they are becoming. As a result of sourcing, or maintaining right relationship with nature, the shamans' increased availability gives them greater access to life force or *kausay*, enabling them to engage with and perceive nonordinary reality or our "trans-temporal" nature. The process of sourcing from Pachamama to feed *kausay* is called a *karpay*. For the shaman, *kausay* is the recovery and expression of luminous nature developed through remembering and awakening to our true essence, which transcends linear time and space. They have made peace with their personal past and the past of their ancestors, which increases their availability in the present, and, ultimately, their capacity to hold power. Shamans practice power in a way that leaves no footprints.

The Q'ero shamans of Peru are medicine people who function as the technicians of the guiding mythology in their culture and have two sets of responsibilities — to take care of the earth and to take care of the members of their community or *ayllu*. The *altomesayoqs* are the shamans whose primary job is to serve the collective of the land, and the *pampamesayoqs* are the keepers of the earth, the community healers who work with herbs. A shaman, who works with sacred stones, or a *mesa*, is called a *mesayoq*.

The *altomesayoqs*, the most highly respected group of Q'ero shamans, function as the doorways between ordinary reality, Kay Pacha, and the Kausay Pacha or living energy of the energetic collective. Many *altomesayoqs* are cross-eyed, the result of being struck by lightning during their initiation. As mentioned previously, a duty of an *altomesayoq* is tending to the *ceke* lines. They maintain the role of stewards of wellness by being in harmonic balance because they honor the connection between all living things. These shamans source their energy from the directors of the holy mountains, the *Apu* spirits, by engaging in an exchange with the energetic collective. They each have membership with a particular mountain and speak directly to the spirits of that location. There are different types of *altomesayoqs*, determined by the spirits they communicate with. The differences are based on functions that include channeling lineage, talking to sacred places, speaking with lightning, or having dialogues with the ancestors.

In ceremony, the *altomesayoqs* have acquired the energetic capacity or power to call the *Apu* mountain spirits into actual physical manifestation. Through their capacity to contain energy or hold space, they serve as a gateway for the aspects of the spirits to emerge. They enable others who are present to enter into direct dialogues with the *Apu* spirits. The voices and energetic quality of the aspect of the *Apu* that appears reflects the temperament of the *altomesayoq* who is serving as the gateway. While sitting in ceremonies with different *altomesayoqs*, I observed the energy and the voices of the *Apus* shift from one of sweet benevolence to one of booming force depending on which *altomesayoq* was performing the ceremony.

Many *altomesayoqs* begin their shamanic path by first becoming *pampamesayoqs*. The duties of *pampamesayoqs* generally involve tracking the future, or the root of a client's or family member's illness. The healing and tracking methods include using bundles of small stones or the entrails of guinea pig to track illness. They also place rod instrument made of silver and gold into hot coals, or use coca leaves, llama fat, llama droppings, or corn to track the future. *Pampamesayoqs* often use herbs in healings and soul retrieval.

10. Learning to Be a Shaman

This is an act of love. This is not a little adventure.
— Dona Bernadina, *pampamesayoq*, conversation 2009

Shamans construct visions for the future well-being of members of their community, themselves, and for Pachamama. In the West, we tend to interact with the world and set goals for ourselves using our heads, not our hearts. In shamanism, crafting a vision requires using all three of the energy centers.

During one of my trips to Peru, a shaman recounted a story about a vision that has stayed with him for many years after he was given it as a young apprentice. He and several other young apprentices were studying with an older shaman, an *altomesayoq*, who was greatly respected for his wisdom and ability to speak with the spirits of the land. The *altomesayoq* gave the group of young apprentices the task of creating visions for each other. The shaman who was telling the story said that at the time, he had hoped that the powerful *altomesayoq* rather than one of the other apprentices would give him a vision. He assumed that a vision given by the older shaman would be much more potent, and likely to come into manifestation. However, another apprentice approached him instead and told the young shaman that he had a vision he would like to give him. Although dissatisfied, the young shaman realized that he must accept the vision being given by the other apprentice.

The other apprentice told the young shaman that he imagined a beautiful hummingbird[11] landing and drinking from a pond that was deep and crystal clear. The water would cleanse and purify the hummingbird, and give it strength as it made its journeys to the realms beyond in the otherworld.

The young shaman accepted the vision but was still disappointed that he had received his vision from an apprentice rather than his great teacher, the powerful *altomesayoq*. The *altomesayoq*, aware of what had transpired, looked at the young shaman and laughed, telling him he was a fool not to appreciate the gift that was being given to him. The *altomesayoq* said to the young shaman, "The vision this apprentice has given you carries strong medicine because it has been created with love and strong intent."

Years later, the shaman who was telling the story said that he again saw the young apprentice who had crafted the vision, who by now had grown into a powerful shaman in his own right. The shaman that was telling the story, who had received the vision, thanked the shaman he had known as an apprentice, who gave him the vision, because the vision had come true. Over the years, the shaman had become the hummingbird in his journeys to the upper world, and the vision dream had given him wisdom and clarity that had enriched his life.

Exercise 3: How to Craft a Vision

Begin by finding a comfortable position, lean back and close your eyes. Bring yourself fully into your body by taking several

---

[11] In Quechua, the word for hummingbird is *siwar qenti*. This powerful hummingbird is reported to have looked the creator in the eye.

deep breaths. After you are settled, find a deep place in yourself, shifting into a body-focused awareness as described in Exercise 2. From this relaxed state, direct your thoughts on clearly defining your intention. Open yourself to your intuition, allowing an image what it is you would like to create to gradually emerge and develop. In shamanism, a vision is crafted in service of the collective and for healing, always with the intent for the highest good. Feel and breathe, bringing yourself into the actual experience. Give yourself time to allow this to occur. If you are patient, an image or symbol will eventually appear. A vision can be created by either imagining it literally or working with it symbolically, whatever comes most naturally to you.

After a vision has formed in your Mind, adding detail and embellishing the image will help the vision image come into clearer focus. Pay attention to the lighting and texture of the image you are seeing. Notice the color. Imbuing it with feeling by directing your breath into the image from your Heart center will help it to become more alive. Shamans use all of their senses to mold and shape their visions. Smelling, tasting, hearing, and feeling a vision, as well as seeing it, will give it power. Breathing into the vision from your Belly will help to strengthen it as well. A vision grows stronger when you hold it in your mind and nourish it with psychic energy on a regular basis. Repeat this procedure as often as you wish. Allow the vision to grow and develop according to its own course over time. In Peru, shamans "feed" the visions they create by loving and tending to them with their thoughts and prayers, and always asking Pachamama for assistance. Shamans also reinforce their visions by creating ceremonial fire offerings called *despachos*, which will be described in Chapter 14.

Calling Sacred Space

When preparing to engage with nonordinary reality, it is important to begin with the sacred ceremonial ritual of opening or calling sacred space. In shamanism, ceremony refers to the practice of entering the spirit realm of nonordinary reality and asking the spirits to respond. Calling sacred space is the way we ask the spirits for their attendance, guidance, and support — always with intention for the highest good. Entering into sacred space enables us to facilitate the perceptual shift into experiencing nonordinary reality. This is especially important when working in groups.

Some shamans call sacred space from each of the four directions — north, east, south, and west. The Q'ero shamans call sacred space by following the movement of the sun, which is the method I use and am most familiar with. When calling sacred space, it is helpful to have a rattle or drum to create a rhythmic sound that will help you to shift into a meditative state. The Q'ero shamans usually work with rattles. Although using either a rattle or a drum is fine, my personal preference is to use a rattle. I have found listening to a drumbeat extremely helpful in facilitating journeying into the otherworld, but I have discovered that using a rattle is less cumbersome to manipulate during a ceremony. I have grown accustomed to working with the rattle, and now associate the sound of the rattle with sacred ceremony and connecting with the spirit world.

Along with using a rattle, most of the *pampamesayoqs* have their own particular song that is a rhythmic, repeating melody, which they whistle and sing to open and hold sacred space when calling upon the spirit world. Anyone who has worked with the Q'ero in nonordinary reality settings or participated in fire ceremonies with them becomes familiar with their songs. Hearing a melody we recognize often elicits an emotional reaction in us and may remind us of the feeling of coming home. Facilitating these kinds of emotional responses may help us to open and connect through our Heart centers.

In the Amazon jungle during ceremony, *ayahausceros*, the shamans who work with the plant medicine of *ayahuasca*, weave the threads of their song into the experience as a way of guiding various stages of the journey into and out of the spirit world.

Michael Harner, the well-known anthropologist and shamanic practitioner, also uses songs, as well as a drum, to help to facilitate the deeper states of receptivity necessary in journeying to the otherworld. You should use whatever works best for you.

Exercise 4: Calling Sacred Space

Calling sacred space is an active process done from a standing position with your eyes wide open. Q'ero shamans began calling sacred space by asking Pachamama to bless them with her presence. The way you call sacred space should feel meaningful and natural to you. You are offering a prayer and asking for blessing. It is important that you always call sacred space from your Heart.

The word-chant used in calling sacred space may sound something like this, "Pachamama, Pachamama, one who has never left us, one who will never leave us. Please come. *Hampuy, hampuy.* Come, come, help us to hold sacred space. Amaru, all the beings who live deep inside the earth or crawl on her surface, or walk on her surface, please come and give us your aide. *Ayaya!*"

Next, following the direction of the sun, shift your attention toward the East. "Lands of the rising sun, great ones of wisdom, wise ones, divine beings, ones that have gone before us, ones that will come again, please come, please come. *Hampuy, hampuy.* Give us the wisdom of your teaching so that we may grow in the old ways and bring your light into our world today. Please come, help us to create sacred space. *Ayaya!*

Then facing toward the sky, call sacred space from above, making sure to include all the deities and collective mountain spirits you would like to work with. Shamans on a pilgrimage to a holy mountain always call the name of the mountain. For example, "Father sun, grandmother moon, great *Apus*, and winged beings, Pacha Tucson, Ausangate, Waquay Wilka (including names of any mountains or mountain ranges near your home where you live). *Hampuy, hampuy.* Please come, please come. Help us to create sacred space. Please give us your love, support us so that we may learn from your ways and grow. *Ayaya!*

Finally, facing the West. "Great ones who swim in the vast oceans, who live in the seas, and who move swiftly through the jungles. Great jaguar Chocachinchi, *hampuy, hampuy.* Please come and hear our prayers. Please give us your powerful strength that we can then give to others. *Ayaya!*"

I have described the way I have learned to call sacred space. Q'ero shamans call sacred space using their native Quechua language. I have heard Westerners who have learned from the Q'ero shamans intersperse Quechua words with English words. It does not really matter which words you use as long as you are using the language of your Heart.

11. The Shaman's Medicine Body: the Mesa

When that mesa *is connected to those higher powers, nothing in the land will touch you. It will always protect you.*

— Don Andre, *pampamesayoq*, 2011

At the beginning of Jose Luis's instruction, he helped us start to build our *mesas*. This is the living representation of the shaman's medicine body. A *mesa* anchors us in the land during vision deep states, and stores the energy downloaded to us by the spirits of the mountains in Peru.

A *mesa* is a collection of individual stones, or *kuyas*, assembled over time, that the shaman uses in all sacred rituals and ceremonies. The *mesa* is the Q'ero shaman's connection to the energetic collective (Kausay Pacha) and the world of consensual reality (Kay Pacha). It serves as a bridge or gateway, linking the shaman to the lineage of ancestors from the past and children of the future. The more availability and conscious awareness shamans have, the greater their power and capacity to shift from ordinary reality, or Kay Pacha, into numinous experience, or Kausay Pacha. The *mesa* is the living embodiment of the shaman's lineage, and the medicine that claims him or her. For the shaman, the *mesa* is the portal into nonordinary reality. It is not just the physical object.

A *mesa* is comprised of *kuyas* that the *mesa* carrier is drawn to intuitively, or has received during an initiation ceremony. A full *mesa* is usually comprised of about twelve stones wrapped in a *mestana* cloth, which is a square piece of material that carries the stones. (See Figure 5 in the color section.) Although chosen individually, the *mesa* stones must ultimately function as a unit or energetic matrix for the *mesa* to have the capacity to hold power. It is customary for the *mesa* carrier to attune to how the stones harmonize with each other energetically when determining whether a *kuya* will actually become integrated into a *mesa*.

There is an Andean myth that the great Condor, Apucheen, brought the first *mesa* into being as a stone that could heal all living things. When it was time for Apucheen to leave the earth and return to the creator, the Condor left a stone that carried his sacred lineage and *ayni* (Heart energy) for human healers to work with.

When *p'aqos* (apprentices) begin to build their own *mesas*, they usually receive the sacred lineage carried in the shaman's *mesa* through a ceremonial ritual of initiation. In Peru, *karpay* refers to the shamanic initiation rites given when the shaman's body of knowledge and the power of the shaman's ancient lineage are passed to the apprentice through the *mesas*. The *karpay* is integrated by the *p'aqo* into conscious awareness through a process of recapitulating and remembering, which occurs in the luminous body by working with the *mesa*. After receiving the initiatory rites, it becomes the apprentice's job to continue developing a relationship with the *mesa* stones that have been activated by the shaman's lineage.

Working with a *mesa* starts by opening the *mesa*. An open *mesa* is a group of stones arranged in a circle that together create sacred space, connecting the personal and transpersonal. First, the *mestana* cloth is carefully laid open on a flat surface, preferably somewhere in nature in a spot where an affinity is felt. The *mesa* stones are placed in an arrangement, often circular, that intuitively feels right to the *mesa* carrier. Next, ceremony begins and sacred space is called. Calling sacred space involves asking the spirit world for assistance in each of the directions, following the rotational movement of the sun as it circles the earth, as described in Exercise 4 on page 64. The *mesa* carrier sits facing the *mestana* cloth with the opened *mesa* and gradually begins to shift the focus to second attention by intentionally dropping awareness into the Belly, breathing into and feeling into the earth and the stones.

Gradually, the *mesa* carrier enters into a receptive, meditative state — often using the repetitive sound of a rattle or drum. An image of scuba diving comes to mind — being underwater, slightly above the ocean floor, and watching and waiting for dirt that has been "kicked up" by rapid movement to settle slowly back down to the bottom before visibility returns. In these circumstances, other than softly breathing, one must remain quiet and motionlessly suspended. Any attempt to rush through the process will inevitably slow it down. This process of slowing down and waiting, known and used by dive masters, is similar to the process the shaman uses in shifting states of awareness.

Once in a quiet state of receptivity, spirit symbolically becomes matter by weaving the *mesa* stones into the subtle body using breath and intention. This process is not an intellectual exercise — it is an intuitive act of focusing intent and energetically weaving the land into the Belly. A point of connectivity between the shaman and the land is established by then weaving the medicine body held by the *mesa* stones into the land.

The Initial *Mesa*

Initially, the work begins with a wounded *mesa*. In this stage of the work, the *mesa* carriers learn to understand, or track their mythic purpose by connecting with the personal lineage of their past. Each stone is given a pattern of memories associated with past relationship wounds. By using intent, and imaginally placing negative patterns into the stones, the charge of the wound is transferred from the luminous body of the *mesa* carriers into the stone. This process initiates the conscious process of separating from, or being claimed, by past wounds. Perry and I began building our *mesas* in the fall of 2005.

Using intention, the *mesa* carrier engages in the process of recapitulation, consciously remembering by bringing greater compassion and understanding to personal narratives tied to the past. By opening to somatic experience through the Belly, one merges with the energy of Amaru, the great snake of Pachamama, Mother Earth.

Movement into a process of dying to the old way of being occurs, and the process of letting go begins. This results in a separation from identification with the personal life narrative and *persona*. Eventually objectification of the psyche — beyond personal limitation — begins to take place. The question, "What will you die to?" meaning, "What personal issues are you ready to face?" is asked. After a period of engaging in open dialogue and self-reflection, while sitting with the *mesa*, the *mesa* carrier prepares to release embedded shadow patterns with a fire ceremony.

During the time between my second pacha and going to Peru I used my *mesa* to deal with shadow issues that were tied to my dream with the black snake — breaking the pattern of being identified with my *persona* and financial security in the world, fear of abandonment as the result of all the loss, not trusting the "unknown" — and all of the issues that came up between Perry and me as the result of both of our lives being blown up. (During my annual meeting with my analytic training review committee I told them I was going to start wearing a T-shirt that said, "Fuck the unconscious!")

Over time, the size of a shaman's *mesa* increases as the capacity to hold power also increases. The individual *mesa* stones change. Some stones may disappear when the *mesa* carrier no longer has an affinity for the woundedness that has been held by the stone. New stones replace stones that symbolized personal complexes. The new stones often hold power, the imprint of the Great Mother, and the mountains of the land. Relationships or membership to the great mountains begin to form and gel as the qualities of the mountain spirits are downloaded into the *mesa* and begin to emerge in the stones. Celestial *mesas* are the *mesas* bestowed directly by the *Apus* only upon the highest *altomesayoqs* with the greatest capacity to hold the power. There is movement from the personal to the mythic collective as energy sourcing shifts from the *hucha* (dense energy of past trauma) into *sami* (the collective light energy of the great *Apu* mountain spirits).

When shamans are no longer claimed by personal history, they become open and available — and their capacity to engage in direct dialogue with the holy mountains increases. The shaman's *mesa* then connects to the reality existing outside of time and space. Forming a connection with the sacred mountains through the *mesa* brings the capacity for prophecy and establishes membership with the various mountains.

The medicine body of the *mesa* serves as the intermediary between the energy centers located in the luminous body and Pachamama, opening the gateway, or veil, between ordinary and nonordinary reality. The relationship between these fundamental components of energetic experience determines the shaman's capacity to hold power, ability to shift between worlds, and dialogue with the spirit realm.

Exercise 5: Creating a *Mesa*

If you were drawn to reading this book, you probably already have an affinity for collecting rocks and stones when you are in nature. Anyone can build a *mesa* by using right intent and working with *mesa* stones. When shamans begin to work with a *mesa*, they start with the practice I will be describing here.

Begin building your *mesa* by finding three rocks or stones in nature that speak to you. Try not to pick stones because they are flashy or beautiful (although they might be). Instead, choose stones that you are intuitively drawn to. When you pick a stone up and hold it in your hand, it should feel good to you. Stones chosen for your *mesa* should feel comfortable or energizing. Besides holding it in your hand, you might also test your affinity toward a particular stone by holding it against your temple. It is easiest to find stones for your *mesa* by not over-thinking your decisions. Using your intuition and going with your initial "gut" response is the best way to select your *mesa* stones.

After you have found the three stones, use a paper and pencil to map out three major life relationships that you would like to work toward healing. The people you choose may be from your past or present and may include parents, siblings, friends, teachers, and/or relationships with significant others. It is important to choose people in which you have had some repeated pattern or struggle throughout the course of the relationship. Perhaps you felt abandoned by this person or betrayed; perhaps you acted in ways toward the person in which you are not proud. You might also have had difficulty being yourself around a particular person, or staying present. Pick people whom you feel an emotional charge toward when you think of them. You should spend quiet time alone reflecting on the people you choose based upon the patterns in your life that you are ready and willing to let go of. Working to release negative patterns is always done for the highest good of everyone involved.

Now, feeling the charge for each person, pick the stone that most closely resonates with that particular person and hold the rock in your hand, closing your eyes. Sit quietly with the rock for a moment until you feel the charge in your body, as you hold an image of the person in your mind. You may remember an experience or event that happened in your relationship. As you start to track[12] your attachment to the pattern in your body, you may notice tightness in your chest or some other part of your body, a knot in your stomach, or observe that you are beginning to feel spacey and/or numb — maybe not knowing exactly what you are feeling. These are signs that you may be disconnecting from your experience and are leaving your body — usually because what you are feeling is becoming too uncomfortable for you to stay present[13].

Next, using your paper and pencil, begin to map aspects of the pattern cluster, writing them down and noticing how they link together. You want to track the pattern back to erroneous assumptions or beliefs you adopted. It is important not to assign blame or fault to yourself or the other person. Try to understand how the relationship pattern has affected and influenced you, and how the pattern has anchored your thoughts and feelings. Spend time recapitulating the memory to learn what you have gained from having this experience. You can only help others heal the inner psychological demons or emotional complexes that you have already wrestled with and gained understanding from in

---

[12] Tracking refers to following and reading an energetic thread to gain information through connecting in nonordinary reality.

[13] If you have frightening trauma memories that you have not dealt with, it is best if you do this with the support of another person such as a therapist, sponsor, shamanic practitioner, or close friend while undertaking this exercise.

yourself. These experiences are gifts because they have brought you the chance to gain wisdom and insight.

The shaman's *mesa* is a vehicle for psychic transformation and a way of healing imprints held in the luminous body. To gain power, energy that has been tied up in the past memories must be reclaimed. As you are feeling the charge in your body, bring the stone to your lips, and using your intention, blow the charge of the pattern you have identified into the stone three times. Repeat this entire process three times, pairing each relationship pattern with one of the stones. You may notice feeling a connection in your body with the charge you have blown into the stones.

Placing your woundedness into the stones will provide you an opportunity to separate from a negative pattern you may have been unconsciously carrying for many years. Working with a *mesa* offers a method to confront psychological patterns, both symbolically and energetically. A shaman apprentice's *mesa* always begins as a wounded *mesa*, with the sole purpose of healing. The psychic process that results in energy splitting off to defend against feeling pain is referred to as soul loss. The shaman brings missing soul parts back by reclaiming the energy that has separated from the luminous body in reaction to the shock of past trauma.

When you have finished mapping the patterns that you have invested into your *mesa* stones, find a cloth to wrap your stones in for safekeeping. In Peru, these are called *mestana* cloths. The *mesa* is a shaman's altar and should be treated with the same respect that you would give any sacred object that is meaningful to you, symbolizing your spiritual connection. Usually the *mesa* carrier is the only one that handles the stones in his or her *mesa*, to prevent the stones from taking on other energetic charges. It is courteous to ask permission before holding *kuyas* in another person's *mesa*.

Now, it is time to feed your *mesa*. Working with your *mesa* will strengthen your connection and give your *mesa* power. Find an offering such as grains or flower blossoms. In Peru, *k'intus* or dried coca leaves are often used. In western countries outside of Peru, bay leaves or leaves from indigenous trees are used instead. When you have gathered your offering, find a place in nature where you can comfortably sit. Open your *mesa* by placing each of the stones in a configuration that feels right to you and call sacred space from each of the four directions. Next, feed your *mesa* with the offering you have brought while holding the intention in your mind of honoring Pachamama. A *mesa* is fed by giving it offerings that you have blessed and are giving for Pachamama and the highest good. Sit quietly in front of your *mesa*, noting any thoughts or images that come to you. Concentrate on sensing the earth underneath you and your *mesa* in your Belly. Try to feel your Heart opening as you focus on moving into a state of compassion for all living things around you.[14] When you feel complete, thank Pachamama for her assistance and carefully place your *mesa* stones back in your *mestana* cloth. You have begun the first step in working with a *mesa*.

The Relationship between our Bodies, our *Mesas*, and Pachamama

According to Q'ero shamans, the ability to embody knowledge ultimately comes through forming a relationship between our bodies, our *mesas*, and Pachamama. Maintaining this connection requires using our intuitive intent to energetically weave the land into our bodies through our Belly. This energetic connection with the land is also woven into the medicine body held by the *mesa* stones. A reciprocal relationship between the land, our *mesas*, and

---

[14] If you are not feeling compassion, ask *Pachamama* for her help. You may need to start by asking *Pachamama* for the willingness to have the willingness.

ourselves is shaped and strengthened using our Hearts and Minds.

The *pampamesayoq* Dona Bernadina says, "The land, the spirits of the land provide everything to us from the very basics to, to the information of medicinal plants, of different ways that the land gives us gifts to heal others or to transform people's lives."

As our ability to hold power as a shaman grows, the connection between Pachamama, our *mesa*, and our luminous body grows stronger. This increases our capacity to serve as a *p'aqo* (conduit) between realities. Creating a gateway becomes easier. In turn, accessing these states, which are levels between ordinary and nonordinary reality, becomes a more fluid process.

Exercise 6: Weaving the Land into the Belly Meditation

Gather your *mesa* bundle if you have created one, and find a peaceful place in nature that draws you. Take a few moments to locate a comfortable place to sit, preferably where other people can't see you. You might find a spot overlooking a natural landscape, or contained in natural elements with boulders or trees. Quietly sit in front of your *mesa* (if you have one). Using your five senses, take in the nature surrounding you. When you feel ready, open sacred space by calling upon Pachamama. Feel gratitude for her presence and for creating the natural world of which you are a part.

Next, breathe by expanding the air into your belly. Feel this process as it is occurring in your body. Notice the gentle rhythm of your breathing as it is happening. Do not force it. Allow the process to take place naturally. Slowly and mindfully, breathe in and out.

Now, with intent, slowly imagine directing your breath, from your belly, moving down into the earth, forming a connection. You might imagine it as a thread, or channel, or tree root, or something else that comes to mind. As you exhale, move your awareness deeper into the earth using the connection you have formed in your mind. Over time, the image you have formed in your mind will correspond more strongly with what you are experiencing in your body. As you inhale, feel the earth coming up more fully into your body. If you are sitting with an open *mesa*, use your intention to visualize this triangular energy connection extending to your *mesa*, creating a continuous circuit of energy between your *mesa*, Pachamama, and your body.

Feel your connection growing stronger, sustaining the connection as long as you can in the moment. The connection might appear in your mind as an open channel between your *mesa*, Pachamama, and your body. The image may begin to grow into a web of light connecting you and your *mesa* into the living environment around you. You may begin to see the image you have formed in your mind transferring into your outer world. Again, do not try to force it. Gently use your focus to experience whatever is happening in a relaxed, receptive state, using beginner's mind. If you begin to notice your thoughts wandering, gently bring your focus back to the sensations you are feeling in your body, through your connection with Pachamama. Using your intent, see if you can move this connection up into your heart, becoming open to feelings that may emerge. Continue this process as long as you like and feel comfortable.

When you feel complete, thank Pachamama for her presence and close sacred space. To give thanks and express your gratitude, you may leave a (biodegradable) gift if you have brought one, and/or you may take a moment to visualize the earth surrounded in light, in a state of perfect wholeness.

12. Shifting Attention States

In life, in this search, in this journey — whatever that is — a little journey or a big, extensive, epic journey, one of the first things we need to recognize is how clear have I been? What are my attachments that I bring with me — particularly those attachments that have not been able to allow me to grow?

— Adriel, *pampamesayoq*, 2011

In addition to the various ways we can interact with the world using the energy centers of the Belly, Heart, and Mind, we can also experience shifts in perceptual states of awareness, which correspond to different levels of psychic engagement. These were the other lessons I have been taught by the Q'ero in my journey to become a shaman.

As we transfer our focus from the outer awareness that we use to interact with the ordinary world into deeper meditative states internally, it is possible to shift progressively from attending to ordinary world experiences into higher states of extra-sensory or nonordinary perception.

Through developing and increasing the capacity to hold power, shamans learn to move into the realm of imagery and far beyond, into energetic states of formlessness. Our ability to expand our perceptual awareness depends largely on our ability to comprehend and connect at different levels in the inner world.

Perception may range from only accepting consensual reality — a concrete world with discreet shapes and form — toward "seeing" in more fluid, energetic states. A gradual shift from physical form into an energetic state occurs, as movement is made further along the perceptual continuum. These levels of psychic engagement include: (1) the literal level, (2) the symbolic level, (3) the mythic or archetypal level, and (4) the essential or energetic level.

The *literal* level is the first level of psychic engagement, and refers to normal awareness, as it exists in the concrete world of everyday, out-in-the-world experience.

The second level of psychic engagement is the *symbolic* level, and is more comprehensive. This level is experienced through metaphor and dream imagery. It is the domain of symbols, imagination, and the realm where visions are crafted. When we enter the world of dreaming and fantasy, we are relating at the symbolic level.

The third level is the *mythic* or *archetypal* realm, existing outside of linear time, where synchronistic events are connected and there is energetic fluctuation in and out of manifestation. Carl Jung explored developing a relationship with the collective unconscious at the third level. This is the psychic realm in which the winged beings and mythic beings visited by shamans manifest.

The fourth level is the *essential* or *energetic* level of spirit or collectivity, which corresponds to the idea of a world soul. This level is often experienced as a state of ecstasy. It is the deepest level that shamans source from. In this writing, I refer to this level of nonordinary reality as the energetic collective.

Negotiability, Intention, and Shifting the Assemblage Point

The ability to facilitate the perceptual change into nonordinary reality depends on three variables: our negotiability, the focus of our intent, and our ability to shift the assemblage point in our luminous body. Each of these factors and their relationship to one another will be described next.

Negotiability

Our ability to make greater perceptual shifts between psychic levels of engagement is a function of how available and negotiable we are in the world. Over-thinking what we think we see and assuming that we already know what we see will keep us trapped in the experience of consensual reality. The statement, "don't confuse me with facts — I know what I know," illustrates this point.

If we slow down and take time to pay careful attention to our thoughts, we may learn that we have made fundamental assumptions that determine how we perceive and interact with the world. We can usually track the inception of these assumptions, which influence our thinking, back to our experiences at an early age. They usually started at a time when we were young and in the process of forming an internal cognitive map to make sense of our external world.

Frequently, as time has progressed, we have unknowingly come to accept these assumptions as being absolute truth and no longer question their validity. Upon closer examination, we may discover that we are operating from a system of beliefs that has little bearing on our present circumstances. Sometimes, these assumptions are projected onto others around us, and we draw conclusions that may not necessarily be true.

There is a story about a young woman cooking a roast that illustrates how assumptions can be erroneous. According to the story, a girl was getting ready to place a roast in the oven. Before placing the roast in a cooking dish, she cut off both ends without thinking, as she had always done. Her friend who happened to be watching her cook asked the girl why she cut off both of the ends. The girl replied to her friend, "This is the way my family has always done it. My mother and my grandmother always prepared roasts in this fashion, and now this is the way I do it." Later, the girl gave her friend's question more thought and realized that she really did not know the reason why the ends of the roast were cut. The girl went to see her grandmother and asked her grandmother why it was necessary to cut off the ends of a roast before cooking it. The grandmother laughed and replied, "It isn't! We only did that when our oven was too small to fit the roast inside of it any other way!"

The more open we are to cultivating a beginner's mind and willing see the world with fresh eyes, the more we will be able to experience what is actually going on around us. Many young artists struggle with becoming negotiable when they are learning representational painting. They are told to "paint what you see, not what you know." Learning to paint requires slowing down enough to observe what you are literally seeing.

Visually translating a three-dimensional form into a two-dimensional image on a canvas requires making adjustments. Color is no longer expressed as being absolute because it is directly affected by the surrounding atmospheric conditions (e.g. "whites of the eyes" are more often brown or blue rather than white), and the shape of an object is altered depending on the actual position (e.g., foreshortening). Eventually, artists learn to anticipate these alterations when approaching new subject matter, because they have formed a new set of assumptions based upon actual visual experience. Shamans also make modifications in the way they see the world and create a new set of conjectures that more closely matches their actual experience.

Body Centered Intention

When I was studying ceramics and learning how to center clay on a ceramics wheel, my instructor suggested I use a blindfold and stop relying on eyesight. This technique helped me to learn to feel when the clay was becoming centered with my hands. A similar example occurs in the epic movie *Star Wars*, when Obi-Wan tells Luke repeatedly to "feel the force."

As we develop the ability to move into deeper states of awareness by learning to direct our intention in our body, we learn to facilitate greater perceptual shifts into states of heightened awareness. Accessing greater states of heightened awareness using intent is a somatic process occurring in the body. It is not only a mental exercise. Active intent is a function of creative will, located in the Belly. Creative intent is a force with momentum that provides structure to creative vision. Combined together, intention and creativity form the vessel needed to contain and make it possible to achieve a shift into perceiving nonordinary reality. The stronger the focus of our intention, largely determined by our ability to be available and actually present, the greater our range of perception will be.

Shifting the Assemblage Point

In addition to the necessity of adopting a negotiable attitude and learning to focus intention, I have observed that loosely attending to current body sensation increases the capacity to shift into positions of heightened awareness in the luminous body. Carlos Castaneda described this phenomenon as "shifting the assemblage point." Entering into states of nonordinary perception requires sinking into a non-thinking state of somatic awareness. This change in perception is accomplished by dropping awareness deeper in the body, sensing through the Belly, and connecting energetically with the earth by feeling into it kinesthetically. When the assemblage point shifts, perception moves into the realm of nonordinary reality, the focus of experience transfers from discreet thoughts and images to somatic *energetic* experience.

Shifting the assemblage point is a function of the luminous body. Shamans acquire this skill through experience. While participating in an *ayahuasca* ceremony at the end of my first journey to Peru, I had an experience that illustrates this phenomenon. During the first stages of an *ayahuasca* journey, there is often a great deal of mental stimulation and activity. As someone who does not enjoy the increased brain activity associated with using hallucinogenic drugs, I was finding the increased neural action in my brain annoying, wanting it to end. Similar to diving under a large wave to avoid being pummeled while body surfing, I discovered that by shifting my attention state or awareness into my Belly, I could drop underneath the Mind experience and feel my way deeper into the energetic experience. Even though I was aware that my brain was still engaging full speed, I was able to drop into a calm centeredness, enabling me to connect energetically with the jungle around me by using the perceptual change of feeling it with my Belly instead of my brain.

Pacha 3: The First Journey to Peru

It is necessary to weave harmony between the Belly, Heart, and Mind. The universe will be more discernible if the Heart and Mind are in a harmonious state — 50% matter and 50% spirit. Westerners spend more time in their heads while in Peru people live more in their Hearts. There is a re-enactment that occurs in the experience of daily living in the modern world, fill the void through your Belly.

— Dona Alahandrina, *altomesayoq*, conversation 2011

I have heard both *altomesayoqs* and *pampamesayoqs* say that we attract to us whatever we have an affinity for, and that whatever we are carrying in our luminous body will manifest in our life. I have also heard the Q'ero say that the myth of the hero is a false myth — our lives unfold according to the *pacha* we are creating. Heroes assume positions that they defend with their lives. If we do not assume positions, we stop creating causes — and live reactionary lives. The causes we create need to be taken to the fire. I agree with the Q'ero shamans. Perhaps taking it to the fire is an aspect of the dismemberment initiation process that most shamans face in some form or another.

Many mystics and shamans have said when we decide to follow the call, time and the lessons we are given through life challenges begin to speed up. I don't pretend to know why things unfold in our lives as they do for each of us — or why we face what we face. My hunch is that we are here, living the lives we live, to learn something greater. Some of the *Apus* have said that they lived as humans at one time. Perhaps when we have learned what we came to learn as humans, we become part of a greater collective. This feels true to me but I can't be sure.

I realized some time ago, based on the life lessons I have faced since beginning the practice of shamanism, that my journey into shamanism has been a warrior's journey. It is not everyone's journey. Much of what has happened to me has felt beyond my control — or at least the control of my ego. Many of the events that have occurred in my life are not what I would have chosen consciously for my loved ones or myself. Most of the shamans (and some Jungian analysts) I know would say we can only heal the demons in others that we have wrestled with ourselves through a process of initiation and dismemberment. Facing the personal shadow is usually the first phase in any deep analytic work.

From the time I made the commitment to follow the path of shamanism, I have held the intention to face and act on what was required of me to continue on the shaman's spiritual course. It has often not been pretty or graceful. Sometimes this process has gotten down and dirty — and has frequently been frightening.

I realize that shamanism — like Jungian psychology — is not everyone's way of self-discovery. Some people seem to have an easier time staying grounded in their bodies and perhaps there are more gentle spiritual paths, although I do not really believe the latter is true. Personally, I believe no committed spiritual path is easy, and that we do not really have a choice as to whether we follow our spiritual calling — whatever our individual journey may be.

Is the path we follow determined by our nature? Do we choose it — or are we born with it? Current psychological research supports the premise that we are born with a particular temperament that influences how we encounter the world. My hunch is that our individual nature at least partially determines our destiny, and that what we experience often becomes intensified if we decide to follow the call of shamanism. My astrological chart is heavily weighted in fire and air signs, with little water and no earth — and my life path has been extreme and passionate. I came into this life as a warrior.

I am letting you know that I have followed a warrior's path — called *tupay* in shamanism — because I want you to know that my path may not be your path. A *tupay* is a warrior's way of resolving internal shadow conflict through challenging and initiating a ritual battle, and meeting both the positive and negative aspects of one's Self face to face. It is not the course every shaman follows. I am telling you this because I do not want to scare you as I tell you parts of my story. Your journey may be easier, if that is your nature — and perhaps your destiny.

Jung said that we carry archetypal motifs in our psyches. The personal myths of other people may be as Lovers, Sages, Tricksters, or Magicians — to name a few. Is this a self- fulfilling prophecy? Maybe, but the awareness that I have followed the path of a warrior did not come to me until I was looking back. With all this being said, I have not regretted following the call of shamanism, even if it has been down the warrior's path. I would make the same choice again.

After two years of lessons, I was finally ready to meet the mountain spirits in Peru. That brings us to the story of my third *pacha*.

13. The First Journey to Peru

In any transaction, in order to be in right relationship with a dream, with a universe, with God, or a vision, there's a process of healing. And after the healing takes place, there is transformation. And transformation is structural. And once you're done with that transformation part, that structural part, there's free flow. That's embodiment. And embodiment is not just your mind, like a piece of knowledge — you already know it.

— Don Alarijo, *pampamesayoq*, 2011

I landed in Lima airport with my son Colin, in June 2007. Perry had planned to accompany me on my first visit to Peru, but days before what *seemed* to be a potentially profitable opportunity developed, requiring his building skills and expertise. Perry elected to stay behind to work on the project. Colin, my sixteen-year-old son, was able to use the nonrefundable tickets and accompanied me instead. In Peru, I had a break from the dismemberment going on in my life at home.

The first part of the trip is a bit of a blur because I did not keep a record of it. As I try to remember, I have trouble recalling the actual events of the first landing — but the impressions remain clear to me.

Flying to Cusco, Peru, can be a long, tiring process — even though there is no time change. International flights land in Lima late in the evening and flights from Lima to Cusco do not depart

86

until 6 AM. Unless you decide to stay in a Lima hotel, you spend the night in the airport.

In recent trips, I have actually come to enjoy my late night ritual in the Lima airport. Waiting in the brightly lit ice cream and coffee shop, I sit in one of the red vinyl booths, spending my hours reading, writing, and reflecting, in preparation for the upcoming journey to the mountains. Sitting as close as I can next to the wall outlet where I can plug in my laptop, I drink my first cups of coca tea or strong Peruvian coffee — both of which I have also come to appreciate — although I have noticed I always feel physically better a couple of hours later if I choose the tea over the coffee.

The first trip was not comfortable. I recall becoming uneasy as soon as we stepped off the plane. Walking into the airport terminal, we immediately encountered all of the airport personnel wearing white sanitation protection masks. They nonchalantly greeted us in a welcoming manner as we entered the airport, and seemed somewhat oblivious to the fact that it might appear alarming that they were *all* wearing masks.

Apparently, a deadly virus had been spreading through Mexico and the Peruvian government felt it prudent to take extra precautionary measures. I remember I felt protective of my son. I insistently questioned employees about safety and where the masks were sold. I asked if we should be wearing masks as well, and they patiently explained that there was really no need. They reassured me that it was safe and that they were following a procedure. I cannot recall if we actually found masks or not — I think we probably did. Given the protective "Mama Bear" energy that had been kicked up in me, I doubt I would have settled for letting the mask situation go and trying to relax. I also vaguely recollect that Colin had not seemed particularly concerned with the situation, and, if anything, had been somewhat annoyed with me for being anxious and over-protective — and refusing to drop the safety issue.

A couple of years prior, when Colin had been caught in the jaws of his struggle with a dangerous addiction, I had taken him with me to India. I had hoped that spending extended, uninterrupted time together might somehow bring out a "reset" on the trajectory that had taken over our lives. In Calcutta, shortly after arriving at the airport, while waiting for the luggage, Colin disappeared. I found him outside drinking chai tea with the local street vendors — a practice that he continued throughout our travels. India is an amazing, but challenging country concerning cleanliness. Colin ate anything and everything — and never got sick. So far, Colin appeared to be adopting the same laid-back attitude on this trip.

As the night wore on, both of us became more tired — and slightly irritable. I remember that we both did our best to try to get along with each other as we attempted to sleep in the small, uncomfortable chairs outside of our departure gate. At about 5:30 AM bright lights promptly flipped on and finally at 6 AM the next morning, our flight to Cusco took off as scheduled.

I found my spirit also beginning to lift, looking out the window and seeing the beginning sunrise. The breathtaking view of the sun coming up over the Andes Mountains at dawn captured our attention, and we were suddenly wide-awake. By the time we landed in Cusco, the sanitation masks had disappeared and the mountains had entered the forefront of our minds.

June 6, 2007

Early morning in Cusco, even in July, is cold. My initial feeling while climbing down the steps of the plane, breathing in the brisk mountain air, and seeing the mountains surrounding us, reminded me of the way I felt when I first landed in Nepal years ago. I felt I

Figure 1: Dona Bernadina dancing

Figure 2: Dona Bernadina

Figure 3: Don Francisco

Figure 4: Adolpho

Figure 5: A shaman's mesa

Figure 6: Jose Luis and the altomesayoq Santiago creating a despacho

Figure 7: Perry's celestial despacho

Figure 8: Despacho for Pachamama

had come to a remote place in the world and sensed that I was beginning to leave the stressful challenges of my busy life behind.

As Colin and I walked into the terminal building, we responded to the sudden drop in air temperature by quickly pulling parkas and hats out of our duffle bags, and were ready to go. Almost immediately, we saw Eta, our travel coordinator, standing patiently at the gate waiting for us. She greeted us with her warm and friendly smile. I felt a sense of relief that we were where we were supposed to be and that it was now okay for me to relax. Meanwhile, Colin, who had been reasonably calm the entire time, was happy to be leaving the airport.

Cusco is a charming place, built on several hills. The older section of the town has a couple of large plazas with narrow, winding cobblestone streets leading in and out. The older, white stucco buildings have tile roofs and windows with wooden shutters that open out to the street. Although walking on the sidewalks can be tight, Cusco is generally an easy city to hike.

After dropping our bags off in our rooms, Colin and I returned to the lobby to schedule a coca leaf reading with Adriel, a shaman who was highly respected by other Q'ero shamans for his tracking abilities. As we sat drinking our coca tea, attempting to combat fatigue and acclimate to the increase in altitude (11,200 feet or 3400 meters), a woman with long blond hair and a big smile enthusiastically bounced into the room and ran over to give energetic hugs to people she had not seen for awhile. After exchanging greetings with a couple of other people standing nearby, she came over to us introduced herself as Julie.

Julie announced that she was heading for the shaman's market and I asked if Colin and I could tag along. She said, "Of course!" Minutes later Julie, Colin, and I had flagged down a street cab and were zipping down winding streets toward the market. Julie informed me that we would need to pick up a couple of *despacho* kits to prepare for the upcoming fire ceremonies, a bag of dried coca leaves to make *k'intus,* and a couple of bottles of Florida water[15] for cleansing rituals.

I learned that before beginning "the work" with the Q'ero shamans, it is customary to visit the shaman's market, also known as the "witch's market," to pick up the necessary materials. The process reminded me of picking up school supplies before meeting teachers on the first day of school.

After about ten minutes, our taxi ride ended as our cab pulled up next to the curb across the street from the market. Colin, Julie, and I climbed out of the cab and crossed the street to the market. The shaman's market is actually a long street with a series of neighboring vendors with small, indoor stalls, opening out on a sidewalk. The sidewalks are usually crowded and, during the day, it is a hubbub of local activity. Peruvian women dressed in traditional clothing made of dark wool with brightly colored embroidery, carrying large bags over their shoulders; marched by at a vigorous tempo. They intermittently stop quickly to inspect fruits and vegetables on sale, displayed by one of the street vendors lined up near the sidewalk. The sporadic sounds of traffic and busy commerce are often heard against the backdrop of someone standing on the side of the street playing a wooden flute. The produce smells fresh, and the cool air feels alive.

Prior to visiting Peru, I was warned to be careful wandering through the market because of pickpockets and sorcerers looking to "acquire psychic energy" from unsuspecting shoppers take advantage of the distractions. Maybe this is true, or perhaps this is

---

[15] Florida water is bottled, scented water with an alcohol base that is used for purification in rituals and ceremonies. Rose, lavender, patchouli, and naranja are other types of water less commonly used that each have unique properties with specific functions. For example, rose water elicits a Heart response, while naranja water is used for heavy clearing.

part of the allure of it being the "witch's market." I suspect both are partially correct. As I think about it today, after countless visits to the market with no mishaps, I have had contact with only one person, most likely a *bruja* (female witch), with a dark menacing stare and seemingly ill intent, who attempted to capture my gaze. In the split second I felt her gaze locking onto mine, intuitively I somehow knew to close my eyes — and did. With my eyes closed, I ask the spirits for protection, and the woman quickly disappeared into the crowd.

This encounter happened the day after I had returned from participating in *ayahuasca* ceremonies in the jungle. The field of my luminous body had been wide open and my spirit had not fully returned to my body — in retrospect, probably not the best time to be wandering around in public crowds anyway.

With a determined gait, Julie walked over to the stall that she said was her favorite. She explained to us that this vendor usually had the freshest coca leaves. Walking into the small stall, I was struck by how much there was to look at. Even though the space we were standing in was almost too small for the three of us to fit comfortably, I felt somewhat overwhelmed by everything I was seeing and trying to take in. Glass jars with seeds, shells, starfish, feathers, colorful candies, llama embryos, and amulets lined the wooden shelves against the walls from floor the ceiling. Whips, feathers, dried plants, and strings of seeds hung from the ceiling, with buckets filled with water holding fresh red and white cut carnations on the floor at the entrance. A small television that had been turned on was tucked away in a corner, close to the ceiling.

It took me more than a minute to notice the older Peruvian woman camouflaged behind the counter. As we exchanged friendly greetings in Spanish, the woman gave us a warm smile. I noticed that her teeth were very white. Julie politely inquired in Spanish whether the woman had celestial *despacho* kits and *despacho* kits for Pachamama. Julie explained to Colin and me that we would be making celestial *despachos* for the *Apus*, while the *despachos* for Pachamama would be given to Mother Earth (as described on page 98).

The woman sitting behind the counter reached up onto a shelf behind her and gathered several packages wrapped in butcher paper tied with string. In Spanish, she informed us which ones were the celestial *despachos* and which ones were for Pachamama. In addition to buying a couple of *despachos* each, we bought bottles of Florida water, as well as additional items that we planned to bring back with us to use in *despachos* we would make when we returned home. When we had our supplies, we went back to our hotel to wait for the trip to the Sacred Valley.

14. *Sacred Offerings:* Despachos

Whether we are creating the big celestial despacho *or the individual* despachos, *it's your time, your time to speak to God, speak to the mountains. Your faith and your intent and your Heart are very necessary in this transaction. And all of this that we are going to do is for our families; it's going to be for our health, for our bodies, for our journeys.*

— Adriel, *pampamesayoq*, 2011

The purpose of making a *despacho* is to establish a channel of communication with Pachamama and the *Apus*. Feeding the relationship with intent through open dialogue is more important than the actual size of the *despacho*. The practice of consistent ritual is what is important in maintaining the spirit connection. Many people practicing shamanism in North America form *ayllus* that meet monthly on the full moon to perform fire ceremonies with *despacho* offerings — or when they want to bring about change and create new vision. During my last visit to Peru with the shamans, we created over 30 *despachos* in ten days!

As mentioned previously, a *despacho* is a ceremonial offering given to the spirit world, usually either by placing it in fire or burying it in the earth. A *despacho* consists of three basic elements from the mineral, plant, and animal world. Because resonance and aroma are very important in attracting spirits in the Andes, *despachos* always include parts that bring sound and smells. Every *despacho* is offered with prayers that are said or sung aloud. After completing a *despacho* and blessing it with prayers, the shaman brings the *despacho* upright to the fire after wrapping it carefully in paper. In fire ceremony, the fire comes "alive" by calling the *Apus* and Pachamama through songs, sung as a group in sacred space with intent.

Before placing the *despacho* offering on the fire, it is customary for shamans individually to approach the fire to clean their *mesas* and energy centers.

Cleansing the energy centers occurs by making circular rotating movements with both hands clasped together directly over each of the three energy centers of the Belly, Heart, and Mind. Using intent, the shaman directs the fire into each of the three energy centers. First, cleansing and release by counter-clockwise movements open the three chakras. Next, balancing, the fire is pulled by reaching into the fire (but not touching it) and holding, packing each energy center with the fire's spirit energy, followed with filling and imprinting the centers with circular clockwise motions that close the chakras. Finally, the shaman holds the *mesa* over the fire for cleansing. At the end of the ceremony, the shaman places the *despacho* in the fire, turns his or her back, and walks away from the fire. The shaman does not look at the *despacho* after placing it on the fire to avoid reversing the effect. [16]

---

[16] In the fire ceremonies we participated in, Dona Bernadina and the other shamans watched over the fire after we had left, intermittently spraying the flames with rose water, reading the fire to insure that our *despachos* had been received and were burning properly.

Exercise 7: Fire Ceremony Purification Ritual

Starting with the Belly, hold both of your hands closely together and begin making a continual rotating movement in a counter-clock wise direction (moving from your upper left toward the right and around to the lower right and then toward the left). Next, visualize your Belly being opened and anything you have been carrying in your Belly being cleansed and released into the fire by making a forceful exhale using your breath and an outward thrusting motion with your hands into the fire. This set of actions is done to open the energy center and release *hucha*, or negative energy. While using your intention to open, cleanse, and release anything stored in your Belly, again ask the spirits for help. Repeat if necessary until it feels empty. Repeat this same process with the Heart and Mind centers.

Next, balancing, the second phase of the cleansing ritual begins. Again, using your intention, place your hands over each center in a way that represents balance, pulling the purifying energy from the fire and balancing each of your centers.

When you have completed the process of psychically balancing your energy centers, fill in and imprint the healing energy of the fire into each of your energy centers with intention. First, gather the fire energy toward you using your hands to make gathering motions, and then closing each center making the opposite motion you made to open the center, this time in a circular, clockwise direction (moving from the upper right toward left and from the lower left toward the right). Repeat if necessary until the center feels full. If you have brought a *mesa*, circle your *mesa* over the fire (holding it far enough away to be safe and not burn yourself), while looking up to the sky, and thanking Pachamama and the *Apus* for their guidance and assistance.

The actual physical *despacho* is a circular arrangement of coca leaves (bay leaves are used in the United States), resembling a mandala. The leaves are carefully separated into groups in three, creating *k'intus*. The *k'intus* are then often grouped in multiples of three to hold prayer offerings. These are embellished with grains, candy, and other colorful objects that symbolize gifts to the upper, lower, and middle worlds.

After *k'intus* have been created, the shamans transfer spiritual intent into the leaves using breath. Each group of leaves takes on a specific prayer (*saminchasqa*) or pattern (*phikhuy*) to be let go of and given to the fire. In addition to being a method of downloading a charge into *mesa* stones, the term *phikhuy* may also apply to the ritual act of blowing an intention three times into the leaves of a *k'intu* to release a pattern. *Saminchasqa* refers to the act of blowing prayers in order to establish an energetic connection linking the three worlds, known as a *sami* exchange.

The leaves surround a central symbolic object (most often a large, symmetrical seashell). The most important element in all *despachos* is the use of *k'intus*, because the spirits are called through the intention given to the leaves through prayer. The *k'intu* is made with the coca leaves facing up, stem down.

There are many different kinds of *despachos* depending on the intent of the ceremony and the shaman. Most *despachos* are sacred ceremonial offerings made to the *Apus* and Pachamama, such as the ones we would be making. Although some are for releasing *hucha* or negativity, and some are visionary *mesas* asking for blessings from the *Apus* before initiation ceremonies. Other *despachos* are prayers to the spirits asking for help in various aspects of life.

For example, *venta despachos* are used for going into business and creating relationships about services. This is one of the smallest *despachos*, and is created to serve as an amulet. *Venta despachos* are neither burned nor buried. They are kept at home or in a pocket. Sometimes *venta despachos* are made in conjunction with asking the *Apus* for assistance.

Kuti despachos are used for protection against psychic attack. According to the Q'ero shamans, if an energy bundle is prepared for the purpose of attack, the person who created it establishes an affinity with negativity. A *kuti despacho* resets and reflects back, stopping the momentum of the energy of the attack by returning it to the sender.

Most of the shamans I have worked with do not bother using *kuti despachos* because they believe service to Pachamama and the *Apus* provides natural protection — and they prefer to work with positive intent rather than negative intent. In all, there are about three hundred and sixty-five different types of *despachos* with a variety of specific ingredients created for special ceremonies, entities, etc.

In addition to different kinds of *despachos*, they are made in a variety of sizes. Some are very small, while others are very large. I have heard that when shamans are preparing to renew their rites as *altomesayoqs*, some of the *despachos* frequently take two weeks to prepare. Extravagant celestial *despachos* made as fire offerings are often created on tables made of plywood. These elaborate *despachos* are sometimes as large as 4 feet by 6 feet.

Celestial *despachos*, commonly created in preparation for an initiation, are comprised primarily of ingredients symbolic of the upper world used to attract vision and clarity (such as candles for illumination, cotton for clouds, gold and silver for transformation, and the sun and the moon respectively, thread to bring wholeness, and found condor feathers *never purchased as they are frequently taken directly from the birds!*).

The ingredients of *despachos* created for Pachamama, often for the purposes of positive manifestation and healing, include a variety of indigenous resources that are grown and come directly from Pachamama (such as seeds, grains, tobacco, clay substances, and llama fat to attract the spirits). For a more detailed explanation of the symbolism of each of these materials, please see Appendix A.

Despachos made in North America and other parts of the world will usually contain different components from the ones traditionally used in Peru. The components are indigenous to the areas in which the *despachos* are created. This is done to attract the spirits of the land in that particular location — and because obtaining and using coca leaves and llama fat would most likely be problematic. The qualities of each of the ingredients are activated and invoked through prayers.[17]

Figure 6 in the color section shows the preparation of a ceremonial *despacho*. Figure 7 and Figure 8 in the color section show completed *despachos*.

Exercise 8: Creating a *Despacho* to Pachamama and the *Apus*

Necessary Ingredients
Tissue gift-wrapping paper
Sugar cross in center
Bay leaves or tree leaves
A large seashell placed in the center
Candy (M & Ms, jellybeans, Gummy Bears, hard candy, or any other small colorful candies such as Easter candy may be used.)
Dried grains, rice, or beans (which may include peanuts, garbanzo beans, lima beans, quinoa, peas, almonds, etc.)
Rainbow-colored string or yarn
Cotton (cotton balls may be used)
Red and white carnations or other fresh flowers

---

[17] A special thanks to Julie Palmer and Stephen Alexander who generously shared notes with me.

Optional *Despacho* Ingredients
Crackers, sugar wafers, or cookies
*Masculine and feminine candy dolls
Alphabet or other noodles
Small birthday cake candle
Fig
Communion wafers
Gold and silver rods
Colored rods
Confetti
Gold and silver foil
Tobacco
Sage
Incense
Glitter
*Tin circle of symbolic archetypal manmade objects
*Mica dust (a shiny mineral)
*Magnetite dust (a black magnetic mineral)
Small colored pieces of paper
Any other dried plant or food
A small amount of red wine
*Ingredients found in Peru

Before beginning to make your *despacho*, you will need to gather the ingredients. After you have collected all of the items, begin the ritual of making your *despacho* by opening sacred space. Next, fold the tissue in four quadrants and form a cross between the quadrants with the sugar. Place the shell in the center of the cross. The llama fat (if you happen to be using llama fat), masculine and feminine candy dolls, and one or two of the flowers are placed inside of the shell. If you are using mica and magnetite, set them in the shell as well, followed by the tin circle with the objects. Next, create *k'intus* with the leaves in groups of threes by using intention and blowing prayers into each of them. Place each of the *k'intus* around the shell creating a circular mandala, resembling a flower with pedals. Position the rest of the flowers around the shell, on top of the *k'intus* and the other ingredients.

For the next step always begin by placing things that come from the earth such as grains, rice, or beans on the bottom, representing the lower world of Uhu Pacha. Next, manufactured, synthetic items such as paper, confetti, and candy should be distributed around the shell, representing the middle world, called Kay Pacha. Candy should be placed in the shell as well. Add incense in each of the four directions. Now, pull apart the cotton, manipulate it into a large flat shape, and place it on top of the *despacho*. The items of the upper world are put on top of the clouds. Items such as glitter, silver and gold foil, candles, and string, symbolize Hanaq Pacha, the upper world and the sky. Finally, a large round cracker is put on top of everything, representing unification and wholeness. If you have decided to add wine, sprinkle a small amount in the shell and over the entire *despacho*. By the time you have gotten to this point, the shell is buried under about four layers!

When you are ready, carefully fold the edges of tissue paper together first right to left, followed by bottom to top. When you have created a package, tie it together with string to hold it in place. You may want to add a flower or two in the bow for decoration. Always keep your *despacho* facing upright.

The *despacho* you create is a work of art that should smell nice and be visually pleasing to attract the spirits. Your *despacho* is ready to be given as an offering to the fire, or buried in the earth. Many people make it a practice to create *despachos* on a new moon or full moon, or on the eve of the summer and winter solstice.

15. Sacred Valley

We have a long journey ahead of us, our lives will provide other venues of learning, of challenge, of interaction — but with the medicine of Q'ollorit'i, the vision, the estrella, *the guiding star, and the presence of all these* Apus, *you'll be successful.*

— Don Andre, *pampamesayoq*, 2011

June 7, 2007

We visited Machu Picchu, accompanied by the shaman Adriel who often works as a tour guide on the side to support his family. After wandering around the stones of the ancient ruins, we sat down at a grassy point on top of the mountain, opening our *mesas* to begin ceremony. I sat cross-legged in front of my *mesa* stones that I had organized in the familiar circular arrangement on top of my *mestana* cloth, which was laid on the grass. I looked out over the expansive mountain view that stretched on for miles. Inca shamans have gazed upon these same mountains for centuries.

I felt myself beginning to shift into an altered state as I felt into the energetic field of the land surrounding me. I began seeing a field of light energy superimposed on top of the mountain view. I became sleepy, and my eyes began to lose focus and gradually close. As I relaxed deeper into the trance state that was coming upon me, the particles of energy became brighter and more vivid

Figure 1: Early morning view near Macho Picchu

and the sharp outline of the mountain silhouette began to fade into a haze in the background.

I began to feel surges of energy moving through my body and I felt myself falling into a vision:

> *I saw an old woman weaving a web of light from the mountaintops to my mesa and me. As I began experiencing the connection I saw an opening emerging and knew it was the entrance to the upper and lower worlds. I felt a black jaguar at my side.*

I felt energized as the ceremony ended and my vision cleared. I returned to my present reality and opened my eyes. My son Colin had been sitting and talking with Steve, another member of our group who, like Julie, had begun to take Colin under his wing. He was patiently answering Colin's questions about urban shamanism sparked by a book he had been reading.

The group gathered and it was time to begin the arduous hike to the Temple of the Moon.

The hike to the temple of the moon consisted of a vigorous walk up and down a steep mountain path. This hike was perhaps not as challenging or as long as some of the pilgrimages to sacred mountains in later visits, but it definitely was the most strenuous exercise at high altitude I had experienced in a while. I began to focus on my breath, repeating the chant in my mind, "Pachamama, carry me, carry me." I used my intention to feel Pachamama's strength and support coming up through the ground into the soles of my feet as I tried to keep up. Like young mountain lions, Julie and Colin raced on ahead, waiting patiently for me to catch up at various intervals. I learned that Julie taught art in high school and she seemed to be taking a special interest in Colin. I was pleased to observe that Colin was bonding to her as well.

When we arrived, the two *pampamesayoqs*, Adriel and Don Sebastian, who had gone on ahead, greeted us with smiles. They were preparing a space inside one of the caves to create a *despacho*. After we had sat with our open *mesas* thanking Pachamama for her love and assistance, we entered the cool, dark cave and silently began preparing our own *k'intus* to add to the *despacho*. When the *despacho* was complete, we silently made our way back up and down the mountain. After leaving Machu Picchu, we boarded a train back to Cusco.

The next morning, bright and early, we climbed on a bus with Jose Luis and made our way to the Sacred Valley where our work with the consortium of Q'ero shamans began. A couple of hours later, our bus descended down the road entering the Sacred Valley, which was surrounded on all sides by the snow-capped peaks of the majestic sacred mountains. We drove through the quaint village of Urubamba and continued down the two-lane highway passing farmland and homes. Soon after, the bus turned into a driveway surrounded by a stucco wall and came into a pleasing landscape of bright flowers, stopping at the largest building in a compound of one story buildings with tile roofs, which was the reception area of the place we would be staying. Courtyards connected a series of small cottages. The shamans, Adolpho, Adriel, Dona Bernadina, Don Francisco, and his son, Juanito, greeted each of us with warm smiles and affectionate hugs, asking each of us how we were. In her usual friendly demeanor, Eta gave us room assignments and keys. We quickly found our rooms, dropped off our duffle bags, grabbed our jackets and *mesas*, and headed for the church nearby.

Jose Luis had gathered *pampamesayoqs* and *altomesayoqs* from all over the Q'ero nation to speak to us and work with us over the next several days. When we entered the church I felt mystified — and in awe. I was moved to tears and I did not exactly know why. I saw a group of about eight or nine inconspicuous, neatly groomed Peruvian men and woman standing in the front of the church conversing among themselves. I looked at them and experienced an overwhelming sense of love. I remember feeling safe and wanting to connect with them. Jose Luis formally introduced each of them individually by telling us their names, where they were from, and each of their respective "job descriptions."

Shamans and shamanas are addressed as Don and Dona respectively. The shamans that had been introduced as Don Sebastian and Don Francisco were dressed in traditional Q'ero clothing, which is what they have worn each time I have seen them. Traditional Q'ero clothing for men consists of beaded hats that hang over the ears, sandals, dark wool shorts, and a brightly colored and embroidered outer garment, usually with a sweater underneath — regardless of the temperature. In colder temperatures, beautiful hand-woven ponchos are usually worn as an outer garment. As usual, Adriel was wearing a western shirt, trousers, and leather shoes. Adriel, is also about five feet tall but slender, with a handsome, long, narrow face with a mustache. I often see him laughing as well.

The traditional costumes Q'ero women wear consist of sandals, dark wool stockings under gathered dark blue or black wool skirts, embroidered jackets, and colorful hats with large rims. Their long, shiny black hair is usually in two braids, either hanging down their backs or worn up under their large hats. Like Dona Bernadina, they carried their *mesas* in large cloths carryalls that they slung over their shoulders.

Over the years, my feeling of being wowed by the Q'ero shamans has settled into healthy respect. The shamans I have come to know are playful and love to joke when they are not involved in their work as shamans. The quality in each of them that stands out most is their big Heart — and intense love for Pachamama.

After introductions were made, Jose Luis announced that it was time for dinner. I looked over at Colin and Julie, who was sitting next to me, and we smiled at each other. I was excited about what lay ahead of us over the course of the next week. We gathered our belongings and headed to the dining area. As we entered the room, Julie introduced me to Dona Bernadina, a tiny Peruvian woman with quick, bright eyes who was wearing traditional clothing. After greeting us with a big smile and a warm handshake, she grabbed Julie's hand and began dancing with her to the flute music that was playing. I watched them waltz around the room together for several minutes as I found a table for us to sit and eat.

After dinner, Colin and I met in the lobby with Adriel for the coca readings we had arranged earlier that day. Without knowing anything about me, in broken English, Adriel told me that Perry had "problems with consciousness," and that he was "regaining health," and was of "importance to the spirit world." He told me that in two to three years I would be "writing a book blending shamanism and western medicine." Adriel told Colin what he would most likely be doing over the course of the next couple of years.

Our readings ended and it was time to meet for fire ceremony, which became a nightly ritual during our time in Peru. Fire ceremonies are held for many reasons. First, they are a way of honoring Pachamama and the mountain spirits through songs and *despacho* prayer offerings. In addition, they are a means of gathering as an *ayllu* or community, and serve as a vehicle for personal cleansing through ritual. The fire ceremony is a process of purification. The phrase "taking it to the fire" refers to the purification of releasing old patterns and beliefs into the fire by creating a fire offering such as a *despacho*. The procedure of creating a fire ceremony is described below.

Exercise 9: Conducting a Sacred Fire Ceremony

The Q'ero shamans say never to come to a fire ceremony empty-handed. They frequently start by creating a *despacho* for Pachamama and the *Apus* to bring to the fire. You may also bring a food offering or flowers if a *despacho* has not been prepared. Find a location, preferably in nature that is suitable for a fire, and gather the wood and other materials needed to start and maintain the fire. Before beginning the actual process of building the fire, remember to open sacred space, asking the *Apus* and Pachamama for their presence and assistance.

After the fire is burning, shamans often blow a spray of flower essences with Florida water or rose water over the flames to purify and prepare the fire for the ceremony. The use of flower water is not essential. What is most important is that your purpose is clear and well intended. A fire ceremony is a sacred ritual. It should always be conducted holding the mindset of honoring the spirits, and/or healing.

If you have brought a rattle, begin to shake it in the rhythm of the songs you will sing, calling each of the spirits by name. Singing songs to the spirits helps a fire to become friendly. A song sung by Q'ero shamans is provided below, with the phonetic pronunciation directly underneath (In this verse of the song, the *Apu* Ausangate is called):

Ausangate muraya kumu paisita kaya
Aus-an-got- ay — mura — yaku — mupa — sita — kayah
Sisay puntay mariri
See-sigh — pun- tie — mar-ree-ree
Kayay puntay mariri
Kai-ake — pun-tie — mar-ree-ree

After calling each of the spirits by name and having the fire burning well, approach the fire with the offering you have brought, placing it on top of your *mesa* (if you have one). Set the offering and your *mesa* gently on the ground next to you, so that you will have your hands free. Now it is time for the ritual of clearing each of your energy centers, the Belly, Heart, and Mind (Please see Exercise 7 on page 95). There are three basic actions in fire clearing rituals[18] — releasing, balancing, and imprinting. *Llank'ay* (will or intention), *munay* (unconditional love), and *yanai* (vision) will be imprinted into your luminous body through intent by using words or imagining this taking place in your Mind's eye — and asking the spirits for their help. In larger groups, it is customary for four people to approach a fire at a time, from each of the four directions.

---

[18] This same ritual for clearing energy centers may also be performed using water instead of fire.

Finally, place your offering or *despacho* on the fire, blowing prayers of thanks into the offering, and walk away. After placing a *despacho* on a fire, it is customary to turn away from the fire and not look back, to avoid undoing the prayers you have made.

After, the fire ceremony we returned to our rooms and retired for the evening. That night I had the following dream:

> *The black jaguar told me he was my ally. I felt a lot of love. He said he would go into an area of blackness with me and blast it with light with his intention. He told me not to hide and that it was okay to face what was coming at me.*

The Shamans

June 8, 2007

The next morning we met in a large meeting area and listened to the stories of how the shamans came to be shamans and to the other speakers that Jose Luis had invited. Jose Luis served as the translator through all of these sessions and introduced each of the speakers individually. The *pampamesayoq* Dona Alexandrina Escalante has served as a consultant in hospitals and an adviser to the president of Peru. Dona Maria, who was about 70 years old at the time, was the only female *altomesayoq* to join us. The young, crossed-eyed *altomesayoq* Adolpho Tito was introduced as the *altomesayoq* who would be calling the collective spirits of the *Apus*, the winged beings, into manifestation later during ceremony. He told his story of how he became an *altomesayoq*. Dona Bernadina Katari, a *pampamesayoq* originally from Lake Titicaca, was formally introduced as a master with plants and soul retrieval. Professor Carmona, the Dean of Anthropology at the University of Cusco, was joining the group to provide a history of the Inca civilization. Don Francisco Alpasa, who had brought his son

Juanito, was introduced as the president of Kuna, the Q'ero Nation, consisting of six villages surrounding the Sacred Valley.

First, Don Francisco told us about the Q'ero Nation. There are 130 people in the Q'ero nation, with about two thousand people in the area. He explained that the Q'ero nation consisted of five farming communities, the main crops being corn and potatoes. Part of the Q'ero nation land borders the Amazon jungle. Because of a new regulation in Peru, the Q'ero have reclaimed some of their land, which will become an ecological preserve. Q'ero have one schoolteacher, in Munaypata, who provides education up to the fourth grade. There are no roads, electricity, or running water. Don Francisco said that it is a "good day and a half hike" to the nearest medical post, which is only open on weekdays.[19]

Next, the *altomesayoq*, Dona Maria Apasa Achaka, from the village of Kico, began speaking. She said,

> The mountains and the *Santa Tierras* of this land have called you. This is your land and our land. We all live on the belly of the mother. We just need to create a new dialog of return. We come from many places but we all belong to the same place. There are many spirits throughout the world. I would love to meet your spirits. With the grace of the *Apus*, we are here.
>
> There is a need to create new places. It is not just personal power but who is going to hold it for the collective. We must work for the collective, not just the personal healing. All we have to do in our dialogs, in our ceremonies is ask for assistance. The *Apus* have always been there, they will be there after us. Ask for the Pachamama, the *Santa Tierras* to

---

[19] Part of the proceeds of this book will be given to aid the people of the Q'ero nation and *Pachamama*. If you would like to contribute an additional donation to the Q'ero people, please contact the address in the back of this book for more information.

hold you. *Calpi* is to retain, to receive. It rearranges your medicine body, rewires you. All you have to do is open up. Be available. The spirit of the feminine, the different expressions of fertility, the Goddess, the *Nusta*, Pachamama are constantly feeding us so that we can be creators. It is when that connection is broken that we get sick.

There is the domain of the heavens, the stars, that organizes time. We can be blinded only seeing the past. We need to see what is taking place. You must build a direct relationship with the land. You must not invest the personal into the collective. An *altomesayoq* is a person who is absolutely claimed by the land. You must map the land, those features where spirit is present. Spirit is connected to these places of power through *ceke* lines.

(The *Apus*) are spirits that belong to the land and there are those spirits that belong to higher realms of consciousness that know the future. Some of the *Apus* have been human. Those people that were of great power and service may choose to come back as a hill or mountain at passing and continue to be of service. Everything is in the process of evolution, even the *Apus*.

It is the affinity of power and service that the *altomesayoq* attracts. You can honor the *Apus* with your breath and an open Heart. Open Heart is not just a happy place. It is being in full disclosure. Be in your body and connected. Shape shift into the place. Merge your body with the body of the place.

Mountains are repositories of information, the human drama, and the human expression. They are also repositories of expressions of nature. A seed that was planted a century ago and has grown is the collective of the mountain. They contain the seed of our destiny.

If you want to tap into a particular lineage, you need to find which mountain holds that lineage. Each mountain is a different mini-collective but at the *kollana*, essential level, it is all the same. It is the application over time that differs.

The land where you were born is imprinted in your luminous body. You journey through the land and develop a medicine body. When the presence of nature makes its mark on your medicine body, it means the land is holding you. As a medicine person there comes a time when your *mesa* peaks and you move past the personal. When you are assigned a guardian spirit from the land, this guardian is called *sayaq*. It is the mountain that watches over you. A guardian benefactor for you that defends you, that claims you. An *Apu* takes bullets for you.

Every place has a spirit. Every place has a spirit benefactor that is in charge of the well-being of the land. The director of the *mesa* has the ability to channel those spirits. The spirits of the land are the same everywhere; it is the manifestation that is different due to the ruling cosmology. In North America, the spirits leave you gifts; they leave footprints. They may talk to you in a different way. In Peru, it is a tradition of dialog.

Q'ollorit'i was originally a *huaca* (place) dedicated to the well-being, fertility, and creation of animals and seeds. Human needs then showed up. During the time of the Inca, human need was not scarcity. They had plenty. Scarcity was foreign. The Spanish came with scarcity and greed. As time passed, they went to Q'ollorit'i to heal their woundedness. Some *p'aqos* have said that Q'ollorit'i has changed its job description and has taken on so much human woundedness and scarcity that the *huaca* dedicated to fertility may move to an undisclosed place.

After Dona Maria Apasa Achaka finished speaking, she sat down and the *altomesayoq* Adolpho told us his personal journey of becoming an *altomesayoq*:

I began this journey by being an assistant to an *altomesayoq*, called a *winayu* (why-nee-u). The mountain spirits told me that becoming a *winayu* is a process of maturation, of growing a medicine body. I started as a *winayu*. I didn't know anything. It has become apparent to me that a pool resided in me — love for the mountains.

I was so impressed with the capacity of my mentor to love and embrace the mountains and *Santa Tierras* he would bring to his *mesa*. That first mentor had doubts about my ability. Luckily, for me, I was still accepted. I was blind at that time. I did not see reality. It was a process of uncovering my blindfolds. I released my family and followed him wherever he went. I got scared and thought it would be difficult. He told me you must have a strong heart to talk to the spirits. Over the years, I realized I was not prepared. The speed at which my mentor took me, that was probably the best learning.

What was becoming very evident to me is that I am learning to create meaning from the experience. You must have the experience to create meaning. You cannot create the meaning before the experience. It has been very difficult. The first stage was my own clearing and purification. The cleaner I was, the more the angels looked at me. My mentor took me to his *mesa* and I met his director and second director. The female director of that *mesa* is Santa Tierra Avanti. All these beings sitting at the *mesa* started calling all these different *Apus*, angels. The director of that *mesa* was able to call different spirits from where I was born. They liked my presence and told me to release anything that would distract me from this work.

Ausangate told me, since we were going to be working together, that I needed to call on him on Tuesdays and Fridays. Ausangate said there is a body of knowledge to learn and that I had seven months to learn it and that I would be tested in seven months. I was given difficult tasks. One was to prepare *despachos*. Another was to serve my mentor faithfully. So I began traveling with my mentor to remote villages and met many people. We did many healings and services.

The first three months of this journey was very sweet and soft but on the third month the *Apus* changed and tested me. It became difficult. On the third month, I was told to recite a prayer I had been given, but I could not. I was then told to prepare a *despacho* in total darkness with them watching. I did not do well. They told me I had a week and if I did not do well, things would change. The day came. There were many people who needed healings from me, but I froze. The result was harsh and they severely beat me. Penance is not to cause pain but to clear sin. This was a clearing for possibly fear or lack of focus. The way my ceremonial beating took place, it was a baptism. They were welcoming me. I had to go past any pain that may come to me. I became busy because my mentor was sending me all over the place, and I did not have any time to do my own work. That is part of it; you have to be everywhere at once. So that was just the tip of the iceberg. That was when the real beating began. I carried so much inside me about who and what I was. So much to release that sometimes I needed the ceremonial beating. It was very tough. I learned to write in the dark and prepare *despachos* in the dark. At the end of the year, I was tested.

I was invited to Waquay Wilka to see if I would receive something. I had to learn through routine, through repetition. My mentor said that after a long process of training, I was looking ready and I was taken to Waquay Wilka. So before going to the holy mountain I had to prepare a few *despachos* to show that I could depict landscapes of healing. But when it came to the prayer part, I failed again. I had to prepare a *hucha despacho* to undo a force of nature but I failed to do it. Much later, I was told there would be another opportunity. On this day, all the *Apus* showed up. Things shifted around. Things turned upside down. The *Apus* addressed my mentor and told him he was not teaching me well. An *altomesayoq* can give two to three *mesas* in their lifetime because they are giving away part of their power so it takes careful selection.

I realized my affinity was not for Ausangate, that that had been the voice of my ego. I found that a mountain from my home called to me, and wanted to be my benefactor. A lot of time had passed. Four years had gone by and they felt I was ready for the *karpays*. There was my evolution and my studies and my mentor thought I was ready for the rite of passage. Sadly, my mentor did not want to give away part of his power in my receiving the rites so he put more tests before me. One of the tests I was given was the *halpi*. That became tedious to me because I thought it was about homecoming and feeding each other. This took me into learning the *halpi* of the right side of the *mesa* and the left side. The left side has to do with protection and the unknown. I had to learn the *halpi* of the Southern Cross. Once I learned the map of the Southern Cross and bringing the Southern Cross to villages, I had to learn my own body.

Another venue of challenges was that I had to take *despachos* to remote places. My mentor said perhaps by going alone to those remote places, the *Apus* would smile on me and I would receive a *mesa*. If that happens, face east, get on your knees, do your *k'intus*, and see what happens. I think it was my love for the *Apus* that helped me make it through the challenges. I came to a place where I really wanted it, but couldn't, and my mentor would not take me to the mountain. I had a vision of a mentor in Bolivia, but I was broke and could not travel. I felt there might be another chance.

The day came when my mentor showed up and he recognized the markings in my luminous body that I was prepared. I had been six years in training. In that *mesa*, I was asked to get a condor's egg and that was out of the question. Then I was told to get a pigeon's egg and I couldn't find one, so I ended up with a chicken's egg. I was told to go to Waquay Wilka to a lagoon. I was told to be present at 7:00 PM. It was a large *despacho* for the Pachamama and the *Apus*. Also, we had to depict the *cocha*, the waters that would give me birth. There had to be three mountains depicted in the *despacho*. I had to have three fetuses, the unborn, one llama, and two alpaca. All in all, there were about seventy items in this *despacho*. I was poor. I didn't have a large entourage. I had a few mortals who decided to come with me.

We arrived at noontime. My mentor took me to the lagoon, and dunked me in the water. I was baptized in freezing cold water and I knew I could die. But I was okay. That was my initiation from my mentor. I was dunked three times, and on the third time, I had to wait for the *Apus*. While in the water, they laid out *mestanas* filled with flowers and *k'intus*. When I got out of the water, four men with ponchos welcomed me. It's a birthing process.

When I came out of the water, they smoked me to cleanse and clear me. My mentor smudged me with smoke. Then my mentor looked at me and said I am giving you my power and it was an act of love because I knew he was dying for me. There were many tears. They were not supposed to look at me so they looked down. The whole afternoon was spent on the *despacho*. I changed clothes again. The humongous *despacho* made me understand the nature of my own soul. I was different. It has been a long process of learning.

Dusk was descending, and it was time for the evening meal. Adolpho told us that he would finish telling us his story the next day. By the end of the day, Colin had become bored sitting and listening to long lectures and told me so. He said he was going to spend the next day in our room talking with his girlfriend whom he was missing, using the phone card he had been able to acquire.

June 9, 2007

As promised, the next morning Adolpho continued telling us his story of becoming an *altomesayoq*.

I was afraid but we had some alcohol. The secret is to drink the first drop of liquid from the bottles with this. I had little shavings of meteorite and a white rock. The ceremonial part of the *altomesayoq* is done mentor to student. This is the first part. The second and most important part is done spirit to human. You cannot receive the full *altomesayoq* rites from a person.

My mentor told me, "Take the *mesa*, go down the mountain, and don't look back." Q'ollorit'i decides which spirit will become the director of a *mesa*. I knew not to show up empty-handed because there is always an exchange.

The high mountain rites were to be held on *Apu* Waquay Wilka. The rites of passage at Waquay Wilka usually take place in August. There is a trail from the back of the ridge to the glacier. You prepare a *despacho* while the *p'aqos* prepare *despachos* to weave conduits to this place. On the mountain, there are no "plan Bs." It is communing with the mountain or not. You must weave your medicine body into the mountain. What is it that is important to you?

With the *karpay despacho*, you create new pathways so you have direct assistance. You are no longer solo. Through the dialog of your *mesa* and your *despacho*, you commune with a mountain that is in charge of giving the *karpays*. Go beyond fear, woundedness, and stories. Go into the collective. Let the consciousness that resides in this mountain live inside your *mesa*. This is a *tupay*. Disclosing yourself to your bare bones, beyond that which separates you from the rest of the personal. The future will show up. We want to exercise these gifts. Anchor them into your *mesa*. With time, you will create meaning. You will go through processes. Right now, we do not have the framework. You must create meaning. There are five lineages that reside in this mountain. They each have a job description. These rites are the high mountain rites. The rites of the lineages of the *p'aqos* who are giving them. With ceremony, you will germinate these seeds.

When Adolpho had finished speaking, he sat down next to Don Sebastian and Jose Luis introduced Dona Paula as the next speaker. Jose Luis said,

Dona Paula has two mountain lion paws in her *mesa*, and works with two bells. These bells bring Illapa, the spirit of thunder. Dona Paula's knowledge comes from oral traditions. For thirty-two years, she has worked with *despachos*, herbs, etc. She uses the mountain lion paws as a last step after prayers, *despachos*, etc. She uses them to rub the people. With prayers, she rubs from the head down to the feet and she feels it leaving. Then she blows it out. Her training and experience is an inheritance. When her mother was pregnant, she was struck by lightning. When she was thirty-two years old, a woman brought a bottle of rum to her home and asked for a coca reading. Dona Paula told her she didn't know how but the woman was convinced she could. The woman was sick and said she needed the reading. This is when she uncovered her gift. She gave the reading and the woman left. A neighbor then came to her for healing. She didn't know about medicinal herbs but she followed her heart, bought, mixed them, and healed the lady.

Dona Paula then added:

I work with *despachos* for love, for the *Santa Tierras*, for the *Apus*. I have made *despachos* to help with very old negative spirits living outside in farm areas. When the spirit attacks, first it attacks the legs. It is not something someone sends you, it is a living energy. It catches you by the legs, a bad energy that touches your leg. If you do a nice *despacho* with special elements, it will leave the person and they will be healed. Sometimes the people don't believe in this energy and it is hard to work with the person. It is important in how hard you pray. It is how strong your power is. Through *despachos*, you can do many things. Through *despachos*, you ask for assistance.

The speakers continued describing their work with plants and healing. A female shaman described her process of performing soul retrieval. I noticed that her approach seemed to be more focused on the concrete steps of the ritual versus an energetic exchange of connection. Little did I know that during this trip, both Colin and I would each have our own experiences with this process.

Colin's Soul Retrieval

June 10, 2007

At 6 AM, I awoke to a rapid knock on the exterior door to our rooms. I was concerned, not knowing who would be knocking on the door at this hour. I jumped up and quickly opened the door, wearing my flannel pajamas and sweatshirt, and was surprised to find Dona Bernadina standing outside with a serious expression on her face. I noticed that she was, as usual, fully dressed in her traditional clothing, carrying her large medicine bundle over her shoulder. She looked at me and announced (in Spanish), "I am here to see your son Colin." I invited her in and motioned that I would get Colin. I leaned in to the bedroom and announced to Colin, that Dona Bernadina had come to see him. Colin, who had also been sound asleep, woke up and said in a strong whisper, "Mom I didn't ask for this." I gently advised Colin that it would be rude to refuse a visit from Dona Bernadina and that it was an honor that she had come to see him. (Soul retrievals are usually conducted at sunrise.)

Colin was slowly starting to get out of bed as Dona Bernadina entered the room. I noticed that she had opened her medicine bundle and was now carrying a cloth whip and a chili pepper in her hand. I was aware that drug use often opens the energetic field, leaving it undefended, and, somehow, I understood that Dona Bernadina had come to perform a soul retrieval to help Colin. Intuitively, I trusted her and although Colin (who has never been a morning person) seemed mildly disgruntled with being woken up, I knew that he felt comfortable with her as well.

Dona Bernadina asked Colin to lie down on the bed and then she had placed the chili pepper over his heart. After calling upon Pachamama, she began burning the same sticks of myrrh incense that are used in creating *despachos*. In a small bowl, she added cinnamon, sugar, cloves, and moved it three times over Colin's body in the four directions of east, west, north, and south. She then swept a lit candle about 18 inches above his actual physical body, over the entire length of Colin's body making repeated motions. On the table next to the bed, Dona Bernadina placed red and white carnations and a dish of holy water. She than began to repeatedly call Colin's name, whistling in between. This was followed by repeatedly hitting the floor in a pathway between the bed where Colin was lying and the door, apparently to clear away any uninvited guests. She then said another prayer to Pachamama in Spanish, gathered the chili pepper that she had placed on Colin's chest, repacked her medicine bag, threw the bag over her shoulder, and quickly left the room. Colin reported feeling more relaxed and wanted to go back to sleep — which he did. I left the room, now dressed in blue jeans, hiking boots, and a sweater, and headed toward the breakfast area.

Adolpho's Reading

That morning, I met the *altomesayoq* Adolpho for an individual reading. As usual, Adolpho was dressed in western clothing, in a button-down shirt, sweater, and dark slacks, wearing a leather sombrero on his head. He has well-defined features with high cheekbones, and like many *altomesayoqs,* is cross-eyed — the result of being struck by lightning during his major initiation. He greeted me quietly in a reserved manner and motioned for me to sit down in front of him. He spoke slowly, using hand gestures so that I would be able to understand what he was saying to me.

Adolpho described an angel lighting my path, and I felt a rush of energy opening my Heart as I listened to his words. He told me that I would be writing a book about the spirit world and that it would be important for me to harmonize what I am learning with what I am experiencing. Adolpho said Perry would gradually become better over time, and not to worry. He advised me to focus on my own spiritual path instead. Adolpho used his hands to motion that my "anima," or spirit, was very large when I was in Peru but that it became smaller at home. He told me that I was connected to the *Apus* and needed to make an *Apu despacho* when I returned home, to strengthen my relationship with the Rocky Mountains.

At the end of the reading, Adolpho opened my *mesa* and placed a starfish in the center of the stones. He blew into the top of my head. As I felt my head beginning to tingle, he gave me three *k'intus* of coca leaves and instructed me to drink them in tea in 30 minutes. The reading was finished and we left for lunch.

Fertility Ceremony

Later that day, the shamans went with us to Moray, a large natural clearing in a crater near the town of Maras, to conduct a fertility ceremony. The general public believes Moray was an Incan agricultural laboratory. For shamans, it a major *waka*, or "power spot," and a place where ceremonies in honor of Pachamama are held.

As we walked around the circular ring of the large crater, the afternoon sun was setting and it grew colder. We could hear a breeze whistling through the tall grass surrounding the exterior rim, and the wind began to grow gradually stronger. Huddled in ponchos, together we made a large *despacho* offering for Pachamama. Next, the shamans prepared an area for the upcoming fire ceremony for our *despachos*, while the rest of us dispersed around the area, spending time by ourselves in dialogue with our *mesas*. I found a spot and comfortably nestled into the soft earth behind a large rock that blocked me from the wind. I was grateful to feel the heat of the sun still radiating off the rock's surface. I felt myself shift into an altered state, and the following images came to me:

I felt myself being pulled into the earth and was buried. I felt myself becoming dirt and saw an old woman I had seen in other vision states sitting cross-legged in front of a bowl with an "umbilical cord" of light going up into the sky and down deep into the earth. I realized I was seeing an aspect of Pachamama. I felt beings of light working energetically on my body. I felt an upward pull on my heart three times and felt myself shaking.

As I returned to my outer awareness from my vision state, I heard the shamans calling, telling us that the fire was now ready for ceremony. Something about this scene, seeing the shamans working together in ritual against the backdrop of Pachamama touched me and I felt tears coming to my eyes. These rituals had been performed years ago by the ancestors. (They are believed to be our ancestors as well since we share the same lineage.) I approached the group and Dona Bernadina flashed me her warm, beautiful smile and motioned for me to stand next to her. I felt humbled to be part of this sacred process and honored to be in the presence of these amazing people.

June 11, 2007

Today was a busy day. Early in the morning, as the sun was rising, our *ayllu* boarded a bus and headed with the shamans to the base of Waquay Wilka for the *karpay* ceremony, the initiation during which Adolpho and the *pampamesayoqs* would pass their ancient lineage to each of us from their *mesas* into our *mesas*. A couple of hours later, after climbing up winding mountain roads, we reached our destination. As I left the bus, I noticed that we had stopped in a flat area surrounded by several mountains. I saw a condor flying above and heard the shamans say that this was a good omen.

The midday sun approached its peak as we stood quietly in a circle, calling sacred space and listening to the shamans offering their prayers to Pachamama. I heard each of the shamans thanking her and asking for her blessing. As I listened to them speaking their native Quechua language, I was once again struck by the love expressed in their voices. Adolpho began the ceremony, followed by Don Sebastian, Don Francisco, and Dona Bernadina. I watched Don Sebastian raise a bell in the air, ringing it in each of the four directions, while asking the spirits to come, and thanking them. I could only pick out the meaning of a few of the words, but their implication was clear. They were paying tribute and conveying their devotion and life commitment to the spirits they served. I felt my Heart expanding in response to their message. The *kausay* behind the words was powerful and no literal translation was needed.

After each of the shamans gave prayers, the members of the *ayllu* stood respectfully in front of one of the four shamans giving the rites. I waited silently for Dona Bernadina, hearing the intention in her tone. She approached me and motioned for me to hold my *mesa* bundle next to my Heart. Then she lightly pounded her *mesa* on top of my head as I knelt down to receive her blessing, followed by thumping her *mesa* against my Heart, and then my Belly. Finally, Dona Bernadina motioned for me to extend my *mesa* out about six inches away from my body and she firmly tapped her *mesa* on top of my *mesa* three times, as the stream of words she was uttering continued. I felt a surge of tingling energy move through me, and the process ended.

I found a sunny spot by myself on the side of the mountain, above where the ceremony had taken place, and I opened my *mesa* to begin recapitulating and integrating into my conscious awareness and luminous body the lineage that Dona Bernadina had given me. As I sat in silence in front of my open *mesa,* feeling the energy moving through my body, I held the intent to remain open to the experience and thanked Pachamama.

After some time had passed, I came back down the mountain and sat next to Dona Bernadina, waiting for the *ayllu* to return. Dona Bernadina smoothed out a patch of ground in front of her and picked up a handful of dried llama droppings that had been lying nearby. She tossed the droppings in the area she had cleared and carefully inspected how they had landed. In Spanish, she asked if I wanted to hear what she saw. I agreed and asked her if she could tell me how I could help Perry and Colin.

Dona Bernadina said that Colin would be fine and that his luck was changing. She shook her head as she looked at the llama droppings and a concerned look passed over her face. She said that Perry had been shocked as a little boy and made a buzzing sound through her teeth. He needed to call on Pachamama and that I should help. There was a lot of stuff going on at our house and it needed to be cleared. She told me that I needed to work with the Birdman, that he was the one that gave me spoken language.

Several hundred yards away, the *ayllu* was gathering and preparing to leave. We made our way back down the mountain to the bus and headed for lunch.

16. Meeting the *Apus and* Santa Tierras

You are a living embodiment of ancestral memory. It is necessary to explore that primordial identity. To find out where core energy resides that feeds the soul. Blood, culture, and karma are the three ingredients that make up lineage. We need to identify the history of our lineage. We need to create a new paradigm of fulfillment, joy.
— Dona Alahandrina, *altomesayoq*, 2011

After lunch, we gathered warm coats, hats, and scarves — along with our *mesas* — and headed by bus to Moray to meet the *Apu* who is the director of Adolpho's *mesa*. Moray is a small village about an hour drive into the hills above the Sacred Valley. This would be my first actual meeting with the *Apu* spirits and I was not sure what to expect. I felt nervous anticipation.

Adolpho quietly greeted each of us as we stepped into the courtyard from the street. We were asked to remove all metal objects, including coins and jewelry — as well as cell phones and watches, which are known to interfere with the *Apu's* ability to come through. I have heard stories of cell phones and watches actually being "fried" by the electrical current given off by the presence of the *Apus*. Not removing these objects is a sign of serious disrespect. We entered a small, dark, rectangular room, containing a large table at the head, which served as an altar, and wooden benches that had been arranged in rows in the formation of church pews. As our eyes adjusted to the darkness, we brought our *mesas* to the front of the room to be placed in a row on the altar. I noticed that sealed glass bottles of soda pop lined the back wall and fresh bouquets of flowers had been placed in vases and were arranged symmetrically toward the middle of the table. I saw that Adolpho's *mesa*, containing several large, rough crystals, lay open in the middle. Candles were lit on either side. I noticed a small bench in the upper right corner of the room, which was the customary seat of the *altomesayoq* who was leading the ceremony.

After we had placed each of our *mesa* bundles on the table, we quickly found seats as close together on the benches as possible, toward the front of the room. Blankets were tacked along the sides of the door, and the room was double-checked to make sure that it would be pitch black after the door was closed. Jose Luis explained that it was customary to greet the *Apus* by saying *Ave Maria Purisima* upon their arrival. Adolpho blew the candle out and we sat quietly in the cold, dark room waiting for the ceremony to begin.

I noticed I continued to feel slightly anxious and hoped that Colin was not becoming freaked out by all of this. Hours before, I had asked Julie to persuade Colin to leave the room where we were staying and he had agreed (even though later he told me not to ask Julie to try to recruit him to attend ceremonies because he could not say "no" to her). I wondered if my decision to bring him had been the right one. I could feel his shoulder next to mine and heard him breathing evenly.

Prior to arriving in Moray, Julie had "briefed" us on what to expect. She had told us that *Apu* spirits assume a male form, and that their arrival is announced by the sound of wings flapping. The *Santa Tierras* are the feminine spirits that come up from the earth through the floor. Their entry into the ceremony is usually accompanied by feeling a gush of air from the floor in the front of the room, if you happen to be sitting in the front row. She said that the voices of the male spirits were unmistakably masculine while the voices of the *Santa Tierras* have a high pitch. Apparently, mountain spirits usually communicate in both Quechua and Spanish. This is a reflection of the cultural paradigm of the *altomesayoqs* who are in contact with them.

As we sat in silence, I heard Adolpho quietly reciting prayers at a rapid pace in Quechua, followed by a long, slow whistle. A couple of minutes later, I suddenly felt a breeze coming from the direction of the wall I was leaning against and heard the loud sound of flapping wings. Heavy pounding that was presumably taking place across the front of the table followed. Next, a loud bellowing masculine voice, greeted us in Quechua. We quickly replied with the greeting, "Ave Maria Purisima," as Jose Luis had instructed us.

Next, I heard a clicking sound, which I later learned were two of the large *kuyas* crystals in Adolpho's *mesa* rubbing together. This is the method the *Apu*, who is the director of the *altomesayoq's mesa*, uses to call other *Apus* into the ceremony. Sitting in the room, the crystals make clicking noises, which often occurs intermittently throughout the ceremony. Occasionally, I have seen the crystals light up as they come in contact with each other. I heard more thuds and sets of flapping wings and new voices entering into the room as the *ayllu* greeted each of the *Apus*. I heard voices with both high and low pitches speaking. Adolpho explained that these particular *Apus* were the collective entities or composite spirits of the sacred mountains surrounding us.

I heard Jose Luis introducing Señor Ausangate whom we greeted in the same manner as we had the other *Apus*. In ceremony, it is customary to address the *Apu* spirits with the title "Señor." Later, after the ceremony had ended, Jose Luis explained that the mountain of Ausangate was considered one of the holiest mountains in Peru, and most evolved of the collective mountain

Apu spirits. Jose Luis said that when Ausangate visited us, we were being visited by an aspect of the mountain collective, similar to how in Christianity Christ is not God but an aspect of God. After the *Apu* spirits had arrived, members of the group were encouraged to ask questions that would help us to understand ways of serving Pachamama and the collective.

As the exchange continued, and the immediate shock began to settle (slightly) for me, I found myself becoming increasingly distracted. My mind was trying to come up with explanations of what was actually happening. I reasoned that the room was kept dark so that we would not be able to see that Adolpho was a ventriloquist who had a wide range of pitch. I thought maybe one of the other shamans sitting in the back had somehow created the sound of the wings flapping — although it did not explain the location of sounds coming from the wall up above. Yet another part of my brain questioned why a group of shamans would go to this much trouble to try to make us believe that spirits were flying through walls, if they were not.

Intellectually, I struggled to wrap my brain around what had just taken place. No sane person would actually believe that mountain spirits fly through walls and speak. My supervisors in graduate training would have diagnosed me as having delusions. What had just happened? Then, unexpectedly, I heard the sounds of bottle tops popping and felt a mist of soda pop in the air, and the ceremony was over.

Before ever coming to Peru, my Jungian analyst had asked me if I could define the intention of my trip, and after pondering for a minute or two, I had replied, "to find out if the realm of nonordinary reality actually exists." I got my answer.

Looking back now, I do not remember when I came to believe that *Apus* actually were manifesting, but I do remember how. My sense now, looking back, was that the tipping point for me didn't actually occur until my second trip to Peru, during an initiation when I experienced firsthand an intense download of energy from the mountain Alancoma, described in Chapter 20. As a general rule, what I experience in my physical body has always seemed the most real to me.

Over the years, as my relationships with the shamans became stronger, I realized that fabricating the presence of *Apu* spirits was completely incongruent with who the shamans were as human beings. Although the concepts I had been exposed to were beyond the outer limits of anything I had ever experienced in the past, and — in addition to what I had physically experienced during a waking state — I eventually came to realize that what appeared to be happening was most likely true. I have always trusted my intuitive ability to read people — and if the shamans were inauthentic, I would have felt it.

As my understanding of their deep connection and commitment to Pachamama had grown, I gradually settled into accepting things as they were. After the ceremony with the *Apus*, I did not push Colin to talk about what we had witnessed. I sensed that it was best not to interfere with his process. I decided that he needed the opportunity to leave what he had seen on the shelf — indefinitely if need be. I have come to believe that we accept our reality as we are ready, and pushing another person before they are ready is never helpful.

That evening after the ceremony with the *Apus*, we had our final ceremony as a group and said good-bye.

Pacha 4. Reentry

In order for our societies to change, a new paradigm needs to be created. Nature is in process of deconstructing itself to be reconstructed. It's a process. This new cultural paradigm is out of personal choice. Need to erase ideas of good or evil — that is a concept that only lives in the Hearts of people. We have polarized our understanding of love. A new alignment is needed with a spiritual paradigm. We then begin again.

— *Apu* Señor Chauipicaro,
ceremony through Juanito's *mesa* 2011

The people I have talked with from Western culture who have entered into the energetic realm of nonordinary reality have all agreed with me on one thing — reentry and ego reintegration is a difficult and painful process in the early initiatory phase of becoming a shaman. The way we perceive our world becomes fundamentally altered when we move back and forth through the veil between ordinary and nonordinary reality.

Carlos Castaneda said, "When a man learns to *see,* not a single thing he knows prevails. Not a single one… Once we *see,* nothing is known; nothing remains the way we used to know it when we didn't *see*" (*A Separate Reality*, p. 235). We may feel confused when we realize that what we had assumed about our world no longer feels true.

131

My first major intense initiatory experience in Peru occurred during my final phase of training to become a Jungian analyst. Before my initiation experience, I had relied heavily on Jung's work as a primary source for understanding dream symbols and visions.

I had often heard Jungian analysts comment that the explanations of all theories of human experience are found underneath the framework of the Jungian umbrella. I had also heard it said that Castaneda's writing was symbolic metaphor. I now disagree with both statements based upon my own reentry experience.

When I returned from Peru in a state of confusion after the initiation, I was disappointed — and alarmed — to discover that Jung's theory did not correspond to the kinds of preverbal experiences I was having. Jung focused on using symbolic imagery as a method of synthesizing archetypal experience, which was not particularly helpful in my initial reentry state. I was trying to manage the intense waves of energy that were flooding through me. I was feeling overwhelmed and disconnected from my life and everyone around me.

I could stay present in my work with my clients — which were the only encounters that actually felt real to me. At the time, Perry and I were separated and I was living in the middle of the city without a yard. Engaging in casual conversations felt like idle chatter and deciding what kind of pancakes to order in a restaurant seemed completely irrelevant.

17. Back Home

The actual responsibility that is taken on in the Mosoq Karpay *rites is one of co-creation — sourcing from the mother through the reactivation of memory and creating maps through culture. This is the responsibility you embrace. The metaphor of mother awakens within you — pivotal energy of the mother that anchors from the Belly into the land. It is a reactivation of the memory of returning to where we always return — remembrance of timeless memory of this planet.*

— *Apu* Huascaran,
Dona Alahandrina's *mesa*, 2011

As I was returning from my first visit to Peru, I learned that even stranger and more disturbing things had begun happening at home. The day I was leaving Peru, I received the most upsetting piece of news while standing in the lobby of a hotel in Cusco, using a public phone. When I called Perry to inform him of my travel arrangements, he sounded shaken. He began the phone conversation by telling me that a couple of nights before he had dreamt he was wrestling with a Chinese knife master all night, and that when he awoke in the morning the bed sheets were actually split down the center. He said that in the morning when he had gone outside, he discovered that the 30-foot Austrian pine tree sitting in our front yard had turned brown and died during the night. After that evening, Perry said he found himself dropping into a very dark state. The next night, he had heard a voice continually instructing him to kill himself. At one point during the night, he had found himself lying on the couch — still half-asleep — with the barrel of a gun in his mouth. Fortunately, Perry had managed to come to his senses. He had locked the gun in a gun safe that morning. Perry said he had not been feeling suicidal, and that something had been trying to kill him. Intuitively I sensed that what he was saying was right. In the midst of all of the turmoil we had experienced during the last couple of years, Perry had never given any indication of feeling suicidal or of being paranoid.

When Perry told me what had happened, I did not know what to think. If nothing else had led up to this event, I most likely would have concluded that he was having a psychotic break. When I later consulted with Jeff, our analyst, who was familiar with mysticism and nonordinary reality, he said Perry was facing something dangerous in the other realm that was trying to harm him. Perry needed to call on protection to defend himself.

Jeff told both Perry and me that often when people begin to acquire power, they encounter energy-hungry beings from the other side. At the time, this conversation had seemed a bit fantastic, but unexplainable events continued to occur. One evening shortly after returning home from work, I decided to perform a ritualistic house cleaning using sage, calling on the spirits I had begun working with in the inner world. I walked slowly through the house, room by room, calling on the light and asking any presence that was not drawn to the light to leave. I continually called upon the spirits I had met in Peru for protection.

During this process, I had not felt afraid, but energized by the positive presence I was sourcing from. About an hour later, shortly after going upstairs to retire for the evening, Perry and I heard a loud crash in the kitchen area. When we raced downstairs to see what had happened, we found that our circular Plexiglas kitchen table (which had not previously had any cracks or objects sitting on it) had split in two, and folded inside the table frame in two pieces. There was no logical explanation for this occurrence.

Other unexplainable things followed the event with the splitting table. At various times our TV, which we rarely watched, began turning on and off — without anyone touching it. We noticed dark soot beginning to form on the wall behind Perry's side of the bed, directly behind his head. The "soot" also began to build up along the windows and on the fan above the bed. Occasionally the bedroom door would also open and close for no apparent reason. In the basement, we noticed for the first time that the baseboard wood behind the bottom stair had split away, leaving a large gap.

Related to this, I had a nightmare that a dark fire substance came up through the floor and grabbed Hannah, our pet Labrador retriever and pulled her away. Hannah, incidentally, escaped with our other dogs out of our backyard gate a couple of months later and permanently disappeared. The other dogs returned, but we found no sign of Hannah, even after days of looking. As our dogs, even the two that were about two years old at the time, began growing white hair on their muzzles, I became increasingly alarmed.

Something definitely needed to be done, but I was not exactly sure what. Since moving again was not a financially viable option, I was in a desperate state. I contacted a woman in Pennsylvania whose name I was given by a friend I had met in Peru, who specialized in long-distance energy clearing. She checked our situation intuitively and agreed to help us clear the negative energy surrounding the house. About a week later, we arranged for a session the next Saturday afternoon and were instructed to leave with our pet animals.

Minutes before the session was starting, Perry ran back in the house looking for me, not realizing that I was already waiting in the car. The time to be out of the house for the scheduled clearing started while Perry was still in the house. When Perry joined us, he was visibly upset.

After getting in the car and driving away, Perry described his experience. He had run up the stairs, leaping three steps at a time trying to find me, thinking I was still in the house. On the way up the stairs, he heard the bedroom door slam closed. After racing to the top of the stairs — assuming that I had been the one to close the door, he bolted down the hall to our bedroom, As Perry was running to our bedroom, the carpet in the middle of the hallway bunched up, causing Perry to trip and fall hard, face first. Perry said he had felt a bit dazed — and shocked — but had jumped up and had pushed open the bedroom door.

No one was there. Instead, a filmy blue haze was spreading throughout the room. Perry felt the wind blowing through the windows as a thunderstorm began to build outside. Perry went on to explain how he had run back down the stairs, out the door into the backyard to the garage, still looking for me. He then saw a lightning bolt strike the alley behind the house. Perry had opened the garage door to see if I was inside, and pinched his fingers when he slammed the door down. When he finally made it to the front yard, he found me there waiting for him.

After the energetic house clearing, the unexplained disturbances went away, and we went back to dealing with the other set of ongoing circumstances we were facing in the day world. As a psychologist and, more importantly, as his wife. I had known for a while that Perry and I were in serious trouble — both in how leveraged we were becoming with the growing debt of Perry's real estate endeavors (based upon his unilateral decision-making process), and with how Perry's ongoing psychological condition was affecting our relationship. I was scared and angry that my life was being turned upside down. Most people whom Perry encountered initially thought he was brilliant and then eventually assumed he was crazy — and distanced themselves from him. Perry did often sound crazy. Jeff said Perry was not crazy but rather was in a constant state of vision. Jeff said Perry was in the midst of a spiritual experience that medication or a hospitalization would not help — it would only make it worse because what he was going through was not pathological.

Of course, other friends and professional colleagues disagreed with Jeff. While grasping desperately for a solution, I convinced Perry to undergo an evaluation for psychotropic medication. Perry, who has no affinity for Western medicine, never believed he would benefit from medication. He went to make me happy. He actually began to take the prescribed medication but stopped after a couple of months when there were no noticeable changes in his condition.

Today, I still try to make sense of what actually happened — although as time continues to pass I struggle less. I now agree with Jeff's interpretation. Yet, even though I am aware that Perry was in the midst of a life-altering visionary experience, I would not wish what we went through together on anybody. Although I would still have made the decision to work with the black snake, I do not feel the exhilaration some people feel after completing a strenuous ropes course. What we went through caused destruction and turmoil in our day world. Perhaps the Q'ero shamans were right. Is the hero's journey *really* necessary? I want to believe in happy endings.

The psychologist part of me believes that Perry's manic behavior was a compensatory reaction to the severe trauma he had experienced as a child. What I experienced firsthand reaffirmed my belief in the need for veils between realities — as defenses in trauma — and as protection against being flooded by intense archetypal energy.

18. Moving through the Veils

Collective doesn't necessarily mean that it's your group of people, or your family, or your country. It doesn't mean that you need to understand how they live and deal with each story — draw conclusions of all the common denominators of everyone, no. Collective means living a life in which you're no longer your own person, but you are collective. You are the land; you are the people.

— Dona Alahandrina, *altomesayoq*, 2011

As the result of two synchronistic events in the summer of 2008, veil symbolism suddenly became very important to me. During this particular time of our life, Perry and I spent every possible weekend camping in a remote desert spot we had discovered by accident. In this secluded place, we felt as if we had entered into a liminal zone between ordinary and nonordinary reality, and had the sense that we had gone back 100 million years in time, into the dinosaur era.

Perhaps, it seems a bit odd that we were compelled to return to such an out-of-the-way place almost every weekend. The drive took eight hours and the mid-day sun could become extremely oppressive — over 100 degrees in desiccating heat. Yet, the area felt incredibly powerful and mystical for both of us. I wonder now if the allure of the desert was because it had become the only place

Figure 2: Perry's Digging

where it was possible for us to slow our rapidly spinning world down.

As I remember being there, I am struck by how overpowering the soundlessness of it was. Sometimes intense heat can become soothing because it slows everything down and it intensifies silence — at least for me.

The summer we spent in the desert was the summer when we were both actively building our *mesas*. Perry had discovered hills of sand speckled with gastroliths, rocks from the gastrointestinal tracts of dinosaurs that aided their digestion. We were both drawn to the biomorphic shapes and smoothly polished patina of the rocks.[20] Before or after the severe midday sun we spent hours

---

[20] Larry, the archeologist from University of Denver, verified that the rocks actually were gastroliths.

collecting stones. During the hours of heat we explored in the shade of slot canyons. I spent hours reading in the shady solitude of the tent — drifting in and out of dreamy states.

One weekend, Perry had become unusually captivated by the activity of an "archeological dig." He had stumbled upon what appeared to him to be prehistoric bones, and had been working alone, digging for several hours. Meanwhile, after the customary gastrolith hunt, I had returned to the secluded shade of the tent and had fallen into my own state of reverie.

I had recently developed an interest in the Qabbalah, and had begun reading Gareth Knight's book, *A Practical Guide to Qabbalistic Symbolism*. In this particular book, Knight explores the concepts of the tree of life and the veils of negative existence. In the Qabbalah, these veils symbolize the separation between existence and nonexistence, or what is manifested from what is unmanifested.

Knight (1978) wrote:

> A veil is something you can see through but dimly, if at all, so one must not expect to come to an easy understanding of the concept of negative existence. It is veiled from understanding because our understanding is part and parcel of positive existence. But it is by no means entirely futile to try to come to some understanding. Some dim glimmering can be obtained. If one likes to try the experiment one might obtain some realization by watching crystals materializing out of a saturated solution as it cools. Alternately, one could visualize a spider's web, symbolizing the Unmanifest mind of God, upon which dew begins to form from the atmosphere in shimmering crystal globes until it is a radiant network of light. In such a manner might these worlds have formed (p. 28).

I was intrigued by the concept of the veil, and curious about how it might correspond to states of reality and shamanic experience. The construct of the veil had given me an image to work with, and I suddenly became very excited by the onslaught of new ideas being generated in my mind.

I immediately went to share them with Perry, who was still actively absorbed in his project of digging and sorting dirt into various piles. As I crouched down beside him in the large indentation he had carved out in the side of a hill, Perry announced with authority that he was "in the veil."

In response to my puzzled expression, Perry informed me that being in the veil is a common phrase used by archeologists to describe the practice of intuitively sifting through dirt to locate remnants of ancient bones. Because the differences between dirt and bones are very subtle and almost imperceptible, it requires dropping into an intuitive, meditative state and relying on a felt sense — outside the perimeter of the ordinary five senses. While in the veil, the filtering process requires the archeologist to feel into the earth using touch because the visual variations are so slight.

I curiously observed Perry's movements as he persistently, but patiently, scratched away the dirt from the side of the mountain using his hands. I watched him gently placing piles of what still appeared to me to be dirt carefully to the side. He seemed to be acutely aware of discreet differences in the piles he was arranging, while I remained unable to detect the faint variations that he adamantly claimed were there.

I could not see any of the differences in the patches of dirt that he was earnestly trying to point out to me, yet to him these variations were apparent. Although nothing seemed out of the ordinary to my naked eye, I became very excited about the idea of the veil — and by what seemed to be a meaningful coincidence.

I was struck by the realization that when I am in the desert, I often have the feeling of being in my own kind of veil — a subliminal realm where things are not quite what they seem. To me, it felt like a heightened awareness, something ephemeral that can only be noticed as a fleeting afterimage in the corner of the eye. Had both Perry and I inadvertently fallen into our own versions of a cosmic veil? Were we both in the midst of it, traveling through it in our own way?

Crossing over into the veil that lies between ordinary and nonordinary states of consciousness is a visit to another realm. The veil is ephemeral, appearing in plain sight in one moment, and then suddenly disappearing. It lies in the shadows just beyond our reach, ultimately unattainable in normal states of awareness. The veil can be ephemeral at times, yet thick, opaque, and impenetrable at others. It can cast a spell on those who enter it — similar to falling asleep in the poppy fields on the way to the Emerald City — or bring brilliant insights through connection. Being in the veil can feel oddly comfortable and relaxing like flopping into an over-sized easy chair.

The veil remains an enigma. Once outside of it in ordinary time we may strain our minds trying to remember what it feels like, and may continue searching for it like the Holy Grail, even after it has become a faint memory. Then suddenly, out of nowhere, a doorway to reenter the veil suddenly appears and it can feel that we never left it — the entrance was right beside us all along. Finding our way back into the veil can also feel like reconnecting with the long-lost home that we have spent our lives searching for without knowing it, that we discover again in dreams when we have finally forgotten to look for it.

These vacillations take place because the veil is living energy. It is vital and essential for consciousness to exist because it provides containment. Yet, like the unconscious, it is unknowable, infinite, and alien.

What makes traveling through the veils difficult is not the actual numinous experience — most people describe numinous experience as a state of ecstasy, feeling they are one with the universe. The actual pain occurs in the experience of transitioning into and out of the warp speed of numinous experience. Shifting *between* states of connectivity and separation, through the veil between nonordinary and ordinary reality, can feel like a death and rebirth process. In this writing, I refer to the transition into nonordinary reality as dismemberment, and the transition back to ordinary reality as reentry. After my first trip to Peru I put together these thoughts to help me understand what was happening to me.

The Veils of Negative Existence and the Qabbalah Creation Myth

One of the functions of the veil between the energetic realm and ego conscious is that it fosters the initial separation that babies experience at birth as they leave the symbiotic state of being part of their mothers. This separation is necessary for healthy ego formation and developing a sense of who we are in the world. These early childhood experiences can be traced back farther still, before the symbiotic state, before birth, before the time when our soul comes into our bodies, and before our souls were formed — back to a state, which Qabbalah mystics refer to as unmanifestation.[21]

In Sanskrit, the word for this condition is *Prabhavapyaya*. It is the beginning and the end, the place or plane everything originates from and into which everything returns and is

---

[21] I am introducing Qabbalistic references because they provide a helpful framework of differentiating the veils of manifestation at the essential energetic level.

resolved.[22] The Unmanifest is also understood as God or the Creator or infinity. It is a state of undifferentiation, before and after opposites exists and separation has occurred. This state exists at the essential level described in Chapter 12.

According to the Qabbalists, the Unmanifest is separated by the Manifest, in the three stages or Veils of Negative Existence. Through the Veils of Negative Existence, the universe manifests into being. The reality described by the concepts of the Veils of Negative Existence cannot be fully understood through experience in ordinary reality because these realms exist outside of human experience and ego consciousness. That is why they are described as veils. Symbolically, the Veils of Negative Existence are associated with a predawn period, or period of primordial darkness before light actually came into being.[23]

The First Veil

According to the Qabbalah, the first veil or manifestation is called AIN, meaning Negativity. Metaphorically, it is represented as a ring that defines space and is responsible for the creation of the whole cosmos. It is symbolized by a circle, and is the container or vessel that holds the force of creative potential. Verses two to five of Genesis read, "And the Earth was without form, and void: and darkness was upon the face of the deep. And the spirit of God moved upon the face of the waters. And God said, 'Let there be light,' and there was light. And God saw the light, that it was good: and God divided the light from the darkness." This passage in Genesis is a description of the first veil. It is an aspect of premanifestation at the energetic collective level.

---

[22] Blavatsky, *The Secret Doctrine*, Vol. I
[23] Hall, M. P. (2003)

The Second Veil

According to the Qabbalah, the creation of AIN left a vacuum, causing the second veil, AIN SOPH, to come into existence. The second veil, also called the "ring of chaos," is symbolized as a second ring counter-balancing the first ring. The manifestation of the principle of the second veil is the action of dismemberment. In Hinduism the god, Shiva, represents this relationship. The relationship between the first veil and the second veil in nature is development (First Veil) and decomposition (Second Veil) occurring simultaneously. This dynamic is particularly apparent in areas such as the rainforests of the Amazon jungle, where there is vegetation everywhere — growing and decaying all at the same time — even on the same plant.

The Third Veil

The third veil is called AIN SOPH AUR. It is the "Ring-Pass-Not," which transcribes a sphere of limitation for all future development and a place of equilibrium. Symbolically, this represents the process of integration, or union of opposites, which Jung named the "transcendent function." The universe comes into being through the union of the masculine and feminine principles, at inception. It is the point at which a soul physically incarnates into a body or, in alchemy, when spirit becomes matter. In Christianity, this is the Trinity and the emergence of the Holy Spirit. The third veil symbolizes the state of wholeness and completion.

So how does the concept of the Veils of Negative Existence apply to our everyday life? The emergence of the initial separation through the veils into conscious awareness creates the capacity for self-reflection. One way to understand consciousness is that it represents the capacity to reflect back upon one's self. Psychologists who study attachment believe that human beings have a basic need for mirroring, to see reflections of ourselves in others to understand what is going on in the world around us. Experiencing the process of mirroring through interacting with our mothers as young infants enables us to begin to see ourselves as being separate from others. These early childhood experiences contribute in later years to developing the capacity for mentation — the ability to "think about our thinking."

As we go the other direction, moving toward earlier stages of psychic development,[24] deeper into the unconscious psyche into the primal, preverbal states we experienced when we were very young, the lines of separation between others and ourselves blur and disappear.

The Dismemberment Process of Separation between the Ego and the Unconscious

There are three major types of human development that involve a process of dismemberment. The first two parts are the extroverted process of forming and developing a healthy, functioning ego at birth and then again during adolescence. The third type of dismemberment is the introverted process required if the commitment to follow the shaman's spiritual path is made. The third type of dismemberment is the first stage of the initiation process many shamans face. This phase occurs after a sturdy ego has already been developed, and is now being surrendered in service to Pachamama or another representation of a force much greater than we are. Both dismemberment as a function of ego development and dismemberment as a means of developing an energetic connection with the numinous in nonordinary reality will now be explored.

---

[24] Fordham has pointed out that actual stages do not exist but they are useful constructs that provide a framework. Michael Fordham (1961), "Neumann and Childhood," *Journal of Analytical Psychology*, 26:99-122.

The Dismemberment Process in Ego Formation and Child Development

The first type of psychological dismemberment facilitates the development of an ego in early life. At birth, the ego is a "bodily ego," experiencing the world through physical sensation as a function of being in a symbiotic relationship with the mother. Through touch, the baby physically experiences being one with the mother. The infant experiences feelings, thoughts, and sensory perception, but does not recognize them as its own. In this state, the infant lacks the capacity for self-reflection and does not distinguish physical or psychological space between its self and others.

In the first year of life, the infant begins to form a discrete sense of having its own body, as an individual human being.[25] During this period, there is continued movement away from being psychologically fused with the mother — both in behavior and in conscious attitude — toward becoming one's own person. In becoming separate, the infant gives up the sense of having omnipotent control and becomes consciously aware of needing its mother (or primary caregiver).[26]

The myth of Bacchus is a metaphor that describes this process of moving from the unconscious state of no separation into an awareness of having individual ego consciousness through the dismemberment process of separation. According to the Bacchus rite, the Titans tore Bacchus apart when he became distracted and fascinated by his own mirrored reflection. In his initial state of oneness, Bacchus was in a state of self-knowledge. Gazing into the mirror caused Bacchus to fall into the experience of illusion, the

---

[25] Thomas H. Ogden (1989), "On the Concept of an Autistic-Contiguous Position," *International Journal of Psycho-Analysis,* 70:127-40.

[26] A special thanks to Jungian analyst Mark Winborn for his input and clarification of current ego development research.

lower world created by the Titans. Seeing his own image sparked the urge to be like his source and develop into a separate being of his own. The Titans then dismembered Bacchus through different processes. They ripped his body apart, dissolved it in water, burned it in fire, and devoured it, leaving only his essence, contained in his heart. Pallas rescued his heart, which enabled Bacchus to be born again and experience.

The second type of dismemberment strengthens the young, developing ego during adolescence. After developing the ability to experience being a separate entity in the world (as Bacchus did after his dismemberment process with the Titans), the ego requires an opportunity to prove itself to build confidence in being able to function in the world. In this second type of dismemberment, as a function of ego development, the ego becomes sturdier by learning how to survive in the world of ordinary reality, through a process sometimes referred to as a hero's journey.

The transformation of the ego through a hero's journey comes from rites of passage that mark a coming of age. The youth of some indigenous tribes that practice shamanism are required to participate in initiation rituals marking their transition from childhood into adulthood. In ceremonies, they are required to pass from the ordinary realms into the sacred through a process representing death and rebirth.[27]

In the West, children read fairytales about slaying dragons, symbolizing this psychological process of dismemberment. Yet, an issue youths in our current culture face is the loss of actually experiencing rites of passage marking their entrance into adulthood. These kinds of dismemberment experiences are a necessary stage of ego development, needed to form a hearty constitution to live life in the world.

---

[27] Eliade (1958).

The story *The Wizard of Oz* is an example of the need for these kinds of experiences in Western culture in order to develop sufficient ego strength. At the end of *The Wizard of Oz*, after Dorothy has made the journey to the Emerald City and has found her companions representing courage, heart, and brains along the way, she realizes she could have returned home at any time. Dorothy's story illustrates an ego's need to experience itself as a separate identity capable of functioning out in the world — the Western world.

Unlike some other cultures, the hero is not an essential component of the Q'ero experience. The Q'ero shamans say the concept of hero is a derivative of a personal orientation that is no longer relevant when sourcing from the collective expression of Pachamama. Through their connection with their *ayllu* and serving the collective of the land as a living entity, the Q'ero shaman move beyond personal ego expression into the greater capacity of collective manifestation.

Our culture has different demands than the Q'ero shamans, and to live in connection with Pachamama we must grow in different ways, congruent with the lifestyle of the Western world. For those of us living in a Western culture that rewards individual autonomy, we must develop adequate ego strength to withstand the individual journey required to function in the world. We don't need the support of a community to survive harsh environmental conditions. Instead, we require a sense of our place in the world to avoid becoming lost in the over-stimulation of living in a technological world. This is one of the fundamental differences between shamanism and Jungian depth psychology. Jung described the process of actualization as individuation and shamans see it as developing greater capacity to source from Pachamama and the connection that exists among all living things.

So, if this hero's journey is a necessary part of orienting in the Western world, it might explain the need for sequential time and space — and physical reality. Ordinary reality provides the necessary scaffolding to grow and develop our egos by presenting a contextual framework through the tapestry of our individual lives. This structure gives us the opportunity to experience the dismemberment process of separation with the veil of ordinary reality.

A hero's journey is a course of action through personal choice leading to the formation of a healthy ego by accepting personal responsibility as an individual. Not everyone will make this choice. For some, the pain of separation can become overwhelming and lead to movement backwards into wanting to be dissolved and submerged into something greater. It is a desire to return to the womb where there is no personal sense of responsibility. This yearning for loss of identity appears in both addictive behavior and in submissive masochistic urges. In *Lord of the Rings*, the subtle but increasingly addictive influence of the rings of power is an example of this. According to the story, the ring creates the illusion of immortality to the one wearing it, but it turns men into "ring wraiths" who are neither dead nor alive.

Dismemberment at the beginning of life and through the hero's journey was described as a way to develop the ego. A third type of dismemberment involving a spiritual journey is taken by shamans as part of moving into nonordinary reality.

The Shaman's Dismemberment

Unlike the hero's journey, which is an extroverted ego process of confronting challenges in the world, the second form of dismemberment, happens in adulthood as an introverted, intrapsychic process. In our culture, this type of dismemberment usually occurs during the second half of life. Jung called it an orphan's journey or night sea journey, to refer to the often-lonely individuation process of listening to the inner voice and moving toward connection with the Self. It is the shaman's process of letting go of the constraints of personal beliefs and attachments and moving into a more negotiable position of connection with the energetic collective. This activity increases their power and availability in both ordinary and nonordinary reality.

Moving away from defining ourselves by the collective culture (how we are viewed by others) often results in the death of a false self, which is why it can feel like dismemberment. In the beginning, this process may manifest as a midlife crisis or depression. Over time, this often progresses toward developing a profound sense of who we are — both individually and spiritually. Shifting psychic energy from who we seem to be — and conscious awareness — into a period of introspection is an individuation journey that facilitates growth and change.

In the third type of dismemberment, separating from the prevailing attitude of the collective has been described as a descent in many myths and fairytales. Descents often serve as initiations and provide entry into different levels of conscious awareness. These kinds of descents are painful for two reasons — in addition to working with and integrating dark and hidden shadow material, identification with the ego is sacrificed. When we are strong enough for the journey and willing to face our personal demons, these kinds of descents may enable us to gather the parts of ourselves that have been held unconscious in the underworld.[28] These types of descent help to increase the shaman's capacity to hold power in the realms of nonordinary reality.

In Assyrian mythology, Ishtar decides to visit her sister in the underworld and must pass through the seven gates of the underworld, opening one gate at a time. At each gate, Ishtar sheds

---

[28] Perera (1981), p.50.

an article of clothing. When she finally passes the seventh gate, she is naked. Like Ishtar, who must shed her layers of clothing, we are forced to shed layers of false identity that hold our self-importance. Shedding these layers can be painful and even terrifying because these layers are the way we know ourselves. I have often heard psychotherapy clients, who are successful in their external world, entering therapy to discover who they are underneath their social mask, say, "I don't know who I am!" This state of not knowing is common before a dismemberment descent is made — and is common in both shamanic initiation and the first phase of a depth analysis.

In myths and stories, there are countless examples of veils that are created to mask reality through acts of weaving a "web of deceit." The veils of illusion woven by spiders, according to Vedic philosophy in India, are to hide the true nature of reality. Evil witches using fantasy images or unconscious material often weave spells in stories. In the story, *The Lion, the Witch, and the Wardrobe,*[29] the witch casts a spell causing a veil of snow to cover the land. In many fairy tales, such as "Jorinde and Joringel" and "The Frog Prince," characters are turned into animals, signifying that they have become too closely identified with their unconscious nature. In the story "Sleeping Beauty," the witch casts a spell and puts the entire kingdom to sleep, indicating that they have fallen into an unconscious state.

There are many examples of the phenomenon of dismemberment in religions around the world. In Christianity the first commandment says, "Thou shall put no other gods before me." In the Hindu religion, *maya* refers to the limitations created by mass culture that define physical reality, hiding the true, unitary cosmic spirit. The spiritual goal is to "pierce the veil" of *maya* to gain awareness of the transcendent truth, from which the

---

[29] C. S. Lewis, 1950.

illusion of a physical reality, or ego consciousness, originates. Kali was the goddess who cut through the veil of illusion and slayed the demons in Hinduism.

In pop culture, there are many examples of this, often involving guns or lightning where energy is directed at something using linear force. In the *Star Trek* television series, the "phasers" used on the *USS Enterprise* starship could stun entire city blocks full of people and even vaporize entire asteroids. The male god Zeus, and male sorcerers and wizards, such as the Sith lord Darth Sidious, shoot lightning bolts at the victims they are fighting. Besides being a method of cutting through perceptual illusion, dismemberment can be a process of death and dismantling felt in the physical and somatic body. Like Bacchus, whose fate was described earlier, Dionysus, the god of fertility, and the mad Maenads ripped vegetation apart.

Whatever illusion we make our "false god" to distract ourselves from truth — to try and convince ourselves that we are protected and safe — must be sacrificed. The Q'ero shamans sometimes describe this process of letting go of our illusions as "taking it to the fire." In this form of dismemberment, the ego moves forward by giving up the control it has established in running the show out in the world, and consciously acknowledges the presence of something greater.[30] In acknowledging something greater, the ego gives up the psychological defenses it has developed as a form of protection against dealing with unpleasant truths and faces those truths. This is very different from the regressive movement backward in the failed hero's journey, where the person simply gives up.

Dismemberment is also associated with initiation rituals in shamanism. During *ayahuasca* ceremonies in the Amazon jungle, a

---

[30] This coincides with Jung's statement that victory of the Self is always a defeat for the ego.

common initiation experience involves being devoured by Amaru, the giant anaconda spirit of the jungle. The visionary experience in an *ayahuasca* ceremony usually moves through three phases. During the first phase, the personal shadow is encountered. The dismemberment experience of losing limbs and being decapitated by Amaru can be terrifying, if an attempt is made to fight what is happening by holding on to physical existence, as it is experienced in ordinary reality.

However, if the initiate surrenders to the process of being dismembered, movement is made into the second phase. During the second phase, attachment to physicality is dropped and no longer matters. The great mythic serpent Amaru is experienced as the sacred transformer in an ecstatic state of archetypal experience. The second phase involves experiencing at the mythic level. When identification with the physical body is completely dropped and symbols and imagery began to fade, awareness shifts through the veil of the literal to the energetic field of the subtle body. This is the third phase. Moving beyond physical form brings one beyond the mythic realm into the celestial field of the stars. This can be an exhilarating and liberating experience as the limitless energetic connection grows stronger and more intense. It becomes possible to experience oneness with the collective at the energetic level by merging with the elements into states of light, air, water.

Initiations involving dismemberment are usually a process of death and rebirth. The Christian religion is based upon the belief that Christ died and was reborn. Buddha also died to the illusion of his old identity in order to reach a state of nirvana.

"Next Time"

Sometimes the psychic pull to keep things status quo becomes too great for us to let go of personal identity attached to outer world experience. Like the antagonist in *The Matrix*, who misses the comforts of the world of illusion he has been living in, the question is asked, "Can I change my mind and take the blue pill instead?"

This desire to go back to things the way they were before and to leave good enough alone happens because letting go can be so devastating and painful. Whatever stands between the energetic collective and us may potentially be burned up in the process, resulting in a ruthless change in the outer world.

I was reminded of this when a colleague, who was a friend, got very excited when I announced that I was going to travel to Egypt. He exclaimed enthusiastically, *"That's me — that's exactly what I would do!"* When I pointed out to him that he had used the word "would" instead of "will," he replied he couldn't "because he had to work, but he would — next time." In shamanism, as Adolpho and Jose Luis have both said, "There are no plan Bs!"

Castaneda stated,

> Realizations are of two kinds. One is just a pep talk, great outbursts of emotions and nothing more. The other is the product of the shift of the assemblage point; it is not coupled with an emotional outburst, but with action. The emotional realizations come years later after warriors have solidified, by usage, the new position of their assemblage point.[31]

My personal experience has taught me that building the capacity to hold power requires commitment to face whatever it is that we do not want to look at. I do not believe it is possible to follow a path of shamanism, or any true spiritual discipline for that matter, without coming to terms with our personal shadow. We all have shadows. What is most important is that we become aware of them to stop reenacting unconscious wounds. The acting

---

[31] Castaneda, *Wheel of Time*, p. 246.

out of the shadow is a futile waste of valuable energy that could be used constructively. Facing our personal shadow is a way to grow as individuals and strengthen our spiritual connection, enabling us to avoid becoming bogged down in stagnant personal patterns based upon limiting assumptions and behaviors, which we tend to repeat over and over. When we become conscious of these patterns, we are no longer claimed by our shadows and gain the freedom to move forward.

Our shadows catch us in a variety of ways. One of the ways to learn more about our shadow is by paying attention to what bothers us most in other people. Usually whatever bothers us about someone else is something that bothers us about ourselves. Sometimes we begin thinking about something, or worrying, and just cannot "get it off our minds." We are caught in a dead-ended loop. One way to tell if something is related to our shadow is by tracking how we feel about it. Do we feel ashamed, guilty, or angry? Are we thinking about something that we would not want another person to know? Something we do not want to talk about is an indication that it is linked to our shadow.

Exercise 10: Identifying Personal Shadow Material

Sit in a quiet place, close your eyes, and take a moment to go inside of yourself by bringing your outer awareness back to your body. Use your intention to move into a relaxed and receptive state of mind. Take a couple of deep breaths, feeling yourself relax. Ask your spirits and guides for assistance, holding the intention that this exercise is being done for the highest good.

When you are comfortable, observe what is happening in your body. Notice if you are feeling emotional discomfort or tension anywhere. Pay special attention to your torso — particularly your Belly and Heart, as these are areas where people often hold tension. Now, focus on feeling into these areas of your body. See if you can trace the physical sensations to any thoughts or feelings that are bringing you discomfort.

If a situation or person comes to mind, see if you can follow the thread deeper, attempting to sense what about the person or situation is bothering you. Try not to get stuck in a mental loop of blaming. Make an effort to figure it out — focus on the effect it is having on you as it is happening. See if you avoid falling back on any preconceived notions by adopting an attitude of beginner's mind. What is this feeling or image creating in you now? Does it remind you of something that is unpleasant to look at or that you have tried to forget? If you are feeling angry, ashamed, hurt, or scared, you have most likely encountered an aspect of your shadow.

You can begin to work with your shadow by maintaining a receptive mind and noticing if there are any erroneous assumptions you have been making. Are there patterns that you seem to be repeating and not letting go? Shamans work with their shadow through their *mesas* and by creating *despachos*. Ask Pachamama for assistance. Shadow material can be a source of strength and power if we learn to harness it. Working with our shadows can provide us with greater understanding and compassion towards others — as well as insights about ourselves.

19. *Preparing for Initiation*

So, you need to go back home with this newly emerging empowered mesa, an addition for you is that you walk in the world as hanaq qawaqs. *A* hanaq qawaq *is sage, a teacher, a master. One that understands the ways of the land and articulates the medicine of the land as though chewing, chewing, you know, like a condor chews, half chews and gives that knowledge to their children, to their people.*

—Asunta,

daughter of the late *altomesayoq* Don Manuel Q'uispe, 2011

I have always known that Perry is amazingly smart and gifted — which, as is true for most things, turned out to be a blessing and a curse. He had the charisma and personal resources to be able to make aggressive investment decisions by borrowing large sums of money. When his painful childhood memories returned, Perry began to rapidly acquire real estate. It did not take extraordinary visionary powers on my part to realize we were headed for financial disaster.

Within two years, the economy turned, and we lost all of our assets, with the exception of an uninhabitable house that Perry had previously dismantled. Because our finances had always been intertwined, I was unable to shield myself from the pending catastrophe — even after filing for divorce "for financial reasons."

December 1, 2008

The low point of the financial mess for me personally was the morning I left for work to see clients while we were in the process of moving into Perry's uninhabitable house that he was trying to make inhabitable (i.e. with working plumbing and electricity). Weeks before, we had gone without electricity for two months in the middle of winter. We had survived by hooking up a generator — when I was still scraping to make the mortgage payments. The way I had previously shown up in the world, as an upstanding, financially stable stockbroker was long gone — and at this point had ceased to matter. I was doing everything I could to keep our sinking ship afloat — and it was not working.

During the months that followed, I struggled to put back together pieces of our financial wreckage. Oddly enough, my private practice as a psychologist continued to grow and thrive. My practice had remained stable, and I refused to let the chaos spill over into my work with clients. Jeff continued to reassure me that I was not crazy. Perhaps my own experience in darkness gave me greater compassion and understanding for the struggles and life traumas that my clients were experiencing. Perhaps I was gaining some shred of wisdom from all of this. My connection in the spirit world had continued to grow steadily stronger and had become the place that I sourced from. I learned that ultimately this was the only realm I could count on.

There were even more problems with the house we were forced to move into. In the previous year, Perry's collection of building materials, previously housed in various storage facilities, were stored in the rooms of the house. Perry sold what he could to pay what he owed.

For days, I carried building supplies up from the basement and attempted to organize piles of building materials and heaps of debris. Perhaps Perry's accumulation of building materials was an unconscious attempt to create a veil that distracted him from the turmoil of the inner chaos he was experiencing. For me, Perry's chaos had flooded through the veil into my outer world. I did not need it to become more blatant than it already was. Although I still loved Perry, the chaotic lifestyle had finally become too much for me. I reached my limit and moved out.

In the months that followed, my own connection with the figures in my inner world deepened further, especially with the Birdman. My fear of snakes had diminished considerably, and I was growing more comfortable in the solace and the familiarity I found in the underworld. I found it nearly impossible to think of the future without Perry — so I focused instead on my own analytic work, the immediate concerns of my psychotherapy clients, and my relationship with nonordinary reality. During this period, Perry and I saw each other, but I refused to live with him — or intermingle finances. We still cared for each other but found it difficult to spend extended amounts of time together. I felt as if I had been bowled over by an unstoppable freight train that had come out of nowhere at intense speed. I had grown to respect his acquired gift of vision, but could not move past my resentment at the toll his process had taken on both our lives.

Invitation to *Altomesayoq* rites

I was invited to return to Peru to undergo preparatory *altomesayoq* initiation rites, and was told by the Birdman that Perry would help me. At the time, we were not able to live well together in the outer world. Yet, our paths continued to be tied together in the inner world — in this realm there was no one I trusted as much as Perry. Perry said he wanted to help me prepare for my upcoming journey to Peru. When I asked him about it later, he told me the Birdman had visited him during a vision state and had offered "a trade." If Perry would help to prepare me for Peru, in exchange he would provide Perry with information on how to build the "energy cone."

In the journey, the Birdman showed Perry what was going to happen to me during my initiation rites. Perry saw that after reaching the place on the mountain where the initiation ritual would take place, I would begin to feel extremely cold and run a fever. Perry said that the other people would want to talk to me to make sure I was okay, but that it was important for me to be as quiet as possible. He said it was important that my focus be directed inward.

Perry informed me that I would experience being hit with blasts of energy. It was important for me to stay conscious in order to hold onto the energy that was being downloaded into my luminous body and integrate the power being given. The Birdman told Perry that I needed to prepare an offering that included cinnamon and tobacco, as these would help to attract the spirits.

Two weeks before leaving for Peru for the second time, Perry and I decided to take a weekend trip to Capital Reef in Utah, and return to our favorite spot in the desert. The purpose of the weekend trip was to help me prepare for the initiation ritual — somewhere in natural surroundings. One of Perry's inner guides had cautioned him against going to the desert with me but for some reason, which neither of us can remember now, we decided not to follow the guide's advice and go anyway — something neither of us would ever seriously consider doing now. Perhaps we were stubbornly returning to the desert because the desert had felt most sacred to us of all the places we had been.

May 24, 2009

After embarking on our weekend trip — and driving all day — we arrived at a motel near Capital Reef. As soon as we drove into the small town where we planned to stay, an unexpected, torrential rainstorm hit the town. Perry's four-wheel drive truck became stuck and lodged deep in the mud — six inches from the paved road! While waiting for someone with chains to pull us out, we realized that we should have listened more carefully to the advice of Perry's inner guides.

May 25, 2009

After spending the night in the motel, we decided to leave promptly at daylight. The flash floods crossing the highway early the next morning made it clear to both of us that we were being forced out of the desert. We began driving east on the highway, with no predetermined destination, and the skies cleared. We stopped on the side of the road to let our dogs out, decided to sit in a rock-cave nearby and "journey" about where we should go next. As we were leaving, Perry spotted a flat piece of sandstone lying nearby with his name carved in it. We interpreted this as an omen that we were heading in the right direction, which at this point happened to be west. An hour or so later, we stopped again at an old trading post and learned that we were about 35 miles outside of Mesa Verde State Park. Since Mesa Verde happened to be a place we had always wanted to visit but never had gotten around to seeing, we decided that this would be our destination.

At the time, both Perry and I could feel something brewing, but we were not exactly sure what we were noticing. After checking into a small motel located at the outskirts of the park, we decided to take a drive into the park at dusk. Sitting in the parked car after it had grown dark, I felt myself shifting into an altered state.

As the wind began to whirl around us, growing stronger and more intense, I began downloading information on how to prepare for the ritual. With my eyes closed, I was shown/told that Perry and I needed to create a *despacho* that included the tobacco and cinnamon we had brought. We were to place the *despacho* under a pyramid structure made from the dried leaves of a yucca plant that we had found while we were leaving the desert. I saw that Perry and I needed to hold space together for the energy to emerge. I would be given the words for the ritual while it was taking place. As the information was coming to me, I found myself feeling very energized by this process. A while later, when I emerged from the altered state, I could feel the energy that had come through. It was still vibrating in my body and I felt oddly euphoric.

May 26, 2009

The next day after eating breakfast, Perry and I headed back to the park and were disappointed to find hoards of people in Winnebago buses cruising along the paved road, stopping and taking pictures. We pulled off onto the most uninhabited side road we could find and parked the car. I noticed a chain link fence that reminded me of the dream that I had months before about Perry and I crossing into foreign territory.

When I entered the landscape I had seen in my dream, something inside of me felt compelled to search out what was on the other side of the fence. Given that there were park rules and regulations posted everywhere, what I encouraged us to do next was perhaps not the smartest decision I ever made. As I had done in the dream, I encouraged Perry to come with me.

Once we had crossed to the other side of the fence, we noticed what looked like ancient cave dwellings in the side of a rock across a canyon — and *no tourists*. We were alone. For a couple of minutes we stood quietly taking in everything around us. I felt my awareness shifting. I noticed that my hearing seemed to be becoming more acute as I heard a bird caw in the distance and subtle sounds of the wind rustling through the grass in the canyon. The sun was directly above, and I experienced waves of energy emanating up from the ground. As I softened my gaze, colors became more vivid and I could see particles of light dancing through the air. I sensed that we had entered into a different time — and were in another reality.

I looked over at Perry and saw that he was paying close attention to what was going on around him. Without speaking, we started to walk down the path through the canyon leading toward the dwellings. At the same time I could feel myself energetically merging with the land. The energy of the earth was moving up into my body while my conscious awareness dropped down into the ground below. Everything around me was alive.

As Perry and I continued our hike down the dirt path, it was becoming steeper and more narrow, I found myself feeling strangely energized — and unusually nimble. I tend to be a bit of a klutz and am accustomed to sliding down patches on rocky dirt paths when I am in the mountains. However, at this particular moment I was surprised to find myself gliding effortlessly along the path at an unusually brisk speed. I had the odd sensation that the pace had been set by a force coming from outside of me. I noticed the energy inside my body building. None of this felt unpleasant to me — just slightly perplexing. In contrast to me, Perry is extremely agile by nature. I was not surprised that he easily kept up with me. In what seemed like almost no time, we found ourselves in the midst of the cave dwellings.

Perry and I looked at each other and then gave thanks to the land, asking for permission to enter. I blew a blessing to Pachamama and to the spirit of the land into leaves I had gathered and then placed the offering on a stone near the entrance. Although Perry and I have struggled with each other out in the day world, in these situations we are more often in harmony, not needing words to communicate. Silently, we both wandered off by ourselves in different directions. We looked to find spots that felt right to each of us to lie down and journey.

I found a spot in one of the dwellings with a cool, gentle breeze coming through the window opening in the wall. As I lay down against the rock wall on the soft red dirt, I closed my eyes, and the energy pulsating through my body grew more intense. I felt myself in a place between two realities — past and present — and sensed I had one foot in each. I asked the spirits of the land for their assistance for the ritual that Perry and I were about to perform. In this state, I was complete. Time passed. I sensed it was time to begin the ritual and I headed back toward the opening of the dwelling to find Perry. He was sitting on one of the boulders near the entrance, waiting for me.

Perry and I silently walked back along the path together, toward the peninsula of land that looked over a vast canyon. As we gradually made our way back down the path we had taken, I took in the scenery we were approaching that had previously been behind us. Colorful red and orange rocks dotted the canyon walls, complimented by scattered sage, cactus, and pinion trees.

As we approached the center spot of the peninsula, I knew this was the place to conduct the ceremony. Again, I had the eerie sense of being back in the surreal world of the dream, where I watched the electrified wheat or corn growing. One aspect of the dream ending had been disturbing to me — the part when Perry had remained the age of two. I hoped for a more favorable ending to the dream we were currently living. I tried to put these thoughts aside and focused on preparing for the task at hand.

With our *mesas* in front of us, Perry and I sat cross-legged, looking across the magnificent valley that spread out in three directions. I sat closer to the ledge, as I had been instructed the night before, while he sat behind me. In the prayer of calling sacred space, we asked Pachamama and the spirits of the land for their assistance. Perry prepared the fire offering, as I had been instructed, in the middle of a large patch of dirt about 16 or so feet in diameter. He gathered the sections of the yucca plant together, creating a pyramid. Underneath he placed materials needed for a fire ceremony.

As I began to shake the rattle I had brought in easy, constant rhythm, I drifted deeper into an energetic state, somewhere beyond experiencing my actual physical body. I had the sense of stepping back in my body to allow another presence to come through me. I felt myself merging energetically with this spirit on a somatic level, while my mind was somewhere far away. The presence of what was coming in felt extremely powerful, yet safe and protective. I knew that it would not hurt me. Because of this, I willingly allowed myself to enter into a passive state of receptivity. I realized I was in the backseat and just along for the ride.

Some of what happened next is not completely clear. I heard myself calling out into the canyon in a tongue I was not familiar with. I could not understand any of the words I was saying, but was aware of urgency in the tone. I had the sense that I, or the presence inhabiting my body, was in the process of calling to awaken spirits living in the earth below the canyon.

Later, Perry said that within this sacred space he could feel power coming in from all directions. With my eyes closed, I observed my arms rising up and moving, as if I were conducting an orchestra of musicians. My body shifted into an expanded state that was not my own. I experienced merging with the canyon — we were the same.

The incomprehensible sounds coming from my mouth grew louder, echoing off the canyon walls. I heard myself making birdcalls. Perry informed me later that twelve ravens answered the calls and came in from all directions. The group soared as one rotating circular motion in a counter-clockwise direction throughout the ceremony. It seemed to Perry that the ravens opened a hole in the sky for the energy to descend upon us. He noted that there was not a raven in the sky when we arrived.

It appeared as though the presence of the ravens made a wall for a column of power. Everything changed. It felt as if time had stopped, as the energy rising from the earth met the energy descending from the sky.

This process must have continued for several hours, although we lost track of time, because the sun was moving close to the horizon when we finally finished. Perry started the fire and we reverently placed our offering on top of the flames. After completing the ritual, Perry showed me how to leave the surroundings as if we were never there.

As it grew dark, we began to walk back to our car, and a strange, unpleasant feeling came over me out of nowhere. I suddenly had a sense of urgency and knew that everything was not right. As I felt myself becoming increasingly more anxious, I encouraged Perry to move faster.

As soon as we had crossed back over the fence, four park officials suddenly confronted us at rifle point. Perry immediately threw his hands in the air. I became frightened, and my autonomic nervous system responded with a "fight" response. Being held at gunpoint — unarmed — felt extremely oppressive to me and I reacted by telling the rangers so in a rather loud voice. The rangers insistently shouted at me, "Put your hands up!" Perry commanded me to be quiet and put my hands up "so we don't get shot." I listened to Perry and complied.

We had unknowingly entered Indian territory — which we would have discovered if we had read the posted signs. We had asked Pachamama and the spirits of land for permission to enter, but had ignored the park regulations. The spirit world taking precedence over the day world seemed to be a reoccurring theme in our lives at the time.

Apparently, the group of rangers that had stopped us at gunpoint had assumed that we were stealing Indian artifacts. After they searched us and discovered that we were not carrying anything other than our *mesas*, water, and our wallets, everything settled down and we all relaxed. The rangers dutifully gave us a ticket for trespassing and politely escorted us out of the park. I apologized to the rangers for my rude behavior and said it would not happen again.

A few days after our Mesa Verde adventure, I said goodbye to Perry and boarded a plane headed for Peru. This was my second trip to the Sacred Valley, and the first time I had been invited to study with the *altomesayoqs*, the group of Q'ero shamans who work with the *Apus* or mountain spirits.

Weeks later, during a ceremony in Peru with the *Apus*, I asked what the spirit that had come through me in Mesa Verde had been doing. The *Apus* told me that the ritual we had conducted in the canyon had been to reopen *ceke* lines in the earth that had been neglected and, as a result, had gone dormant over time.

Pacha 5. Second Journey to Peru

Fun = magic.

— Perry Edwards

After my trip to the desert, I had the opportunity to return to Peru in 2009 to continue studying with the *altomesayoqs*, the Q'ero shamans living in the mountains of Peru above the Sacred Valley. Through a process of initiations, I began to see parallels between experiencing an energetic connection with the land and altered psychic states. At this time my exploration of mystic realms as a psychologist with a Jungian orientation had brought me to a place of needing to grapple with and reexamine my own understanding of the numinous as it related to the veil of shamanic experience.

This trip to Peru was the time when my process shifted from grappling with ideas using my mind to feeling with my heart. I became less concerned with searching for my soul. The exploration of the tension between Heart and soul that had been part of my own spiritual journey had taken on a life of its own. Through my journey of discovery and dismemberment, what I considered "me" at the start of the journey was taken apart and reassembled by my experiences.

My encounters with the energetic collective often brought about an intense rush of emotion in the Heart, an experience of *munay*, the sense of universal love. This blissful state of ecstasy and sense of "belonging" transcends words. The experience of energetic relatedness through being in a state of union with energetic collective is an expression of Pachamama. I associate this condition with numinous experience.

The energy centers of the Belly, Heart, and Mind, which correspond to different levels of psychic engagement, are the mechanisms we use to shift back through the veil from nonordinary to ordinary reality, from the energetic collective to daily living. As we transfer our awareness from deeper psychic states of connectivity to our "outer" awareness, our experience shifts from a fluid, energetic state to the physical world with discreet form. During this phase of my journey I moved deeper into the inner world and learned more about moving back to the outer world.

20. Learning from the Altomesayoqs

This year, unexpectedly, I am returning to Peru. I had not planned to go back until I received the invitation to return to the sacred mountains to work with the altomesayoqs. *The invitation was an honor and privilege that I could not refuse. I had to go — even though I was already going to Egypt. Normally, I would not have intended to leave the country twice in six weeks — but there are no "plan Bs."*

— Deborah Bryon, Journal, June 8, 2009

While roaming through Egypt, I had grown accustomed to traveling light — with a backpack, a few items of clothing, and a sleeping bag. I had come to appreciate not having much to drag around, and had applied the same line of reasoning in preparing for Peru. Shortly after returning from Egypt, with Perry's help, I had begun preparing for the upcoming journey in nonordinary reality, but had neglected the logistics of ordinary reality.

It was not until I met one of my traveling companions, Jeff, in the Cusco airport that I realized I had made a blunder. When we were leaving the airport together, Jeff looked quizzically at my small backpack and casually asked, "You have another bag besides this one — right?" I looked over at his bag. Noticing that it was the size of a small boat — that he and someone else could probably fit in — I grew slightly concerned. When I replied that my pack was it, Jeff kindly reminded me that we would be sleeping on the ground in the mountains at freezing temperatures — and high altitudes — for a week and suggested that I might want to do some shopping in Cusco before we left. I took his advice later that afternoon.

As we arrived by cab at the small bed and breakfast where we would be spending the night, we were greeted by Dona Bernadina's warm smile — and hugs and kisses. Jeff opened up his boat duffle bag to give "Dona B," the gift he had brought for her. In years past, he had watched her carrying her large, heavy satchel over her small shoulders. In response, Jeff had thoughtfully brought her a metal luggage carrier with wheels to help her lighten her load. After he explained to Dona B how to use the carrier, she thanked him — and then opened her satchel, placed the carrier inside, slung the entire bag over her shoulder, and walked with us out into the street — now with an even heavier load.

We were reminded of the futility of trying to change the way things had been done for years by introducing something that we assumed would be better — from our culture. It seemed that things had been working just fine for Dona B as they were. I looked over at Jeff, who smiled and shrugged his shoulders. The three of us took off walking, headed to the restaurant, Jack's, for lunch.

Jack's is a popular restaurant for eating breakfast. Its convenient location, close to the center of the old town in Cusco, makes it a great place for mountain trekkers and other foreigners to hang out and drink coffee. As we wandered in with Dona B, we saw other members of the *ayllu*, and after exchanging hugs and greetings, found a large table that seated a group of about eight. We talked about what had transpired in our lives over the course of the last year, as well as getting updates on what the shamans we knew had been doing.

We were sad to learn that Dona B would not be joining us on our journey to the mountain because she was tending to pressing family matters. Apparently, Don Francisco and Don Sebastian would be arriving tomorrow, as well as Juanito, an *altomesayoq* who worked with *Apus* from Bolivia, and Don Santiago, another gentle *altomesayoq* with a kind heart, who had recently begun working with Westerners.

After breakfast, we made our way to one of the popular streets for exchanging money, and then were off to the witch's market for supplies — and I made my rounds to the local mountaineering stores to buy what I had neglected to bring.

June 9, 2009

This morning our *ayllu* joined the *pampamesayoqs* and headed for the Condor Temple for the first of many mountain hikes. As we wandered around the old stone ruins of Inca celestial calendars, we stopped and listened to the *pampamesayoq* Adriel explain the cosmology of the ancestors of the Land.

The following is based upon excerpts from this discussion.

The Incas had three calendars. These were the solar calendar for human affairs, the moon calendar for animals and agriculture, and the peak calendar for new *pachas* — fresh beginnings and stages of life. The Incas believed that the past always is in front of us. For the Incas, creation is a state of fluid being that we must move into through dialogue with the Land. Living in a state of anticipation is a means of coping, not creativity. Ceremony allows us to reset, entering into a creative state of being. We arrive at each new *pacha* by using our intent.

The *Apus* are expressions of the collective being that manifests in this reality through the paradigm shift created by the *altomesayoq*. The *altomesayoq* brings the voice of the spirit. If we embody love without external participation, attaching it to something or someone, it is possible to move beyond scarcity, into a unifying cosmic vision and understanding of the universe. As Jose Luis says,

> The *altomesayoqs* take it one step further by aiding the *Apus* in physical manifestation. The *altomesayoqs* are highly specialized. They have the ability to create the doorway between realms, between worlds — whatever that is. And the cool thing about this is that these [*Apu*] spirits — all of them — are benefactors. All of them are in charge of providing comfort, safety, guidance. They make sure that there is life force in the little plants, life force in the makeup of the village so everything is in right relationship. So, their job description is guardianship, guardianship of humanity, stewardship of humanity. And they obey as well. Within their realm of consciousness there are also hierarchies of power. There are little *Apus* that are probably more lost than you and I. And there are the big *Apus*. And through the *altomesayoq* tradition, particularly in this area, these spirits have fused themselves so much and so well to our human cultural paradigm that they have even learned our language, to speak and to think and feel and validate exactly the same way we do.

The *altomesayoq's* organization of the knowledge of the land is a configuration to process and hold power. The stories we bring back from communing with the land are ways we validate our subjective experience and remember what has taken place.

The question becomes, can we find a mechanism to reenact direct experience? The process of initiation is a new tradition and convocation. This is a process of entering into a state of envisioning a new trajectory in the time beyond words, through which we are able to bring back a sense of clarity — and a sense of light. All of this happens through right relationship with Pachamama.

Imagine thinking of our mind as an acoustic chamber. This chamber has layers sound travels through. What resonates in these chambers is our intuition — and we remember. The amount of energy we bring back depends on our capacity to sustain what we evoke through our connection with the land.

The ability to shift from one state into another is referred to as exercising multiplicity. Multiplicity requires that we visualize and articulate the energetic expression of the land in our minds. This internal map is the identity of our primordial selves, the aspect of us that has the capacity to step outside of linear time. Our relationship with the land is the way of forming identity and making meaning. Two of the ways of doing this are through revisiting the past through ceremony, and "trail-blazing" as visionaries journeying in the inner world.

In the following section, the sans serif passages are my personal account of my first major initiatory experience on the mountain of Waquay Wilka in Peru, describing my process of remembering through the body. When working with numinous, archetypal material, describing the experience with words will never fully encompass the experience. These verbal descriptions are an approximation of the *direct experience* as I remember it.

Parallel to my personal narrative, I am including Castaneda's descriptions of shifting from heightened awareness to normal awareness that correspond to this experience. (Although I am aware that Castaneda used the sacred medicine of plants in some of his shamanic experiences, none of my experiences described here were drug induced.)

June 11. 2009

Yesterday our *ayllu* met with the *Apus* of Don Santiago's *mesa* in sacred ceremony and were told that the destination of our sacred pilgrimage was to the holy mountain of Waquay Wilka. (Please see Chapter 16 for a more in-depth explanation of this type of sacred ceremony.) After the ceremony last night, we gathered our mountain gear and left early this morning, beginning our hiking journey up the mountain. We carried light daypacks and water with us, while the heavier camping gear and food was transported up the mountain on the backs of the horses that accompanied us on our journey. We walked up the switchbacks for several hours before eating lunch and then began hiking again.

Before leaving for Peru, Perry had journeyed for me on how to prepare for the trip. Our inner guides told us that it was important that I bring sage, cookies, and cinnamon to leave as an offering for the mountain spirits. As I had been instructed, these ingredients were with me in my backpack.

When the *ayllu* reached the destination where we were going to camp for the evening, I noticed my stomach was beginning to feel uncomfortably queasy. Don Sebastian read my discomfort in my face and without words gathered a plant remedy growing nearby, which smelled like mint. He rubbed it on my stomach. My stomach began to feel better, but my body began to grow incredibly cold. I could feel I was beginning to run a fever and I became spacey and light headed. I knew I needed to lie down soon. I remembered that Perry had predicted that this would occur and, based on the information he had given me, I returned alone to my tent, buried myself in layers of clothing under my sleeping bag, and closed my eyes. When members of the group grew concerned and came to check on me, I informed them that I was okay but needed to be quiet and lie still. Per my request, I was left by myself for the rest of the evening.

Dusk came and went as I closed my eyes and slipped deeper and deeper into an altered state — buried in layers of clothes and blankets. The Birdman came and told me to experience communion with the land. I became aware that I was preparing for a dismemberment ceremony. First, I experienced burning in fire and in the process remembered a life in Peru when a village had burnt as a result of my misuse of power. Next, I was eaten by a snake, followed by a bird eating my heart. I experienced myself dying and being reborn, and dying and being reborn again. None of this was painful. It felt cleansing. I sensed I was letting go of old energetic debris that I had carried for lifetimes.

Finally, I fell into a deep sleep. I did not wake up until sunrise. Waking up I realized I felt energized and clear-headed — and was extremely hungry.

June 12, 2009

After breakfast, the *ayllu* began its ascent up the mountain. We walked single file up narrowing switchbacks until we reached a clearing. When we reached a comfortable spot, we sat in a circle and began sacred ceremony. Don Francisco and Don Sebastian offered our prayers and thanks to Pachamama. After the last words were spoken, we each fell silent, entering our own state of reverie. I turned, sitting cross-legged, and gazed over the white-capped mountain range across the valley that lay in front of me. The sun was high in the sky and everything began to shimmer. I saw the great mountain Alancoma lying directly ahead of me in the distance. The range of mountains that stretched in front of me was now appearing to be made up of particles of light. I felt myself shifting into an altered state as the light intensified.

While sitting on the top of the mountain with my eyes closed, I felt myself entering a trance state. I saw a series of doorways or openings of light with five points each that opened up onto each other so that one doorway opened into another doorway, and onto another. I began to experience a succession of waves of convulsions or intense shaking that echoed through my entire body. I heard a voice keep telling me to "hold it." I understood that "holding the energy" meant containing the sensation in my body through a focus of intent. Intuitively I knew that my ability to hold the energy in my body would determine the degree to which I would be able to integrate the energy being downloaded from the mountain.

When the vision ended, it was time to begin the descent into the valley immediately below where we would camp that evening. I looked over at my friend Brad who had been sitting next to me the whole time. He smiled encouragingly at me and said, "Nice work."

As I looked around me, I saw the land, rocks, and plants pulsating and vibrating with power. I could see the energy field connecting everything and actually understood for the first time — in my body — that everything is alive. Coming down the mountain path to the campsite, I had the odd sensation of dancing. My legs felt as though they were gliding on the energy vibration that was emanating from the earth. I moved quickly and effortlessly. As we made our way down the mountain, dusk set in. The particles of darting light appeared effervescent, and seemed to fill up the space in the surrounding atmosphere. After arriving at our campsite, while lying down in the tent to sleep, I could still faintly feel the force radiating through my body. I felt alert, full of life, and serene all at the same time.

In *The Eagle's Gift*, Castaneda (1981) wrote,

> My body began to shake, out of control. I had a sense of duality. Perhaps what I call my rational self, incapable of controlling the rest of me, took the seat of a spectator, some part of me was watching as another part of me shook (p. 70).

June 13, 2009

This morning we made our way to a sacred Inca site on Waquay Wilka and the *ayllu* prepared celestial *despacho* as offerings that would be burned for the initiation ceremony at high noon. The site was located on a mountain ridge that looked out over a valley. A large stone gateway marked the entrance to the site. When we approached the ridge, the wind picked up. I put on my poncho in a futile effort to try to block the wind that was whipping across the ridge.

Don Francisco came and sat next to me and informed me that he would be helping me make a special altar in the *despacho* I was creating. We sat closely together, with our backs to the wind facing toward the mountain. Together, we carefully sorted through the ingredients of the *despacho* kit. Don Francisco methodically began by making an altar for the *despacho*. He formed the llama fat in the shape of a ball, rolling it between the palms of his hands until it became malleable. He then placed the ball of fat inside the seashell at the center of the *despacho*. Next, he added neatly aligned rows of the *k'intus* I had created so that they were standing straight up, until the llama fat was completely covered. Don Francisco then placed the *despacho* upon the paper sheet.

One by one, I opened the paper packets holding the individual ingredients, showing each of them to Don Francisco. Based on the relevancy of the ingredients to the celestial *despacho* we were creating, Don Francisco nodded "yes" to the ones to be used and "no" to the ones that would be put away. He explained that items pertaining to of the upper world were the only ingredients needed. We carefully added each ingredient to the *despacho*. When we were finished, we folded the paper and wrapped the *despacho* in string. I thanked Don Francisco for his help. I then set the *despacho* on my *mesa*, waiting for the ceremony. Don Francisco smiled and nodded.

The purpose of the *despachos* the *ayllu* was making was to help each of us remember experiencing the energetic collective at the essential level. These *despachos* were made as gifts of love to the *Apus* of Waquay Wilka demonstrating our commitment to the great mountain. After the ceremony began, we walked through the gateway at the entrance of the sacred site one by one and were greeted by the *altomesayoq* bestowing the initiation rites. While speaking the sacred words of initiation in Quechua, the *altomesayoq* placed his *mesa* on each of our individual energy centers, the Mind, Heart, and Belly, and then on our *mesas*. He transferred the lineage held in his *mesa* into each of our luminous bodies and *mesas*. While giving the words of the sacred initiatory rite to each of us individually, he "thumped" each of these areas three or four times with his *mesa,* which he continued to hold in both hands. I felt the transmission from the *altomesayoq* as a surge of energy beginning to move more intensely through my body.

After receiving the rites, I found a spot on the ground in an area of the clearing directly in front of the gateway. I sat cross-legged with my back to a large boulder and concentrated on dropping my awareness deeper into my Belly. My body began to shake and I felt myself falling into a trance state. I felt intense waves of energy continually running through my physical body. At certain times, when I experienced contractions in my solar plexus and belly, the process became painful. At one point, I felt I was in labor and giving birth in the process. After the waves subsided, I felt incredibly energized and in a state of euphoria. Throughout this entire process, although in trance, a part of me remained conscious. On some level, I was aware that this was necessary; otherwise, I would not have the intentionality needed to hold the power.

I had the sense of going through the doorways and looking into a mirror reflection. It was not an actual mirror but seemed more like an energetic aspect of myself that I needed to face. I heard a deeper part of my emerging self telling the reflection that I would meet it — because we were equals. I then consciously realized that in this state of connectivity I was an equal with everything I was experiencing. We were all the same. We were all energy. I sensed that I needed to claim my power in order to hold the energy and, through this process, I would be required to face, as equal, whatever I saw and/or experienced. It was necessary to honor the experience, and myself. Intermittently, the reflection I was looking at became dark. I told the reflection that I was willing to look at it "head-on." I then realized that I had encountered an aspect of my own shadow. I was seeing what I needed to come to terms with.

In *A Separate Reality*, Castaneda (1971) wrote,

> As impossible things keep happening to him, he becomes aware that a sort of power is emerging. A power that comes out of his body as he progresses on the path of knowledge. At first, it is like an itching on the belly or a warm spot that cannot be soothed, then it becomes a pain, a great discomfort. Sometimes the pain and discomfort are so great that the warrior has convulsions for months, the more severe the convulsions the better for him. A fine power is always heralded by great pain (p. 185).

Castaneda said that the pain involved in this process is what facilitates a shift of focus into the body where one acquires will. Will is a force or power. Acquiring will is necessary to *see*, in other words, to pierce the veil. What transpired for me on the mountain during these experiences is what Perry had been given in his vision on our trip to Mesa Verde.[32]

Knowing in advance the importance of focusing my intent on holding the energy helped me consciously prepare for engaging with the energy downloaded into my psyche. Rather than questioning what was happening, having prior knowledge of what was taking place enabled me to stay aligned with my purpose. I believe this allowed me to absorb and ground more

---

[32] Please see p. 163.

energy from this experience in my luminous body. Looking back now — three years later — what stands out in my memory is not pain, but the incredible surge of power I experienced. The longing to return to this deep state of connection has also remained. I believe this is the state shamans call ecstasy.

Engaging with these deeper layers of the psyche is sometimes referred to as seeing in darkness. Jung said that individuation is a process of taking the light into the darkness.[33]

Shamans take seeing in darkness both literally and metaphorically. In shamanic journeying, reference is frequently made to an altered state of consciousness of working in darkness. In dream work, darkness represents the unconscious.

June 14, 2009

In the blur of these couple of days, I had faint memories of what I intuitively felt to be a past life. In this life, which had occurred in Peru, perhaps with these same *Apus*, I had misused power. I had the sense in that moment that this was part of my past, and that I could choose to no longer be claimed by it. I was aware that I had returned and was committed to serving the light of the collective. I traced the dark memory to a thread I still experience in myself that manifests when I happen to fall into a

---

[33] An important clarification I would like to make is that this not a symbolic description about the experience, it is the experience. I have heard the comment that Castaneda was writing in metaphor and that Don Juan was a fictitious character. In his books, Don Juan's description of the Eagle has been interpreted as being a symbol for the Self, a representation of the Numinous. Within the context of ordinary reality, it is easier, and perhaps more comfortable, to understand Castaneda's description of the spirit of the eagle as a symbolic metaphor for mystical experience. However, based upon my experiences, I would challenge that perspective. Although his writing can easily be understood and worked with symbolically in the realm of ordinary reality, when one is in the energetic realm of nonordinary reality, it is actual experience.

mindset of scarcity and become competitive. I noticed the dramatic effect in shifting from a personal to a collective perspective. I became cognizant that this shift in awareness can be made by intentionally aligning with the light energy — by focusing on the light. It became clear to me that I could acknowledge the dynamics of my history and then transfer the focus to the energetic level where the personal falls in the background and the collective becomes the primary focus.

Through the process of shamanic initiation, light is the vehicle through which power is layered into the physical body. While I was sitting on the mountaintop in a visionary experience, feeling myself being infused with energy, I realized that my personal narrative was there — and would always be there. We do not get rid of our egos; instead, we move beyond the ego into a state of fluidity by engaging in a dialogue with the land, using our Belly, Heart, and Mind. This energetic flow transcends words, personal narratives, and stories. It is a state of wholeness and abundance.

The stories that we create and bring back from shamanic encounters are how we validate and integrate our experience with the unknown in ourselves. Using language is an attempt at putting the experience into a framework that we can comprehend. Shamans teach that the essence of the true experience is always beyond words. Jung also said that we do not get rid of our shadow and complexes; rather we develop an awareness of these aspects of our psyche so that they no longer dominate our thoughts and claim us.

During this particular experience in Peru, I was continually reminded not to focus on the personal narrative. Like Hercules cleaning out the stables on Mount Olympus, eradicating the shadow is experienced as an impossible feat. However, our personal woundedness becomes smaller in direct proportion to our ability to develop conscious awareness of it. I have learned to experience the energetic realm more fully by shifting from a personal orientation to a much larger perspective rooted in the energetic collective.

As I reflect on my initiatory experience in the collective, I remember that the emanations of light came through the energetic shape of a bird, Apucheen. For me, this bird is the intermediary, the ally, the bodhisattva to the energetic realm.

June 15, 2009

As the process of energetic layering deepened over the course of several days, I was in constant dialogue with my ally, the Birdman.[34] At times, with my eyes closed, I would see an intense golden yellow light that surrounded me. These experiences lingered with me, even after opening my eyes. Within the light, I saw doorways consisting of five points. The energetic outline of a bird with extended wings also appeared — also composed of radiant light. While I was in deeper states in my connection with nonordinary reality, a couple of times the visions shifted into actually experiencing myself in the form of a bird. I felt what it was like to grow wings and to stretch them. I felt myself flying and soaring — flapping my wings aggressively — then gliding with the momentum. I could feel myself circling higher into the atmosphere, and then diving through the air closer to the earth. I do not remember ever before experiencing such a great sense of freedom. I loved the experience of stretching my wings as far out as they would go and gliding with the breeze. I looked down at the earth and noticed how small everything looked. At times, I was reluctant to look down when I realized how far above the earth I was. I remember hearing the voice of the Birdman, saying to me, "If you are asking for visions, you must be willing to see them."

---

[34] I use the phrase energetic layering to refer to the cumulative effect of repeated numinous experiences on the somatic psyche. I experienced this as feeling energetically charged and in a state of heightened awareness.

Shamans often see the archetypal image of the bird, Apucheen, during visionary states. In the realm of the Condor, everything is crafted with intent through vision. Shamans say that it is the place of wisdom and dreams. The large mythic bird has appeared as a condor, eagle, or humming bird, offering wisdom through connection with higher vision. It serves as an ally, intermediary, bodhisattva, and something greater. The mythic bird is a celestial manifestation of the energetic collective.

In *The Fire from Within*, Castaneda (1984) stated:

> The old seers actually saw the indescribable force, which is the source of all sentient beings. The call it the Eagle, because in the few glimpses they could sustain, they saw it as something that resembled a black and white eagle of infinite size....They saw that it is the Eagle that bestows awareness. The Eagle creates sentient beings so that they will live and enrich the awareness it gives them with life. They also saw that it is the Eagle who devours that same enriched awareness after making sentient beings relinquish it at the moment of death (p. 38).

In *Andean Awakening*, Jorge Luis Delgado (2006) has written about his experience with the Condor in Peru, during his apprenticeship with a shaman. In the middle of a ceremony, he described seeing a huge cloud with the shape of a condor as a moment of joy, and heard his teacher say to him, "The Condor was always there. You could not see it because your heart was not yet opened" (p. 60).

Throughout his writings, Castaneda has frequently described his encounters with the Eagle from the realm of nonordinary reality. In the *Wheel of Time* Castaneda (1998) wrote,

> The Eagle, that power that governs the destinies of all living things, reflects equally and at once all those living things. There is no way, therefore, for man to pray to the

Eagle, to ask for favors, to hope for grace. The human part of the Eagle is too insignificant to move the whole (p. 202).

Words or images are not enough for me to "name" exactly what the Condor, Apucheen, or the Eagle is. I know that it exists, it is powerful, and its capacity extends far beyond anything I have experienced in ordinary reality. It is bigger than me on a grand scale, and its awareness surpasses my own by leaps and bounds. I have described how I experienced the Condor through some of my visions. Your visions may be different — perhaps involving other mythic beings. Visions can only be experienced directly through your Mind's eye. The visions will come to you if you are receptive, patient, and clear in working with intent.

The following exercise is one way of beginning to open a dialogue with your own inner figures.

Exercise 11: Using Dream Material in the Visionary Realm

The following exercise is a way of engaging in dialogue with the figures that come to you in your dreams.[35] It is always best to work with a figure that has come to you through one of your dreams. Imagery from your own inner world will be more powerful and meaningful than those from the outer world given by someone else. Shamans enter into visionary states and develop their capacity to hold power by respectfully trusting the sacred visionary experiences they receive. For the shaman a vision is always a gift.

One of the ways of deepening your relationship to the inner world of your unconscious is by keeping a journal of your dreams. It is best to record your dreams, either in writing or on tape, immediately upon waking, as they may fade throughout the

---

[35] Carl Jung developed this process and referred to it as "active imagination."

course of the day, making it harder to remember them. Recording visionary experiences should also be done immediately upon returning to your outer awareness to avoid losing information.

To begin the process, you need to have had a dream with imagery that is emotionally meaningful for you. The dream imagery may be a place or an inner figure. In the beginning, it is best to work with positive figures and/or places that you have encountered in the inner world.[36] Although this process can also be useful in working with aspects of your shadow, it is important to first develop relationships with positive inner figures that you can call on to come to your aid if needed. As your capacity to hold power and your relationship with your ally grows stronger, you will be better prepared to face darker areas of your psyche, always for the highest good.

After identifying and connecting with the dream imagery you have selected, find a quiet, comfortable place to sit and close your eyes. Start the exercise by surrounding yourself in light, asking Pachamama for her protection and assistance. Using your intent, "know" that you are perfectly safe and protected and ask that all that transpires be for the highest good.

Bring your awareness into your body. You may want to use the slow exhale of three long breaths to center yourself. When you are relaxed and in a receptive state, imagine the dream image you will be working with in your Mind's eye. Take yourself back into the dream where you saw the image, paying attention to all of the details of the imagery available to you, as it exists in this moment.

---

[36] It is important not to call on people who are living without their permission, even if the intent is for healing. Shamans never assume that they know what is best for another person. To do so is considered a misuse of power. Rather than trying to direct a course of events, if they want to help someone, they ask *Pachamama* for her assistance or surround the person in light.

If you have decided to engage with an inner figure, ask why it has come to you. What does it want you to learn? What does it want to show you? The first answer that comes into your mind is the answer you are looking for. If your figure is silent, sit with it. Look at it and try to get to know it. If you have chosen a place that you have seen in a dream, explore it. See if you can see and learn more about the place beyond what you experienced in the dream. Look around at your inner surroundings so that you anchor yourself to them and return to visit them later.

Try not to censor or "over think" whatever comes into your mind. In the beginning, you might hear a part of yourself saying something like, "You are making this up — you are imagining this." Tell that part of yourself that it is okay — you don't need to know right now whether or not "you are making it up" — and then gently redirect your attention back to the image in your Mind's eye. Allow the figure or place to present itself to you in whatever form it takes. If the imagery begins to develop and change, allow it to follow its natural process as it unfolds. Do not try to keep it in a certain form or force it to appear in a certain way. Let the image live in your mind in the form it needs.

When you feel finished, thank the inner figure for appearing to you. In your own time, gradually bring yourself to your outer awareness. Slowly open your eyes when you are ready. Record everything that has transpired.

You can go back and revisit places or figures or wait for new dream images to appear. Trust the process by following the path that feels right to you rather than thinking about what it "should" be. Engaging with your inner world will become easier the more you work with it.

21. Pulled between Worlds

The process of observation is a deepening process of awareness through which you develop a clear heart and become a beacon of your own light. Pure observation leads to pure awareness, through holding space with the collective and becoming a steward of your own journey.
— *Apu* Ausangate, ceremony with Juanito's *mesa*, 2011

The Q'ero *ayllu* is a community firmly rooted in a spiritual tradition that values the shaman's Heart connection with the spirit world. A deep respect for the natural world is an integral part of the Q'ero community. This is fostered in the Q'ero nation through maintaining an open dialogue with the land through ceremony, ritual, and service for the purpose of "giving back. This ongoing "right" relationship with Pachamama provides a supportive framework within the *ayllu* that facilitates the transition through the reentry process after a numinous experience. It is accepted in the community that everything living is connected and available. The Q'ero people practice shamanism as a way of living. These key ingredients — intrinsic to the Q'ero nation — sustain the shaman's ability to shift between the worlds of ordinary and nonordinary reality.

These ingredients are often missing in Western society. Perhaps this is because we have become industrialized and have moved away from our understanding of nature. In our modern world, we are living in a time during which individual autonomy is valued over community, causing separation into power blocs to become more prevalent than connection through right relationship.

We are also a culture that tends to live in our heads — predominately outside of our Hearts and bodies. We gravitate toward living in our minds as a way of protecting ourselves. Feeling alienated often results in fear and constriction, causing our Hearts to close. For protection, we may fall into the ineffectual, familiar pattern of prematurely trying to "figure out" what is happening, as we attempt to navigate and regain our footing in the modern world. The problem with this approach — besides the fact that it leads to feeling cut off and disconnected from the actual experience — is that our minds are incapable of processing the energetic experience of reentry. There are no words in the English language that adequately describe the subtle yet significant nuances in somatic and emotional feeling tones associated with the experiences.

Attempting to reassimilate back into an extroverted, left-brained culture may often lead to feelings of estrangement. Before our capacity to hold power and our ability to regulate the intensity of the energy have been developed, reorienting to our modern way of life after undergoing a numinous experience is challenging. Upon returning home the Heart-felt energetic connection must be kept alive. Ways of actively attending to this sacred relationship include activities such as working with a *mesa*, exploring imaginal dream states, spending time in nature, and performing ceremonial rituals to serve the land.[37]

------

[37] Now I recognize the necessity in intentionally feeding this connection. It has become part of my practice — it should be obvious. However, during my first process of reentry, although I reached a state of *munay* during dreamtime, in my waking hours it became almost impossible for me to remember. My initial experience, where everything was changed,

The way we are torn between the ordinary and nonordinary can be seen in many of the science fiction films that have been released in recent decades. In the films, *Altered States* and *The Fly*, scientists cross the threshold of ordinary time and space and physically "morph" as a result of being in this other reality. Readapting to a physical world with discreet boundaries, when emerging from a fused energetic state, requires a flexible, nonlinear way of being in the world. This new world perspective is not the same as what we previously knew.

I am reminded of a story where a space shuttle blasts off into space, reenters the atmosphere of the earth, and lands in a different time and a different place. In science fiction literature, there are many stories about time travelers who visit a different place and time and then are faced with the dilemma of not being able to return home. When we step outside of consensual reality, we begin to perceive the world differently. We can't return to the same world we left — and often begin to feel separate and isolated.

Feelings of loss and separation develop during the reassimilation process into our previous culture — especially after an initiation — for various reasons. Mystical experience is often not shared or valued by the majority in Western culture. The experience of separation after a profound encounter with the energetic collective often becomes linked to feeling like an outsider, along with an incredible sense of loneliness and isolation. Similar to the alien ET's quest to return home, separation is accompanied with a strong urge and longing to find reconnection. Like the people of the Q'ero shamanic tradition, we must learn ways to "grow corn" with our experience. The first

---

was the most jarring and I was the least prepared for what happened and how it changed who I was. Over time, my connection with the energetic collective has grown stronger and so has my ability to maintain my nonordinary energy while living in the ordinary world.

step is finding ways of understanding the process of making the transition back.

As our assumptions and beliefs about reality are stretched, we are forced to adjust our thinking in order to incorporate the new information into our existing map of understanding the world. In addition to being required to adapt to a newly expanded sense of reality, the intense numinous energy that frequently floods our psyche may become challenging to regulate.

A friend and colleague, Joe McNair, commented, "Anyone can drop a couple hits of acid and you're in — it's the coming back which is much more difficult." We are forced to deal with the intense influx of energy, often feeling and appearing as mania to others, as we attempt to reengage in life. Sometimes our narratives of the events we have experienced seem strange, even delusional, to people around us, if we describe what actually occurred.

Models of Reentry

I researched everything I could find that had previously been published by others who had undergone similar kinds of experience in nonordinary reality, starting first with the writings of Jung. I was desperately seeking explanations that could account for the sense of alienation I was experiencing at a preverbal level that could not be held by images or words. In an attempt to gain understanding, I was forced to look outside of the published Jungian literature.

I explored what had been written in the field of analytic psychology, as well as the current research in neuropsychology. I began to spend long hours writing and reading — trying to somehow make sense of what was happening to me. Somewhat surprising to me, during this initial phase of reentry I began to observe relevant parallels between what I seemed to be experiencing and theories of early childhood development. I found similarities between the incredible sense of loneliness —

and loss — I was experiencing from being forced to return from an ecstatic state of energetic connection. I noted similarities between my own experience and the emotional states often associated with early psychological trauma. I discovered that Castaneda's descriptions of his own nonordinary reality experience, the recent findings in neuropsychology, theories of body-oriented therapies, and Object Relations theory on early development seemed to correspond most closely with what I was literally living.

Reentry necessitates adjusting to the day world of Western culture after leaving the numinous state of connectivity. Through my own exploration and process of consolidation, I can now identify three facets involved in the reentry process, with a great deal of overlap between them, which I refer to as (1) Somatic Perception, (2) Imaginative Engagement, (3) Narrative Integration. The first phase of Somatic Perception involves making the actual perceptual shift from the state of "being in the flow" in nonordinary reality back into the time/space continuum of ordinary reality as experienced directly through the Belly.

During the second phase of Imaginative Engagement, words and symbols begin to emerge and materialize within the psyche as a function of the Heart, the domain of Chocachinchi the mythic jaguar. Chocachinchi has the innate ability to connect with its environment as it is happening through experiencing with all of the senses. From this present state of awareness, psychic space for phantasy[38] and imagination can be actively held. As a result, symbolic interactions with the outer world begin to emerge as a new language with words that can begin to describe the experience.

---

[38] Psychoanalysts using the spelling "phantasy" rather than fantasy to denote this as an unconscious as well as conscious activity.

During the Narrative Integration phase, mental recapitulation becomes possible, through developing an overarching structure to use when thinking about and describing what has happened. This process entails using Condor vision with the Mind. Reentry necessitates using the Mind to regulate the influx of numinous energy that has been downloaded. In addition, reentry requires readjusting to the outer world in relationship to others.

I have observed that the process of reentry has become easier with each reentry experience. Perhaps gaining a fuller understanding of the energy collective has helped me to transition more easily, along with increasing my capacity to hold the powerful energy that is being downloaded.

In my description of what I currently understand about the process of reentry, I will touch upon each of these areas as they relate to my own experience. Chapter 22 will focus on the psychological and emotional challenges I experienced during my first reentry experience. Chapters 23 and 24 will focus on the internal processes, which often accompany reentry. Chapter 25 will address the shadow aspect of the reentry experience.

22. Somatic Perception and the Influx of Energy

You are going on a transcendent spiritual journey. A sacred pilgrimage that transcends any consensual reality that informs you. In order for the sacred journey to Ausangate to unfold, you must transcend the personal, meet Ausangate at a higher level. You have to peel off other identities to be embraced by the Apus.

— Dona Alahandrina, *altomesayoq*, 2011

Attempting to bend nonordinary experience to fit into the preconceived notions we use to organize our experience of ordinary reality does not work. This is because experiences occurring outside of consensual reality are impossible to describe in the language of consensual reality. They do not conform to a framework based in linear time and space and as a result become distorted when translated into temporal spatial reality.

A significant perceptual shift happens when moving from experiencing an energetic state into awareness of having discreet physical form. In reentry, movement is made through the various levels of psychic engagement — starting from ecstatic energetic experience, into mythic and symbolic levels of the imaginal realm, and finally arriving at the literal level of the concrete world. Since these kinds of initiatory numinous experiences take place outside of the realm of normal psychological development, as it exists in our collective culture, coming back requires establishing a new interior framework for processing the nonordinary information.

I have heard that the Sami, indigenous people of Northern Sweden, have many different words to describe the characteristics of snow, and that in places in Africa there are eighty ways to describe the characteristics of dirt! In both cultures, a verbal system of communication has been developed that provides a supportive framework to explain an essential element of their environment.

Unlike the language of the Sami and African people, which describes unique aspects of the native external environment in ordinary reality, it is not possible to keep the integrity of an experience of the nonordinary reality intact using linear thinking and verbal language. There is no logical progression. No accurately descriptive words exist and the same rules do not apply. The experience is irrational because one is struck by the experience, rather than engaging in an internal process of rationally thinking about it, or developing feelings that will determine how the experience will be perceived.

Verbal communication is a sequential process tied to causal logic and is a function of our conscious ego. We use speech, both internally and externally, to differentiate, interpret, and assign meaning about what is happening in our inner and outer world. However, the realm of the energetic collective can only be accessed indirectly through intuitive and sensory experience, beyond the boundaries of ordinary mental functioning. The Belly and the Heart do not experience events in the same way as the Mind. Because of this, making sense of an intense energetic experience is individually "felt" as direct experience.

In the later phases of reentry transition, it becomes possible to verbalize aspects of the process — as I am doing now — however, during the initial phase this is not possible because much of the information in the initial phase is coded internally as non-verbal, sensory/somatic experience.

In *The Eagle's Gift*, Castaneda (1981) has described the process of recapitulation:

> ...reaching an unimagined world of hidden memories. {Recapitulation] enabled us to recollect events that we were incapable of retrieving with our everyday-life memory. When we rehashed those events in our waking hours it triggered yet more detailed recollections. In this fashion we disinterred, so to speak, masses of memories that had been buried in us (p. 167).

The reentry dilemma reminds me of an old *Star Trek* episode, during which a series of circumstances have occurred, leaving Dr. McCoy in the predicament of having to transplant Spock's brain. During this particular episode McCoy is downloaded the information to accomplish this amazing feat and marvels about how simple the procedure is. Although he rapidly loses the valuable information upon returning to his normal mental state, McCoy remembers the ease he experienced in performing the complex operation. Shifting from experiencing the energetic collective back to ordinary reality corresponds to Dr. McCoy's situation, only more so.

There are many myths where the hero looks back after a journey to the underworld and, as a result, whatever he was trying to bring back is forever lost. In *Creation Myths*, Jungian analyst Marie Louis Von Franz (1972) explores this issue of coming back from mystical experience and crossing what she refers to as the threshold involving a "relativity of time and space and a temporal simultaneity of the whole content." She wrote:

> For instance, Jakob Boehme, the great mystic, had a sudden enlightenment when looking at a tin plate in which a ray of sunlight was reflected. This threw him into an

ecstasy, and he saw what he said was the whole mystery of the cosmos. All his chaotic stammering and bad style are really the effort to put this one experience into a spatial and logical time sequence, something which he grasped, and by which he had been overwhelmed in one second! Though he did not quite succeed in doing it, he spent the rest of his life trying to work it out, to put it into words and into a conscious system (p. 56).

Making a perceptual shift from a fluid state of deep, otherworld, energetic experience back into a linear time and space is a process that begins as an approximation involving the Mind. The Mind is the mechanism involved in translating energetic experience into analytic constructs using words, as I am attempting to do now.

Being with something energetically requires entering into a state of fluidity in the present moment, while describing something symbolically requires being outside of the experience that has already happened. Images and words are symbols that represent experience but are not the experience itself. The internal dialogue between energetic experience and analytic thought often occurs first as a formless state in the body and then begins to take on form through images, which is why using metaphors can be helpful. The images then become shaped using words. The permutation of energetic experience into images and or words is never exact. This is because the essence of the actual energetic experience can only be accessed as a present state, and only be described as it is remembered in the past.

Taoists and Existentialists have explored the philosophical dilemma related to the experience of disconnection. In Western culture, we tend to think about our experiences rather than relate to them. Describing an experience is a cognitive operation that requires separating from the "I" which is describing it. The operation of transferring energetic experience into a cognitive framework cannot be successfully approached as an intellectual exercise because our intellect lacks the capacity to process the experiences of our other parts. Once something is named, we are referencing something that has already occurred in the past, and we are no longer in the flow of actually experiencing it. We are no longer open to the process — or, as in the story about the rainmaker, in the Tao of the experience.

Imagine a bank of fog settling in along a coast. Although such a phenomenon can occur rapidly— it is linear. Understanding the experience requires global attention. If an attempt was made to draw such an event, the layering of the fog would occur all at once in gestural movements — and it would be impossible to capture the mood with precise, detailed "mark-making."

This metaphor applies to the process of reentry as well. Although developing some understanding of deeper meaning in layers of the psyche closer to conscious awareness is useful in assimilating the experience psychologically, this process is difficult in the early stages of coming back from the realm of the energetic collective. This is because at the energetic level, everything is connected as a web or matrix of light — beyond form in the outer world and mental imagery in the inner world of our mind.

Shamans and traditional native healers have learned to work through relationship with the energy channels of the luminous body as a whole. The means of processing energetic experience occurs as somatic connection in our Belly. In this state of snake perception, through connecting with Amaru, everything is experienced as direct contact and connection. Moving from a state of "no separation" in the energetic collective, into a primary state of energetic potential through the Belly becomes an energetic exchange between spirit and matter — and the beginning of physical manifestation as somatic experience occurs.

In addition to adopting a negotiable attitude in the present, transitioning back from nonordinary reality requires actively using intention. Castaneda wrote, "Intent is what sends a shaman through a wall, through space to infinity."[39] Focusing our intent is a way of finding our purpose. It is the means of directing and reaching the destination of our travel in the otherworld. It is how we track during vision states.

Like Jung with his hearty constitution, our ability to apply our intent is influenced by our capability to focus, and our negotiability, or willingness to let go of limiting beliefs and negative attitudes that hold us back. We create a natural law that we believe. We attract what we have an affinity for. Whatever we focus on becomes stronger.

After we have clearly defined our intention using our Minds, we can use our Belly to strengthen intention by drawing from the energy of our creative will, which is needed to implement actual perceptual shifts into nonordinary reality. By transferring our attention from our busy minds to a relaxed focus of intention, using our Belly, we may experience being fully present in the current moment in our bodies. Being fully and immediately present enables us to enter into a receptive state, increasing our awareness and capacity to track what is happening around us.

The Belly becomes the vessel that contains the energy, and the staging area for processing somatic memories in the present. Unlike verbal concepts, sensation can be experienced, with full awareness of being in the experience occurring simultaneously. Fully being is a process that involves understanding with the body through the Belly. This is because we experience energy through the Belly and use our Minds to describe the energy through images and thoughts. The actual experience, occurring

---

[39] C. Castaneda, *Wheel of Time*, p. 54.

energetically within the body through the Belly takes place at a deeper, preverbal and preimage level, before abstraction.

Infant Research and Shamanic Experience

The findings of early infant research are helpful in developing an understanding of reentry after shamanic experience. As in early stages of infancy, when the ego is in the process of being formed, what takes place during a shamanic initiation lies outside of the scope of ego functioning. To process the experience an internal cognitive schemata must form to accommodate the experience. In his writing on early psychological development, Bollas has stated, "The experience of the object precedes the knowing of the object" (p. 39). In other words, we experience our world before we know our world. In the first stage of cognitive development, sensory motor experience is understood to be a necessary building block.

Early infant attachment research has shown that newborn babies require a secure holding environment for strong psychological growth.[40] The experience of nonverbal, somatic containment corresponds to the shamanic experience of reentry through the luminous body.

In many ways, the first stage of the reentry process is a reenactment of the birth process involving separation from a state of connectivity — for the shaman this is with the energetic collective and for a baby it is a symbiotic relationship with the mother. The shaman's process of reentry involves reexperiencing history related to early emotional trauma as the spirit reenters the energy centers of the body. This is why a sturdy ego is essential in

---

[40] Object Relations analysts such as Rosenfeld, Winnicott, and Klein have all described the need of both infants and adult psychotic patient to find a "safe holding environment" and "space inside the mother" (Summers, 1994, p. 128).

order to engage in this type of work. It is well known that many people who become shamans have gone through early traumatic events or physical illnesses, often associated with dismemberment that would bring about dissociative states. For individuals with a personal history of childhood trauma, the emotions experienced during this process can be particularly challenging, as unresolved early childhood wounds are reopened.

After the spirit reenters the energy centers of the body, as energy experience becomes assimilated into somatic body awareness, the ego transitions through a phase of reintegration when the experience is brought into conscious awareness. Integrating energetic experience to make meaning occurs as a blending and layering process, starting as a nonverbal energetic state that gradually shifts into organized language. Initially — in both shamanic experience and the infant's preverbal world — no language or internal map exists to build upon, so one must be formed.

Our bodies are the cumulative storehouses of our experience, which are accessed in present states of awareness. Past experiences that we are capable of recollecting but are not consciously aware of in a given moment, along with any repressed memories — too traumatic to consciously hold — become stored as somatic memory in our bodies. Our luminous bodies are the templates. They encode this energetic information in the matter of our physical bodies. As described earlier, in addition to carrying the energy of our past and the totality of our ancestral lineage, the luminous body contains the visions we construct for ourselves as well as the blueprint of wholeness of our future.[41]

------

[41] Arnie Mindell (1985) has described processing information from the subtle body through different channels. In *Working with the Dream Body*, he wrote, "The different channels of the process are like the little streams which go off from the bigger river. If you do not know about channels,

By remembering the energetic experience contained in our luminous bodies, our Belly enables us to stay acutely connected with the actual energetic experience. Accessing memories in states of heightened awareness begins with the activity of "swallowing energetic experience whole." As the process begins, the Belly provides the vessel needed to hold the experience in order for it to become metabolized into a form that can be worked with and translated into cognitive understanding.

This process resembles the digestion process of snakes. Snakes ingest their prey completely— in one piece, and then become dormant as digestive enzymes dissolve the nutrients of the food. The process of absorption occurs as the threshold of what is referred to as "the energy barrier" is crossed, causing a reaction. Like snakes digesting their food, by opening ourselves to somatic experience through our Belly we cross the threshold of the energy barrier between ordinary and nonordinary reality. Q'ero shamans call this merging with Amaru, the great snake manifestation of Pachamama. Q'ero shamans teach that experiencing energetically through our bodies is how we become aware of being in the moment.

Rearranging Experience between the Left and the Right Sides of the Body

Assimilating and integrating numinous experience into conscious awareness requires moving it from the somatic state we first experience in the Belly. To do this we rearrange energy in our luminous bodies. During his apprenticeship with the sorcerer Don Juan, Castaneda described shifting between reality states of heightened awareness as a bottom-up process of remembering

---

then you will work only physically, or only with the dreams of your client, and you'll miss the bends and turns in the river, which makes all the difference in the world." (p. 11)

through the body. In addition to involving a shift from somatic experience into cognitive understanding, Castaneda understood the process to be a transfer from the left side of the body to the right side of the body. In Q'ero shamanism the term *collari* refers to the feminine principle of formlessness governing the left side of the body and *inkari* refers to the structured masculine principle governing the right side of the body. In *The Eagle's Gift*, Castaneda (1981) wrote,

> Don Juan had told us that human beings are divided in two. The right side of the body, which he called the *tonal*, encompasses everything the intellect can conceive of in normal awareness. The left side, called the *nagual*, is a realm of indescribable features: a realm impossible to contain in words. The left side is comprehended, if comprehension is what takes place, with the total body; thus its resistance to conceptualization. (p.167)

Castaneda is using sides of the body as a metaphor for the split between ordinary and nonordinary. During his training Don Juan moved him between the states by a blow on his spine, high up between his shoulder blades. Each tradition has its own way of describing the differences. In the Q'ero terminology, the division is between Mind, Heart, and Belly. For me transitions between states come from interactions with the spirits and through the rituals led by the shamans.

For shamans, bringing memories of numinous energetic states into the linear time of ordinary reality takes place through a process of remembering and recapitulating. According to Castaneda (1984), "No one remembers anything while in a state of heightened awareness. Remembering is an act of becoming conscious, or shifting from the left side to the right side" (p. 10).

In *The Eagle's Gift*, Castaneda wrote:

...the richness of our perception on the left side was a post-facto realization. Our interaction appeared to be rich in the light of our capacity to remember it. We became cognizant then that in these states of heightened awareness we had perceived everything in one big clump, one bulky mass of inextricable detail. We called this ability to perceive everything at once *intensity*. For years, we had found it impossible to examine the separate constituent parts of these chunks of experience; we had been unable to synthesize those parts into a sequence that would make sense to the intellect. Since we were incapable of those syntheses, we could not remember. Our incapacity to remember was in reality an incapacity to put the memory of our perception on a linear basis. We could not lay our experiences flat, so to speak and arrange them in a sequential order. The experiences were available to us, but at the same time they were impossible to retrieve, for they were blocked by a wall of *intensity*.

The task of remembering, then, was properly the task of joining our left and right sides, of reconciling these two distinct forms of perception into a unified whole. It was the task of consolidating the totality of oneself by rearranging *intensity* into a linear sequence. (p. 170)

Q'ero shamans have an easier time with this than Westerners because they live in a culture that teaches experiencing the world with all three aspects of the self. By living in close connection with their natural environment, they have greater understanding of experiencing through their bodies. Movement of experiences from Heart and Belly to Mind is something they have experienced their whole lives.

23. Imaginative Engagement and Acts of Creation

If you want to be an altomesayoq, there is the possibility. So it's up to you. It's up to you how you can harbor that power and you can grow that power.

— Don Alarijo, *pampamesayoq*, 2011

The recapitulation process that occurs during reentry begins as a progression through various feeling states. Initially, consciously connecting with deep, nonverbal experiences may be difficult because the cues associated with ordinary memory retrieval are unavailable due to the nonordinary nature of the experience. Feeling and sensation states are the ways numinous experience becomes accessible to our brains during ordinary waking states.

Castaneda wrote,

> For a warrior, the spirit is an abstract only because he knows it without words or even thoughts. It's an abstract because he can't conceive what the spirit is. Yet, without the slightest chance or desire to understand it, a warrior handles the spirit. He recognizes it, beckons it, entices it, becomes familiar with it, and expresses it with his acts ("The Power of Silence" in *The Wheel of Time*, 1998, p. 262).

From these states symbols connected to the feelings emerge. In the creative act of shifting from the energetic realm to discreet form in ordinary reality, symbolic imagery forms the necessary transitional bridge that is useful in describing an approximation of the experience.

During the Imaginative Engagement phase of reentry, symbols emerge into conscious awareness as movement is made from an energetic state into more differentiated states of ego consciousness. Working symbolically with emerging dream images can be instrumental in configuring the energy of the experience into a representational format, which then becomes easier to assimilate using our mind. In the process of actively imagining symbolic imagery, the depth of the connection to numinous experience — or nonordinary reality — varies depending on our present state of mind, intention, and the degree of receptivity.

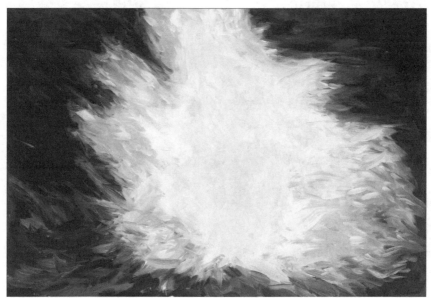

Figure 3: The Energetic Collective

My experience is that a cumulative layering effect occurs. I noticed that when I returned from my first major initiatory experience, I felt compelled to try to paint what I had experienced. I found myself painting images of "worm holes" into a vibrant white light.

Sometimes the faint outline or gesture of a bird would enter the imagery on the canvas. Over and over again, I painted the picture of what I had experienced on the mountain, attempting to find a way of conveying the profound experience I held in my mind. I also wrote about the experience — the original draft of this book.

After my first major initiatory experience, each night in my dreams I returned to the mountain, and once again became immersed in the vibrant light that now felt like home to me — and

Figure 4: Condor Vision

to my soul. I felt the momentum of the energy as a forceful drive that needed to be expressed and given form in this world.

The length of time we carry the afterglow of numinous experience in our luminous body depends on our willingness to engage with our vision of the experience and to keep it alive in our Mind, Heart, and Belly. At deep levels of profound energetic collective experience, a faint thread of conscious awareness is held by being with the feeling. Following the feeling of energetic experience is the only means of connecting with the experience at a preconscious level. This is because these states exist in nonverbal and nonimage centers — and feeling states are the only channel available to us at deeper levels. Once an energetic experience can be felt, it can be recapitulated — and processed.

Shamans believe that healing the past occurs through feeling with the Heart. Telling (and retelling) the personal recollection of the past as it is recalled in a given moment often generates feelings connected to it through the Heart. This is the basis for the healing that occurs during trauma work.

After returning home after one of my trips to Peru, for a period I repeatedly dreamt of snakes. I had dreams of snakes lying by my feet at my computer as I wrote and of carrying them around in my pockets. Snakes became my companions in the inner world. In one of my dreams, a powerful snake split open the floor beneath me. In another dream, I was taking energy from a large snake in the otherworld and giving it to baby snakes that lived in caves in this world. The snake dreams I experienced provided my psyche with a metaphor for working with and assimilating the powerful energy of Amaru associated with the numinous experience.

Inner symbols charged with psychic energy often become accessible in dreams, meaningful synchronistic events, and shamanic vision. The process of remembering by circumambulating around a symbol or image is a top-down approach that eventually may become grounded in the body through an "aha" moment. Moving into energetic states of connectivity usually involves first feeling the experience somatically in the Belly. From this feeling state, symbolic imagery may emerge that provides structure that can contain the energetic experience.

Engaging in this way offers a means of entering a dialogue with nonordinary reality. The constant element in each of these processes is that connection with the experience occurs and is maintained through the body, first somatically, then emotionally, and then in the form of imagery. The sequence of steps involved in the recapitulation process corresponds to experiencing energy through the Belly, the Heart, and then through the Mind.

Working with Symbolism

Similar to the practice of yoga or meditation, recapitulation requires discipline. This may begin to feel laborious if a live connection with the energy of the experience is lost. Using creativity and imagination during the reentry process is useful once the energy has become accessible in the form of images or symbols. For an artistic act to have meaning, it must involve the imagination and become an automatic experience through the creation of a symbol. Usually symbols take form in visual imagery, although sometimes they are heard or felt. Symbols arising from our own psyches are generally the most potent with the greatest capacity for holding numinous energy. Sometimes people also work with collective religious symbols that have become imbued with meaning through personal associations. Experiences in nonordinary reality and the imaginal realm that are not recorded immediately, or expressed creatively may be rapidly lost, similar to the way dreams are forgotten as the day progresses.

Creative expression, actively engaging with symbolism, and using imagination are methods of constructing vantage points to stand on when creating meaning. They are the vehicles for integrating a numinous experience. Activities involving the imagination include working with dream symbolism, waking phantasies, and interacting with visionary experience, and may be carried out either in the inner imaginal realm or as a process involving external objects. Jung referred to this process as active imagination. In shamanism, *mesa* stones provide a symbolic function in clearing past events and/or recapitulating experience. Similarly, in psychotherapy, recapitulation is usually a verbal process that may be augmented through art, sand trays, or through play therapy with children.

The act of creating occurs when we are in the flow of the experience. Being in the flow requires the ability to stay present. Our body's experience brings us to the here and now and opens the channel for creative expression. The creative act is engaging in a process of open dialogue with the energetic collective. The act of creating facilitates the manifestation of energetic experience in an outward expression — and what has been unconscious becomes conscious.

In Western culture, creative expression is a means of working symbolically with numinous energy. Creative activities such as writing, gardening, or painting are ways of continuing a dialogue with numinous experience. The art form provides the context for "the work" — becomes an access point into nonordinary reality. The mode of artistic expression offers the means of solidifying the energetic experience. Creative expression contains the heat of the energy and becomes an organizing agent that is both the catalyst and a vehicle for self-reflection.

Working with imagery gives us the necessary building blocks to transfer the experience into language. This allows us to begin to think about the experience explicitly and approximate it in linear

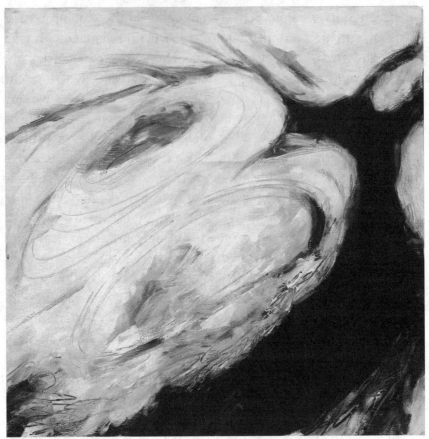

Figure 5: The Birdman

terms. My own transition through the stages of reentry started during my first vision experience in Peru while sitting on top of the mountain. I experienced the intense white light of the energetic collective running through my body as an intense electrical current. I saw the energy emanating from the mountain range in front of me as I felt it pulsing through me. Over time, the vibrant light shifted into an energetic outline of a bird.

Later, as I reflected back on the experience, the bird became my mind's anchor for what I had experienced. After I returned home, I painted the bird that I saw in my mind's eye. In my dreams, I accessed the energetic state through the bird image. The bird images appeared to me in a state of receptivity.

I experienced the prementation phase of recapitulation through maintaining a receptive ego state. This provided a means of mentally holding the energetic experience consciously in the bird image. Having the ability to access the memory of the experience of the bird in my mind gave me the opportunity to process the vision experience. The symbols gave form to the energetic experience, enabling me to think about and reflect upon it.

I am aware that I would have still been able to access the energy of the experience even if had not "morphed" into a bird, but the bird image added dimensionality that made it easier for my Mind to access. The symbolic form of the bird offered a bridge between my Mind and Heart to sharpen my memory of the experience. In *The Eagles Gift*,[42] Castaneda describes Don Juan's practice of having Castaneda interact with certain people in states of heightened awareness to aid in the task of remembering. By creating appropriate conditions for remembering, the "vivid, moment to moment recollections" could be reconstructed from the events. Having some reference point for memory while in an altered state helps in the process of memory retrieval during ordinary states. This process occurs during Imaginative Engagement.

The Symbolic Expression of Q'ero Shamans

For Q'ero shamans, rituals are creative acts of Imaginative Engagement. Ceremonies performed individually and in community with others often involve symbols and words to facilitate sacred engagement with the energetic collective.

---

[42] C. Castaneda, *The Eagles Gift*, p. 170.

Through the *temenos* of ceremony, the rituals function as a bridge between soma and psyche and the energetic collective.

In addition to working with *mesa* stones as described previously, another practice I learned from the Q'ero shamans, which I have found useful during the process of recapitulation, is to sit somewhere in nature and to create a *pacha*. Besides marking an intersection in space and time, the word *pacha* can also refer to the physical activity of mapping personal life history from birth to the present. A *pacha* "life map" is often a circular timeline marked by stones, sticks, and other objects found in nature. These designate significant patterns and events recorded in seven-year increments. Creating a *pacha* presents a means of slowing down, stepping to the side, and seeing one's life from a bird's eye perspective. Working with this kind of a life map provides an overview of our past, with the opportunity to envision the direction of our life path moving forward. This practice can assist us in cultivating a new awareness free from rigid preconceptions that may have limited us in the past. Self-reflective ritualistic activities, such as *pachas*, are ways of drawing meaning from events and situations and creating new life narratives. *Pachas* can also be useful in assimilating experience that occurs in states of heightened awareness.

Exercise 12: Creating a *Pacha*

You may decide to create your own *pacha*. After reading this, plan to put the book down and find a place that you are drawn to in nature, but first, it is important that you find an offering to give to Pachamama. Shamans never come empty handed to a ritual or ceremony with Pachamama. They bring an offering often consisting of grains, flowers, or leaves. In Peru, shamans sometimes bring candy or colorful paper decorations. You might bring some grains you have in your kitchen or cut a flower from a nearby plant that is indigenous to your area.

After you have gathered your offering, find a comfortable spot in nature where you can sit undisturbed. When you have found your spot, clear a space on the ground about two feet in diameter, leaving an area for you to sit. This will be the space for your *pacha*.

Next, gather small stones, twigs, or shells to use as markers for the life map you will be creating. Take a moment to sit quietly, shifting into a receptive state of mind. You may call sacred space by asking the spirits of the land for assistance. Using your intent, gradually begin to feel into your surroundings. After you become aware of your connection to the earth and other living things, take a moment to reflect on the course that your life has taken.

Begin creating a timeline by placing the natural objects you have collected in a design that represents your life from your birth to the present. Starting with your birth, gradually map out the course of your life in seven-year increments. You might create a *pacha* shaped as a wheel with the seven-year periods becoming spokes, or instead you may create a spiral starting with your birth and moving outward. Indicate the significant events that have occurred in your life with other markers. You might mark events such as weddings, moves, or deaths. Include any life event that has been important in shaping who you are today. Using your intuition by following any hunch you might have, pair your life events with markers that feel most appropriate. When you are finished with the map, sit for a moment. Does this feel right to you? Is there anything missing that you would like to add?

When your sense that your *pacha* is complete, feed the *pacha* with the offering you have brought. You may visit the *pacha* as often as you like to rekindle your connection — paying close attention to any changes that may have occurred. Continuing to feed your *pacha* using your intention will help it to grow stronger.

24. Narrative Integration and Condor Vision

Lineage enables us to gain balance. As we serve lineage, we need to be creators of tradition, re-enacting presences before and after, bodies of custom and knowledge. As we undergo our journey, although the person is important, collective identity occurs through the lineage of our becoming — and the ones after us — our children. Here in Peru there are tremendous power places, royal roads, luminous markers here for us. Collective identity we are summoning ourselves to is important for ourselves and our descendants.

— Dona Alahandrina, *altomesayoq*, 2011

During Somatic Perception, the first phase of reentry immediately following an intense energetic experience, the luminous body progressively adjusts to the incoming influx of energy through the Belly. This energy is often experienced as intense white light or a state of euphoria. After a numinous experience, the physical body gradually acclimates and begins to regulate the increase in energy through implicit feeling. Physically, numinous experience may be felt as a surge of energy, or a vibration that can range from ripples to tremors to spasms. The quality of experience is individual and a function of the particular experience, especially if it involves an initiation.

In the phase of Imaginative Engagement, the energetic experience shifts from being primarily sensation-based into a state where words and symbolic mental images related to the experience begin entering the Mind. Over time, these words and images are gradually woven into the framework of a verbal narrative as the transfer is made from remembering the energetic experience implicitly through the body into memory using the Mind. This transition brings the capacity for mental self-reflection as a shift is made to Condor vision. I am calling the third phase of reentry Narrative Integration.

During Narrative Integration, our perception shifts from somatic experience into a cognitive perspective that we can share with others. From a birds-eye view, our minds have the capacity to begin to describe and reflect upon personal nonordinary reality experience. This cognitive operation is called mentation.

Mentation is a form of abstract thinking that involves "naming" our experience of being in the world. Within the context of our experience of ordinary reality, mentation gives us the ability to step outside of ourselves and reflect upon our thoughts and behaviors.

While shifting into a state of normal awareness after a nonordinary reality experience, the process of mentation becomes more complicated. This is because our ego — as the center of consciousness in our psyche — must read and interpret incoming energetic information in order to self-reflect. To accomplish this, ego first must understand what it is reflecting on.

During reentry, the capacity to reflect upon our experience using verbal language is a function of self-awareness in our body. Translating the imprint residing in the body that is associated with deep memories and early experiences into conscious ego awareness begins with implicitly reexperiencing the feeling states associated with the memory. Converting the somatic memory of energetic experiences that have taken place during altered states

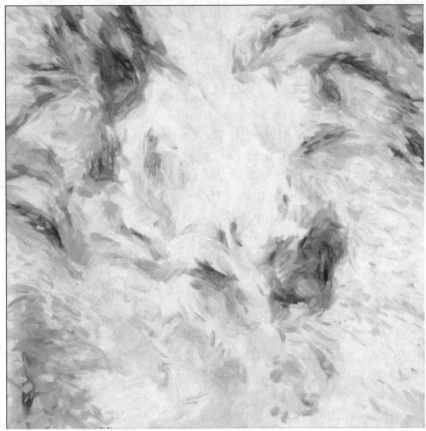

Figure 6: Energetic Collective

in nonordinary reality into a tangible ego language requires arranging the experiences contextually in linear time and space. This understanding develops through linking symbolic imagery with feeling states. Symbolic imagery and metaphor provide us with useful mental constructs that exist outside our inner world. The space that is created between our immediate experience and the symbol we are working with enables us to name what we are feeling and what holds true for us. Anchoring the experience in this fashion is necessary for self-reflection and mentation to occur.

The mentation process of conscious differentiation provides a means of separating from the sensation of our experience so that we may think and reflect upon it, facilitating the development of a personal narrative that is congruent with our perception of our own ego structure. This makes our experience available to our consciousness. Being able to work with an event as past gives us a chance to step outside of the experience and reflect upon it. The act of verbally describing our recollection of an experience enables our egos to assimilate the memory into meaningful personal narratives.

Castaneda wrote:

> The average man also examines the past. But it's his personal past that he examines, for personal reasons. He measures himself against the past, whether his personal past, or the past knowledge of his time, in order to find justification for his behavior, or to establish a model for himself. (C. Castaneda, "The Power of Silence" in *The Wheel of Power*, p. 260).

The recapitulation process of actively rearranging our current perceptions of memories of past events, which form our personal narratives, increases our understanding of who we are in the present. Forming a flexible narrative enables us to remove ourselves from the immediacy of the experience in order to recollect our perception of what has taken place more thoroughly. Creating new awareness creates new understanding in the present.

During the recapitulation process in reentry, the capacity for mentation determines our ability to regulate the incoming sensory stimulation of the energetic experience — as well as our emotional response to an intense influx of energy. Engaging in the activity of mentation can help us regulate our emotional reactions to our experience because it facilitates the opportunity for a more objective vantage point.

A similar process occurs in working through trauma in psychotherapy. Helping clients move from feeling the emotions and physical sensation associated with their traumatic experience into the story of their personal narrative created from the memory of the traumatic event is followed with the act of recapitulation. In this process the interpretive meaning of the narratives that have formed as a result of the experience are explored.

In addition to working through energetic charges that are being carried from the past, intentionally focusing on feelings experienced in the present that stem from unresolved past memories may change our experience of the present and affect our experience in the future. An example of such a scenario occurred several years ago when I was working with an intelligent young woman who was processing the painful memory of her parent's separation that began when she was two years old. As the young woman led me through her personal narrative, she said that she had assumed that she was responsible for her parent's divorce. This woman happened to have a graduate degree in early childhood development — which was probably no coincidence. When she heard herself say aloud that as a two-year-old she had caused the divorce, she instantly became aware of the fallacy of her personal narrative and in that moment was able to let it go.

During the initial phase of reentry and in trauma work, focusing on breathing and attending to physical sensations in the belly are two ways of regulating the potential reaction to the energy charge associated with the experience. Applying these techniques can create a buffer to absorb the shock that may accompany consciously remembering what has taken place and defend against falling into potentially disorganized psychological states. Experiencing somatically requires being in the present and limits the possibility of constructing narrative realities related to an unfulfilled past or catastrophic future.

Psychologists and therapists working with clients who have trauma histories are acutely aware that memories change through the act of remembering. The narrative interpretation of past events becomes fundamentally altered as feelings linked to painful past events are worked through. Through the process of recapitulation, forgotten details are remembered and the assumptions we have made about the world change as we reexperience parts of ourselves that we split off in an effort to avoid feeling pain.

An example that illustrates this progression occurred in my psychotherapy practice years ago. This particular client had described feeling paralyzed as a result of her inability to escape the painful physical abuse she experienced from her raging stepfather on a regular basis. As she recollected the pain associated with the past memories in her body, she began to feel numbness and tingling in her legs. Through reexperiencing the somatic memory of paralysis, the client was able to connect the physical sensations to her personal narrative of the experience, and, as a result, worked through the charge of the past trauma that she had been carrying for nearly thirty years.

Many artists have explored the concept of creating a personal visual narrative. The Abstract Expressionist movement of the 1950s sprung out of the urge to understand art as a record of the artist's experience. Art critics such as Clement Greenberg argued that the artist should be less concerned with *representing* or describing the subject and more concerned with recording the artist's *experience* in relating to the subject. Jackson Pollock's paintings are a visual testimony that tracks the movements and gestures he made while putting paint on the canvas.

Contemporary performance artists have taken this concept one step further. In performance art, the viewer actually experiences the process of art in the present, as it is being created, rather than as a record of the experience of what already occurred.

The narratives we create determine our perception of our own experience. The contemporary psychoanalyst, Christopher Bollas has stated, "I argue that a person's character is a subjective recollection of the person's past."[43] The personal narrative we form can confine us to limiting assumptions we have made about the world or create new ways for us to see and perceive reality.

In *The Power of Silence*, Castaneda (1987) described a process of recollecting with engagement:

> Sorcerers start their recapitulation by thinking, by remembering the most important acts of their lives. From merely thinking about them, they can then move on to actually being at the site of the event. When they can do that — be at the site of the event — they have successfully shifted their assemblage point to the precise point where the event took place (p. 145).

Shifts between ordinary and nonordinary reality states require constructing a permeable personal narrative that can adjust to the ongoing changes of the living experience. Shamans are aware that recapitulating past experience into our personal narratives determines who we are at any given moment in consensual reality. They understand the importance of not becoming overly identified or "claimed" by feelings associated with the memory. Like the wise Jedi warrior Obi-Wan Kenobi in the *Star Wars* film, who passes discreetly through difficult situations, shamans maintain a fluid state of energetic connection through the act of using conscious intention. In remaining unattached to their outer appearance in the world, they are able to "leave no footprints." In this state, it becomes possible to be "in the world but not of it."

---

[43] C. Bollas, 1987, *Shadow of the Object.*

This intentional practice of constructing provisional identities that can be physically altered in ordinary reality is known in shamanism as shape shifting. Shape shifting refers to the capacity to hold the necessary power to make the perceptual leap out of a personal identity limited by a discreet physical form into a fluid state of conscious energetic connection where anything becomes possible. The process of shape shifting occurs through merging with the energetic collective at the essential level.[44]

The process of recapitulation during reentry enables us to mentally reorganize past experience and fill in the gaps, which exist now in our current state of awareness. Creatively imagining or feeling into possibilities with new narratives changes our understanding of what has transpired. Similar to crafting a vision of the future, recapitulation involves altering the perception of the past.

Piaget's model of early cognitive development is useful in understanding how the mental maps we create to understand our world are formed. The cognitive mechanisms involved in early sensory motor processing correspond to the way we assimilate energetic experience in our luminous bodies while we are in the process of integrating numinous experience. In both situations, the ego moves into a state of disequilibrium as it encounters novel, unmapped experience, previously inaccessible using verbal or visual language. As in early preverbal development, integrating nonordinary reality experiences into conscious awareness requires our ego to find a means of coding and assimilating the experience. If no cognitive schemata or body of working knowledge based in consensual reality exists, then one must be created. In this culture, we have a need to explain our experience and as a result will go to great lengths to create a congruent internal mental framework to hold the experience.

---

[44] This visionary state is described in following chapters on initiation.

Learning to put unexplainable events on the shelf is a learned skill. Many choose to forget them instead.

Integrating experiences into a mental map results in the formation of a personal narrative in ordinary reality. The framework of a personal narrative enables the past to be differentiated from the present in a sequential format that can then be described, named, and communicated. It helps us to sort through and differentiate what may have initially felt disorganized or chaotic — what Bollas has referred to as the "unthought known."

The translation of sensory memory into verbal language enables the experience to become "thinkable." Prior to this, no functional structural method of sequencing or internal scaffolding exists. Rather than having an existing map, one must be created in the reentry process.

Adopting a fluid mental attitude of beginner's mind in relationship to the memory keeps our vision of the experience alive. It prevents us from becoming embedded in assuming what the experience should be — or what it was. Energetic visions that continue to hold the numinous charge take on a life of their own, and our relationships with our visions continue to grow and develop after we return to states of outer awareness. Like the shaman's relationship with the *mesa* and Pachamama, this relationship must be cared for and tended. Jung said that the unconscious mirrors the face that we show it. Our connection to numinous experience is a reciprocal relationship that may grow stronger if fed on a frequent basis.

The way we interact with our visions and our *mesas* must carry personal meaning for us in order to be effective. What we do to maintain this relationship is far less important than how strongly we feel about what we are doing. A personal ritual that has evolved for me has become a nightly practice. I have grown accustomed of holding a *kuya* from my *mesa* in each hand as I fall asleep and keep the medicine bundle of my *mesa* underneath my pillow. One of the stones that I now customarily embrace carries the energy of the Birdman. The other is the stone I received during my first initiation on Ausangate. Through the course of this nightly ritual, I feel my way back into the energy of my connection with the Birdman and Ausangate. My spirit finds my way back to the mountain and I drift off to sleep.

I carry my connection with Birdman and Ausangate into the day world as well. Mentally, I ask the Birdman for assistance. In my work as a psychologist and a Jungian analyst I often have the sensation I am channeling the energy and information that I pass on to my clients. During my psychotherapy sessions, I continually feel my energetic connection with Pachamama and the Birdman through my body. Somatically, using intent, I pull from the energy of the experience by consciously bringing it into the energetic analytic field to gain better intuitive understanding of the client's individual process. I source from the purifying energy I have experienced during past vision states when I am working with someone processing difficult trauma memories. Bringing an energetic connection with Pachamama into the room raises the vibrational frequency by lightening the quality of the energy field. Sourcing from Pachamama provides protective insulation to avoid *hucha* and becoming depleted by the intensity of the work.

June 19, 2011

After reading this chapter for the umpteenth time — first to organize it into something cohesive that can be more easily understood and then using metaphors and my own experience to bring Heart into the writing — I sense it still needs more. To gain objectivity, I decide to walk away and I go to the gym. I am using the elliptical machine, listening to music, reading, and occasionally glancing at the television screen that sits directly in front of me. As I look up, I notice that the final scene in the movie *King Kong* is on the screen. Fighter airplanes are firing at the giant ape that is on top of what appears to be the Empire State Building in the middle of New York City. The ape is looking gently at the heroine in a flowing, scant white dress, with pain and sadness in his eyes. The heroine is crying as she stands in front of the ape trying to protect him from the firing airplanes, and, as embarrassing as it is to admit, I find myself crying too. I hope the person next to me does not notice the tears streaming out of my eyes that I continue to wipe away as I adjust my reading glasses. She seems involved in listening to the music on her headphones.

I wonder why I cry every time I see the scene with the ape in this tacky, grade-B movie — I do not think I have ever watched the entire movie — yet I still cry. My Heart hurts as I reflect upon why I might be crying.

The feeling that I had tried to access while writing, flows easily after watching minutes of the movie — and watching the ape fall to his death. Am I crying because there is no place for the ape in our modern world? I reflect upon how, less than an hour before, I was struggling to bring feeling from otherworld experiences into my writing and contending with how difficult traversing between both worlds can be. Perhaps the ape symbolizes the longing I feel to stay connected with the otherworld and that is why I cry. Through feeling my desire for connection, as it is being expressed in the snippet of the movie, I become grounded in the experience. I recognize that the actual symbol is less important than the feeling that is attached to the symbol. I tell the Birdman that using my reaction to King Kong is embarrassing — because it's corny. I note that most self-respecting Jungian analysts would be drawn to the metaphorical content of an ancient myth or fairy tale — while I continue to cry for King Kong. The Birdman tells me that that this is why the King Kong example works — the glamour is taken out of the experience.

As I have done here, we often we pull symbolism from events in our daily lives that symbolically mirror aspects of our experience. Likewise, in dreams our psyche creates metaphoric narratives imbued with meaning from seemingly random events. For me, this came about by feeling struck by the demise of the fictional King Kong.

As my example demonstrates, sometimes silly and seemingly insignificant events can feel unexpectedly intense and powerful. Experiencing the mundane of our daily lives with interest can broaden our connection to our experience beyond the stagnant, preexisting mental framework of our inner world. Activities of open engagement can embellish our inner mental maps with greater depth of feeling and understanding. Ultimately, this is potentially linked to the development of a more comprehensive, ongoing, animate relationship. Staying open to new possibilities brings dimensionality to our intrasubjective relationship with the otherworld. It feeds the experience of the original memory.

By continuing to acknowledge the memory of our experiences we provide them with the opportunity to sustain an ongoing life of their own. Recognizing that our memories have a life of their own brings them alive in our Minds — as well as bringing back lost aspects of our soul that have split off in reaction to traumatic experiences. This is the root of meaningful synchronistic experience.

Our relationship with past experiences changes when we continue to actively engage with them as the children of our psyches that must continue to be cared for. This reciprocal process is illustrated in the numerous stories of puppets and robots that come to life because of the attention bestowed on them by their human creators. The quality of our interaction with the otherworld is always a function of our intent and ability and willingness to maintain a receptive attitude.

A seemingly random symbolic encounter can trigger an unexpected response that holds hidden meaning. As I continue to reflect on my own charged reaction to King Kong, I recognize that, fundamentally, I am responding to an underlying concern and need to protect Pachamama and the other living creatures that are frequently sacrificed in the name of technological "progress." I feel the potential devastation of disasters associated with thoughtless actions that upsets the balance of the natural order and Pachamama. I realize that this is why I feel the compelling urge to cry.

Fundamentally, we are changed through the process of interacting with our memories, and this determines our attitude toward the experience — and ultimately who we are — in any given moment. The nature of the reciprocal dynamic that exists between us and our understanding of our experience affects how each new encounter is experienced. Our present has a give-and-take relationship with our past. Time is not always experienced linearly — even in this dimension.

In *Journey to Ixtlan*, Castaneda (1972) wrote,

> It is best to release personal history because that would make us free from the thoughts of other people.... Take yourself for instance, right now you don't know if you are coming or going. And that is so, because I have erased my personal history. I have, little by little, created a fog around me and my life. And no one knows for sure what I am or what I do (p .32).

When we let go of a fixed narrative that has defined our interpretation of the past, it changes how we perceive ourselves, which changes the energetic field of our luminous body. This affects the quality of the energetic field surrounding all of us. It determines how we experience the present and how others experience us in the present. Experientially, we co-create in our relationships with ourselves, others, and Pachamama. Actively maintaining a receptive attitude in connection with our experience deepens our capacity for mentation — and enables us to use all of our experience as potential "grist for the mill" — even King Kong.

An open state of mind offers greater freedom to escape from the limitations of existing mental images that have held us hostage. An amenable attitude offers new opportunity to engage with the experience of present reality, as it is unfolding, and gives us the chance to source from and feed our visions as an integral part of daily living.

25. The Shadow Side of Reentry

I am in a room at a conference. A giant serpent has moved through the room and the floor has split open along the path it has made. A ball of light emerges, and I hear a voice saying, "They are going to try to contain it from the outside — but it won't work. There will be a second emanation of light that will emerge from the interior that will create the container."

—Personal Dream, November 2009

The first couple of months after coming home to Western living, after undergoing my first set of initiations with the shamans, were painful and extremely lonely. I was not comfortable in my own skin. Perry was the only person who understood what I was going through. He listened to me. Yet, even though I trusted his clarity of vision in the otherworld, our lives together had been fundamentally dismembered in our day world after our shamanic journeys began. I had no idea how to pick up and put the pieces together. I woke up to and lived with a constant ache of intense longing to return to the Birdman and the light on top of the mountain.

I sat with my *mesa* and wrote — and in the inner world I talked with the Birdman. Night after night, I returned to the beloved mountain. What I experienced during these nights was not a dream — there was no plot with a sequence of events. I was simply there. Then, like leaving a dream lover behind, I was forced back into the harsh reality of the day world each morning. Perhaps I was back on the mountain searching for a piece of my soul that had been left behind. If I had a choice, the rest of me would have joined the part of my soul that was still there rather than coaxing it to reenter my body. The truth is, I did not want to come back and I did not want to be back.

A part of me wanted to communicate what I had experienced and was attempting to reground myself. I struggled to find language to describe what had happened to me, yet I felt self-conscious. I felt "crazy" and was sure colleagues would say I was delusional if they knew what was going on in my mind. Perhaps I was paranoid. I know I was scared. Saying that I had experienced spirits flying through the walls and coming up through the floor and speaking seemed over the top. I remained silent and tried to "pass."

I spent days reading what others had written about their experiences in nonordinary reality, and wrote pages and pages myself, trying desperately to understand what had happened. I diagnosed myself as schizoid, and read Object Relations theory written by analysts such as Fairburn and Guntrip. The early primitive states they were describing — accompanied with the need to be encapsulated in a bubble — fit my experience. Even if it was a "severe diagnosis," being able to label myself was comforting because the part of me that was doing the diagnosing was outside of the experience. At least part of me was acting like a psychologist — even if the rest of me was crazy.

I read Thomas Ogden's work on what he has referred to as the "autistic contiguous position." Ogden has described psychological states that occur in infancy, during which everything is processed as sensory experience — before an actual awareness of discreet physical form exists. The analytical part of me understood that a part of me had "regressed" in reaction the intense energetic experience. Part of me had tapped into a time in my psychological development before I had words. I kept reading.

Where Have I Landed and What Is Real?

Carlos Castaneda's writings seemed to speak most closely to what I was experiencing — and I appreciated the fact that he did not sugar coat what his process had been like. Much of what I was experiencing at the time felt like a living hell. As time continued, I became acutely aware of the fact that I had been altered in a significant way that was turning out to not be temporary. I knew I had been fundamentally changed but could not explain how — *to anyone*.

As my friend Brad has said, too often people write about the "love and light" aspect of shamanism and leave out the shadow aspect — which in my case was every bit as real. In an attempt to recollect the pieces of himself, Brad's solution was to board a plane and return to Peru just two weeks after coming home. Since going back to Peru was not really a viable option for me at that time, I began writing. I wrote and wrote — it seemed to me that the only way for me to organize my thoughts was to attempt to track where I had been.

Few people knew what I was actually experiencing. I could not form words that adequately described what I was going through. My thoughts were not well organized and my speech was tangential. Even if I could communicate what had happened, the numinous experience felt too personal — and sacred — to share with anyone who had not experienced what I had.

During this period, I found myself growing closer to Perry. He intuitively grasped what I was going through even though I was incapable of putting it into words. His kindness and understanding felt reassuring and comforting. The intense shamanic experience that had driven us apart was now bringing us back together.

The topic of reentry eventually became the topic of my thesis in my Jungian analytic training. I am extremely grateful that I had an incredibly kind and caring thesis chairperson, Marilyn Matthews. I projected my need for the Great Mother onto her, and she gently tolerated my projection. She said she found merit in the topic "Piercing the Veil," and became an anchor point for me in the outer world. Marilyn seemed to understand the pain I was going through and encouraged me to come back into my body.

In her role as a thesis chair, Marilyn respectfully informed me that my writing was "tangential" and "scattered" — it was. She patiently helped me wade through page after page of my unassimilated writing. I was "flooded." Marilyn said she felt that what I was writing about was important and wanted to help me bring it into a form that people could easily understand. One day she jokingly asked me, "Did you hear about the intuitive that aimed for the ground — and missed?" We laughed. Her joke had "hit home" by accurately describing what I was feeling.

Almost three years later, after working with the experience of reentry by writing — and rewriting — and *rewriting* — I have gained more clarity. My thesis was approved and I completed the long, ten-year process of becoming a Jungian analyst. Now I can write and talk about what I experienced more clearly.

This chapter is the story of my own shadow experience of reentry. The journal entries shown below were my way of returning after piercing the veil and are representative of my thought process at the time.

September 30, 2009 (Reentry Experience at Two Months)

After returning home, I have spent time working in the inner world, trying to recapture and comprehend the essence of my experience. As my journey into the realm of energetic experience deepened, I began to sense that the energetic collective lay beyond what I have understood to be the archetypal regions, into a place where separation and form no longer exists. Alchemists refer to this as the prima materia. Qabbalists call this the "Veils of Negative Existence." Part of my motivation was a need to articulate in writing what I experienced during my initiation in Peru. The other motivator being a strong longing to return to the state of union.

As I spent more time in this energetic state, symbols, images, and even archetypes themselves began to feel superficial, and I sensed there was more. The concept of a continuum of the energetic collective emerged from this state, and I sensed that this might be the essential missing link. The construct of a continuum of an energetic collective conceptually could be understood as ranging from the subtle body into the land. Because this continuum exists at the essential energetic level where no form or separation exists, the idea of a continuum is only a model through which to understand the experience. This continuum may be an expansion of Jung's instinct/archetypal continuum into psychoidal territory and is the point of piercing the veil from the energetic collective back to ordinary reality. My hunch is that what I am proposing is only a superficial description of something that is vast and beyond all human senses.

As I continued to explore the realm of the energetic collective, trying to go deeper, this state of vision of light began to change, or rather, I began to change, and it began to feel like fire. As I attempted to write or describe what I was experiencing, I began to lose the sense of where I ended and where the energy began, and my words stopped making sense. In other words, my ego was beginning to decompensate. I began to feel that I was losing myself and was becoming consumed in the fire. Needless to say, it was very frightening and disorienting. I had to stop writing and I struggled to find my footing in this world again. I sat with the medicine bundle of my *mesa*, and went to see my acupuncturist who put needles in my feet. I tried to feel my body and to remember mundane things like what I had for dinner the night before. I began to wonder if I would actually go crazy and decompensate — and not find my way back.

As I tried to talk to people close to me, I could see the concern in their eyes and I knew that the gaps in my intuitive leaps in my thinking were becoming too great and my speech was becoming too tangential for anyone to follow closely. The fire of the light became increasingly uncomfortable and I found it becoming harder to disengage. Therefore, I stopped. When I visited my Jungian training analyst, he told me that I needed to "will" myself back from the otherworld and close the door to the veil of the otherworld for the time being — to shield my ego and sense of identity. He said that I was in the chaos of the prima materia and that I needed protection.

Although I had spent pages writing about the function of the land in Peruvian shamanism, what I had been writing about, trying to explain, finally began to make sense to me experientially, and I began to embody the understanding. Edinger (1985) has written about coagulating spirit into matter in *The Anatomy of the Psyche*. I felt that the land and the shaman's *mesa* are the shaman's shelter, and way of anchoring the energetic experience. In connection with the energetic collective, the shaman is the *p'aqo* or doorway that the electrical current runs through, and without a way of grounding the experience, the *p'aqo* would be burned up in the fire of the divine. For the shaman who is working with the energetic collective, the land is essential and so is the Great Mother — the *temenos* that holds the energy. It is the protection against chaos and madness.

It was then that the purpose of archetypes and symbols began to make sense, and I began to understand their necessity. Among other things, the images and symbols function as the ego's protection against the chaos of the prima materia. In reentry, the symbolic image becomes the philosopher's stone, the way to come back with meaning. It is the buffer and the insulator — the psyche's way of coagulating energetic experience. In supervision conversations, Nathan Schwartz Salant told me that coming back from the other realms was literally a birthing process. In *The Imaginary Twin*, Bion (1950) described the process of splitting off as the mechanism that allows the formation of symbols to occur.

I started looking for ways to ground myself using my thinking function as a means of separation from the actual energetic experience. I began looking for answers by revisiting psychoanalytic theory, reading material that previously had not seemed to me to be of relevant interest. I started to notice a tie between the development process in early object relation and my own reentry experience. I began to wonder if the shaman's connection of the land through the subtle body provided a *temenos*, or container, that helped to facilitate the ego's process of separating from the energetic collective — similar to what happens during infancy when the ego separates from the symbiotic relationship with the mother and forms as a separate identity.

As I write these words, I feel I am coming back into ordinary consciousness and I once again am able to begin to sense my own boundaries. I feel raw and exhausted as though I have had an intense case of the 24-hour flu for the last three days. Two days ago, I woke up feeling I would faint if I tried to stand up.

Sadly, I realize that I do not live in a culture that supports these kinds of experiences and know that I must find a way to return to and connect with the land. If I were living in Peru, I would have the support of my village, my *ayllu*. Other shamans would understand and help me create *despachos* or fire offerings for the Pachamama, the Great Mother. I am thankful for the mentors I have had that have helped me in this writing project, yet I realize, that I am very, very alone. In our extroverted culture, most of us who have these kinds of experiences have become introverted and spend time in solitude. I realize I must turn to my inner figures or allies in order to digest and metabolize what has happened.

Gradually, in the recent months after my return, I am noticing that I became more interested in daily living, or what a friend of mine refers to as the mundane. As someone adding solid food back into a liquid diet, I have begun to dialogue with my inner figures. I now understand my need for relationship with them. They are a necessary component of the veil, my cloak and protection when going into the otherworld. These inner figures need to be fed, infused with psychic energy, and attended to. They are like Peter Pan's Tinker Bell who needs belief in fairies in order to survive.

Although I am tired, I know that this work is not finished and I will need to venture to the other side again. I ask myself, why would I willingly go into these other realms again? The thought crosses my mind this might be thanatos, the death instinct written about by Freud. I am aware of the toll it has taken on my ego and my physical body. As I write this, I know I will go back, because I have no choice. Maybe it is my myth — or perhaps my fate.

Many writers and artists have creatively described the intense feelings of loneliness that often occur after undergoing mystical experience. Rilke wrote,

> Because we are alone; because we stand in the middle of a transition where we cannot remain standing with the new thing that has entered our self; because everything intimate and accustomed has for an instant been taken away (Rilke, *Letters to a Young Poet*, p. 64).

As Rilke suggested, what is familiar is gone, but perhaps even more importantly, when one returns to their outer awareness, one is forced to separate from the experience of union. Longing to return to numinous connection often brings frustration because the memory is not expressed and communicated easily — although it may become a *raison d'être* or driving force. This desire can be so strong that it becomes an insatiable compulsion. Reentry can feel like trying to communicate through a language barrier in a foreign country — or visually shifting from seeing in color to only black and white while retaining the memory of what it was like to see in color. This process can be incredibly lonely because tools to describe the experience do not exist. Explaining the experience of seeing in color is impossible if there is no common knowledge. Estrangement is an aspect of reentry that frequently must be dealt with. Even if color could be explained in a black and white world, talking about the experience may become risky.

In this culture, the reentry phase of integrating the influx of energy after otherworld encounters potentially creates two sets of relationship problems — the inward experience of alienation and the outward expression of inflation. The particular manner in which the energy becomes manifest is a direct function of the direction in which the energy is experienced. Alienation is an introverted experience of separation, marked by feelings of isolation and the inability to connect with the outside world. In inflation, the energy moves toward the world. In inflated states, the energy often feels impossible to contain, and there is an inability to disconnect from the outward expression of the experience. Both Perry and I have experienced alienation and inflation in various phases of reentry, to different degrees.

Introverted Reentry: The Experience of Alienation

The reentry process is a reenactment of the birth process because it requires separating from a symbiotic state of union. The disconnection is often followed by subsequent feelings of intense loss — which is why a "sturdy" ego is essential. Many shamans have experienced early trauma or physical illnesses, resulting in dissociative states. The intense influx of energy that occurs during the reentry process can be particularly challenging when there is a history of early childhood trauma. Early psychological states are reexperienced; unresolved childhood wounds inevitably become reopened — and must be faced and dealt with. This can cause the process of reentry to look like psychopathology.

Some people do not return to their "day jobs." Intense encounters with the energetic collective are both jarring and transformative and often leave one with the feeling that there is no way to integrate the experience into an existing frame of reference. This may result in an attempt to "move away" from the experience by discounting and dismissing the memory of what has taken place. In following the spiritual path of shamanism, the road becomes narrower and psychological defenses such as denial and intellectualization no longer work as they have in the past.

Compensatory Identification

Shamanic experience can be intimidating and the reentry process can be frightening. From the ego's perspective entering into a relationship with the energetic collective is frequently perceived as dangerous, due to its inability to control the outcome of the interaction. The popular metaphysical idea of "creating anything you want" is a fallacy beyond surface levels of ego consciousness. Movement into the veil is beyond the grasp and influence of ordinary ego functioning. As a result, moving into states associated with nonordinary reality requires the ego to surrender to a much greater energetic force — one which exists outside of the individual psyche.[45]

---

[45] Although Jung referred to this energetic force as the Self, I am reluctant to label it as such to avoid reducing the experience into an aspect of a person's psyche. The collective manifestation I have witnessed directly contradicts this interpretation.

Capitulating to the actual experience of being "dwarfed" by a much greater, independent force, which exists beyond our psyche, can be highly intimidating for a person operating with the belief system that we are ultimately in control. An attraction to shamanic experience may exist, but the fear of losing an established identity in the day world may be too great. In these situations, an attempt is made to return to things "the way they were." Jung referred to this condition as a regressive restoration of the persona.

The practice of "armchair shamanism" is common in Western culture. The need to maintain an established identity based on external circumstances creates illusion and with it the tendency to circle around the idea of the experience, instead of having the actual experience itself. Some people are drawn to the study of mystical experience, while at the same time avoiding opportunities for direct contact with the energy of numinous experience. In these situations, there is a fascination with the hidden mystery of these kinds of novel experiences, but the desire and/or mental endurance to make the actual leap into the other realm is missing. The illusion of the phantasy of the nonordinary reality experience is casually flirted with — as long as it seems harmless and situations that require direct encounters with nonordinary reality can be avoided.

This is one of the major pitfalls of Jungian psychology. Although Jung himself was most likely a visionary, symbolic images frequently become "mind candy" swallowed whole in the Jungian culture. In a couple of past relationships with my Jungian colleagues, I have observed an eagerness to associate with the experience of the energetic collective, accompanied by an unwillingness to "pierce the veil" themselves. Shamanism becomes reduced to an idea that is talked about instead of experienced. Adopting a theoretical stance is often a substitute for making a direct leap into actual shamanic experience. This is what

Q'ero shamans refer to as a "plan B" — in shamanism, there are no "plan Bs."

October 23, 2009 (Reentry Experience at Three Months)

Three months after returning I found myself continuing to process my inner experience of where I had been and noticed changes in my relationships with my children, partner, and peers. I became increasingly aware of a greater focus toward the inner world and greater intensity of the need to connect with the energetic collective. At one point my son said, "Mom, you have been crazy since you came back from Peru!"

I realized that I was different. Similar to what I frequently hear people in the midst of a depression say when they think they are still functioning well, I was surprised. I had thought I had been containing the inner turmoil I was experiencing in my attempt to return to civilian life. A couple of months after my return, a couple of clients commented that I seemed different since I came off the mountain. Surprisingly, I heard my analytic training supervisors comment that I seemed more grounded. In professional settings with colleagues, I find that I tend to censor my thoughts less and say what is on my mind more quickly. Some people seem drawn to this while others seem put off by it.

Personal relationships during this phase of reentry became difficult. Going through a four-year dismemberment process with my husband, who has been on his own shamanic initiation journey, has caused turmoil in our lives — leading to a separation for a period of time. During this period, I have noticed that colleagues seem curious about what I am doing. Maybe they are responding to the energy I brought back with me after my encounter with the energetic collective. Yet I have noticed that they have had difficulty tolerating sustained connection with me. As I have looked into their eyes, I have been aware that they were not relating to what I was saying — although they were trying. I experienced having a desperate need to be understood and to experience a sense of connection at a soulful level. I saw that I frightened them. I wondered if the energy of my experience felt contagious and if facing potential dismemberment became threatening.

I questioned what it was in me that felt compelled to share my experience. I wondered if I had a narcissistic need to be seen as a mystic or as one who "speaks with the spirits." Maybe, but that did not seem to fit with what I was feeling. I reflected on the sequence of events that occurred in my life after returning from Peru. In an attempt to reintegrate myself back into my life, I downloaded the experience into writing. I wrote solidly for six weeks, completing [a first draft of] my required thesis project for analytic training that was expected to take two years [before the project was even approved]. At the time, I had needed a way of containing the energy of the experience. In doing this, I neglected to follow proper training protocol. A couple of my peers commented that my behavior had appeared entitled. Why did I think I had a right to finish in weeks when other candidates had taken a couple of years [including a long approval process]? Did I think I was different? I speculated on whether this was true. I understood that writing had become my creative endeavor, an attempt to separate from the experience by describing it. I heard myself saying, "This isn't about me — it is about the experience."

When I reflected upon the situation weeks later, I realized that I had indeed become inflated by the archetypal energy. It felt as though I — being my ego — had been along just for the ride. I was being dragged along by a momentum of energy that was bigger than I was.

After having undergone a life-changing event through a mystical experience, a sense of being driven and continuing to carry the intense energetic force frequently remains. The unexpected, erratic power bursts are unpredictable and often difficult to manage both physically and mentally. The power of this energy is unpleasantly overwhelming if not channeled in a meaningful and imaginative way. Working with the creative expression of this energy may take on many forms — from the mounds of mashed potatoes Richard Dreyfus builds after his interaction with aliens in *Close Encounters of the Third Kind*, to an artist's painting after a numinous dream.

In extreme cases, reentry can appear and feel psychotic. This is because during reentry, our psyches are trying to integrate an energetic experience that took place outside of the time and space continuum that defines ordinary reality, and this energy is more powerful than our existing ego structure. The ego has no language that describes these kinds of intense energetic experiences because they are beyond its realm of experience. No preexisting algorithmic systems can be used, nor are there previously established road maps with easily identifiable points of references to lead the way. There is no cultural support system.

Prematurely talking about the experience during recapitulation, while still in an uncontained, energized state, may be perceived as arrogance or delusion. A mystical occurrence should not be casually discussed while it is being processed because the energetic field is in a heightened state of vulnerability. In this state, there is greater susceptibility to feeling "attacked" or misunderstood.

In *The Feminine in Fairy Tales,* Von Franz (1972) has described the need to keep mysterious archetypal processes secret "in the realm of Eros (p. 102)," in order to grow. In fairy tales, trolls and fairies live under bridges to protect themselves from light, and in "East of the Sun and West of the Moon," a young woman loses her relationship with her prince because she looks at him in forbidden candlelight. These parts of the psyche require containment and adequate time to develop before they are exposed to the outside world.

Extroverted Reentry: The Risk of Becoming Inflated

The fine line that exists between genius and insanity can seem to disappear during reentry. The aftereffects of a numinous encounter usually require dealing with the abundance of energy. If the vessel of our psyche is strong, this energy can manifest in amazingly creative ways.

In extreme cases, the intensity of the energy can feel like being on fire. It may bring a sense of euphoria — like an uncontainable substance that blasts rocket ships into warp speed. The forceful momentum of highly intense energetic experiences can bring about powerful change and transition if it is harnessed, contained, and channeled appropriately. However, the driving thrust of these energetic experiences can also become extremely difficult to manage. Psychologists frequently diagnose the manifestation of this condition as mania. In extreme cases involving psychosis, when the sense of ordinary reality is lost, it may be diagnosed as affective thought disorder.

Jung described this state as becoming inflated by archetypal energy and referred to it as mana personality. In its intensity, this psychological state of grandiosity "feels like you can do anything." The potential aftereffects of a numinous experience can be extremely disruptive — leading to destructive, dangerous behavior. While Perry was in an inflated state, he made unilateral business decisions that ultimately created a huge financial liability for both of us. Inflation becomes magnified in relation to the intensity of the experience.

Moderate States of Inflation

I experienced the negative effects associated with being in a moderately inflated state during my oral propaedeuticum exams in Jungian analytic training. A couple of days before my exams, I had spent time alone in desert, grounding and centering myself for the exams I had begun preparing for almost a year before. Sitting in silence in the incredible landscape, I entered into an altered state and connected with Pachamama. I felt very connected with nature.

Two days later, I arrived for the exams, confident and filled with the potent energy of the Great Mother. During my first three oral exams, I sourced from the strong connection I experienced with Pachamama, which I had accessed while being in the desert. I felt her powerful energy supporting me. I pulled from my recent desert encounter as a source of strength, while maintaining focus as I presented the details of the material I was orally being tested on. Everything seemed auspicious until I was in the middle of my last exam. I lost the ability to hold the tension between accessing the energy, harnessing it, and channeling it effectively in my exam.

My ability to discern what was actually happening in the room with the three examiners disappeared when I was suddenly overpowered by the powerful energy, and I became inflated. As a result, I lost my judgment and became unbalanced, causing my exam performance to be negatively impacted by my lack of conscious awareness. I had adequately prepared for the exam and could have easily presented material on the chosen topic. I most likely could have passed if I had not let myself become overwhelmed by the energetic force. As in the myth of Icarus who flies to close to the sun, I was blinded by the powerful energy.

In my inflation of what felt like an intensely potent connection with the Great Mother, I stumbled into the illusion of believing I was invincible. In one misguided moment, I threw away a year's worth of study and preparation by allowing myself to become convinced that my connection to the energy was strong enough to carry me through the exam. The forceful energy propelled me, and I tangentially leaped into an unrelated topic. The examiners recognized that I had become ungrounded, and, like Icarus, I crashed and failed the exam.

Another similar experience happened to me later in the course of my analytic training after I had a series of experiences with the powerful energy of the snake. Snakes had begun reappearing in my dreams on a nightly basis, and clients were bringing in their own snake dreams on an almost daily basis. As I had mentioned in a previous chapter, in one of my more vivid dreams, the floor split apart as a giant snake moved underneath it, bringing with it an emerging ball of light. In the dream I was told that a second burst of light would occur and this would be the container for the first blast of light. I continually dreamt of being in the underworld with snakes, and one night I dreamt a majestic white snake visited me. The next morning when I sat down in front of my computer screen to write about the snake dream I had the night before, the AOL news headlines flashed a photograph and story about a 30-foot python that had been rescued and released from captivity. Snakes were suddenly showing up everywhere in a big and meaningful way. I decided to go to Haiti to learn about Damballah, the powerful snake god who resides at the gate of the otherworld.

One day, soon after I had made the decision, I entered my clinical training supervisor's office and enthusiastically shared my recent snake energy experiences — as well as my plans to go to Haiti. After I finished talking, my supervisor, Joe McNair, looked at me intently with his hands folded and then calmly told me that I needed to learn to keep a secret. He said that openly sharing — and impulsively acting upon — numinous experiences often creates problems because "people will perceive you as crazy, arrogant, or they will become envious."

Quickly after our meeting, my plans for the trip abruptly fell through — for some reason I could not make the necessary travel arrangements — even though I continued to make numerous attempts. Then, the day before my original departure date, a tragic earthquake ravaged Haiti, destroying the location I had planned to visit.

Being Bowled Over by the Intensity of the Energy

Many people I have known have described the urge to talk about numinous experiences. Maybe the energy from a numinous experience causes the need to connect, or as one of my clients says the "urge to merge." Talking about an intense traumatic experience in a debriefing situation soon after it has occurred often mitigates the potential for negative, long-term effects. Group support has been identified as a curative factor in treating addiction in twelve-step programs. However, in the case of reentry, sharing the experience with others who have not had the experience is generally not helpful — and can even be detrimental.

The increase in psychic energy can be beneficial during the early stages of a creative or transformative cycle, but the experience will eventually need to be grounded. This unwieldy afterglow can become a Trickster, wreaking havoc in the psychic field. The struggle of the cartoon character *Casper the Friendly Ghost* illustrates this dilemma. In the cartoon, Casper unsuccessfully tries to interact with others around him in the world, but is unable to because he is not fully in the world himself. Casper feels a need to be seen and repeatedly tries to find a friend who will accept him for who he is — eventually, each time, he is rejected. The fact that he is a "ghost" — and not completely in this reality — scares people. Strangers become startled and extremely uncomfortable because he threatens their experience of consensual reality. Casper is left feeling lonely and disappointed.

The Potentially Severe Effects of Manic Inflation

Perry experienced the effects of inflation on a greater scale. For months, while in a manic state after the memories of his childhood became conscious, I watched Perry go through the same kinds of painful experiences as Casper — over and over again. When Perry met a new person who became impressed by his visions and ideas for inventions (which occurred on a regular basis), he became so excited that he would inundate and overwhelm the person with an intense flood of ideas. When the person suddenly disappeared, Perry felt hurt and misunderstood. A few weeks or months later, he would meet another person and the process would repeat itself.

The intensity of energy picked up and brought back from a numinous encounter is often difficult for others to tolerate. In a reentry state, the luminous body is expanded and wide open. The charge often creates a strong impulse to share — while others in close proximity may feel bombarded by the energy blasts and intruded upon. This kind of expanded state often constellates projections in others — as they have the experience of "bumping up against" the energy present in the field.

During his own reentry process, Perry commented to me that he felt as if he would burn up energetically if he did not tell the world about what he had undergone. He said he felt there was no way to contain the energy. Perry believed he had grabbed some important information in his journey into the otherworld and needed to communicate what he had learned as quickly as possible. He said he was afraid he would not be able to hold onto it and would lose it. From the outside, he appeared manic. During this period, his speech was pressured and his thinking was tangential. Perry appeared to be driven by a boundless source of energy. His extroverted energy bursts were difficult to keep up with and others around him began to withdraw.

Psychologically these kinds of energetic states can develop into an unrelenting compulsion that is addictive and exhausting. They are often accompanied by an irrational sense of emotional urgency that becomes uncontainable, triggering the need to blurt out whatever happens to be going on inside. In extreme conditions, the energy associated with these kinds of experiences makes the practices of keeping secrets and/or sitting with the process of the experience seem impossible.

Learning to Harness the Energy

Based upon my personal experience, it seems that the reentry process grows easier with each subsequent initiation. Last year, a month after returning from Peru, I happily noticed that my psyche did not feel as if it were on fire during my transition into my life in the outer world. I noted that my thoughts were definitely clearer and less tangential than they had been during my previous reentry, even though I was again experiencing inflation because of the energy that had been downloaded into my luminous body on the mountain. Last year I knew to channel the numinous energy creatively. I painted, wrote, and gardened for hours, late into the night, when I would have been sleeping under normal conditions.

Pacha 6: Walking in Two Worlds

Ultimately, the greatest capacity for human beings — through intent, through love, through all those wonderful virtues, passion, dedication, focus, or stubbornness, whatever, — those are just a plethora of adjectives describing your capacity to have a meaningful life.

— Jose Luis

After returning home in 2009, I knew that shamanism had become my spiritual path. I had expected that at some point, I would return to Peru but I had not given much thought to when I would actually be going back. Here is where my path led me.

26. The Journey Back In Begins

Let energy move into your Belly and Heart — weave new memories.
This is a process of remembering. Although it may seem foreign, memory
resides within us.
  — *Apu* Señor Chauipicaro, ceremony with Juanito's *mesa*, 2011

As months passed, I found myself still contending with readjusting to the day world. I appeared to be functioning for the most part in the external world, but everything in the ordinary world seemed drab and lacked meaning for me. I noticed that I had fallen into a funk, in stark contrast to the vibrancy I had felt as part of the energy of the mountain collective. My journals from that time show the process of reconnecting to my day world and using it to move farther along my path as a shaman.

January 18, 2010
    Gradually, over the course of months after my return, I noticed becoming more interested in activities related to daily living. Six months after returning to civilian life, and my practice as a psychologist, I have come to understand that there are two aspects to finding the way back. First, through feeling the field in the outer world, and second, through developing an awareness of the introverted, imaginal field in the inner world. Psychoanalysts and shamans have taken the first path, while mystics and monks

have chosen the second. The first path could be understood as connection with the Heart, the second being a path of wisdom.

I am not sure how we end up on one path instead of the other — it could be typology related (extroverted feeling vs. introverted thinking function) or it could be through cultural experience (being part of *ayllu* or community or in an analytic relationship with an emphasis on the transference relationship).

In the imaginal realm of the psyche, the symbol becomes the anchor or coagulating agent. In the external world, memory and connection in human relationships, and the experience of the land are means of organizing the experience. Both symbols and connection are a means of solidification, of bringing spirit into matter. They are transitional zones of the experience that can facilitate movement through the veil. The preverbal, presymbolic aspect of the energetic collective can be described and talked about in the inner mind or outer world through symbols, memories, and connections, but it is not the energy itself. In Jungian terms, this might be conceptualized as the actual archetype. Yet what we are talking about, here, is the stuff that the archetypes are made of, the energetic collective or the prima materia that becomes gold when it is worked with.

The psychological meaning of a numinous experience is derived from the ability to transfer the energetic experience into symbols or connection. Making meaning can be understood as an ego function — the organizing process of transferring energy into thoughts and ideas through symbols or through relational feeling states, which create memories. Psychologically, this is the means of transferring spirit into matter. This movement between energetic states, as an evolution of psychological differentiation, is a process of splitting between thou and I, fusion and separation. During the reentry process, the path our ancestors traveled manifests and is retraced through our personal complexes and history. Coming back requires revisiting emotional states and events that are unresolved, to be worked through again and again. Whether we believe in reincarnation, or repetition compulsion, the process is the same — reentry is a birthing process that involves passing through each of the sequential developmental stages to our present awareness in the outer world.

Maybe the reentry process is not about piercing anything at all, but requires instead that we learn to sit beside and tend to the experience of the collective, moving into it when and where we can. This path would be more consistent with the path of the Q'ero shamans. Is trying to figure it out similar to the hero looking back while returning from the journey and losing what he has gained? Maybe our fate is like the alien E.T., who keeps trying to "phone home." It could be that the reentry process requires us to wait patiently and tend to the fires until we can eventually be beamed up. Instead of "sticking to the image," the opus of reentry could be to sit and hold the energy, which serves as a numinous beacon for the mother ship of the collective. My sense is that what we are actually waiting for in this process of reentry is the emergence of a creative spark, otherwise known as the transcendent function, to serve as an access point or intersection between the energetic collective and the archetypal continuums that occur through the subtle body.

So where do we go from here? We go back in with the memories of reentry that have already been laid down — the guideposts as a means of making meaning. Similar to the therapeutic process involved in helping clients heal past trauma, we move back and forth — in and out of the experience — feeling it and then describing it. This slow process must be built brick by brick, or walked step by step. As the Peruvian shamans say, "poco y poco," little by little.

In February 2010, I went to see the blockbuster motion picture *Avatar*. When the movie ended, I sat with my husband and cried.

The movie mirrored my experience in Peru. The land of Pandora and the state of connection with the "Tree of Souls" reminded me of my communion with the mountain (and seemed to me to be based upon the belief system of jungle shamans). Given that the movie was the highest grossing film in history in the United States and Canada, I am aware that I was not alone. Many people in the Western world had emotional reactions similar to mine — a yearning for deep connection with nature. Perhaps collectively the film touched a universal need for connection that lies buried deep inside of each of us — which most likely brought me to Peru in the first place.

Just before seeing *Avatar*, late in the winter of 2009, while sitting with my *mesa* on a large rock, I drifted into a state of reverie and entered into a vivid vision. In the vision, I recognized the smiling face of Don Sebastian and heard his voice telling me that I needed to return to Peru to gather the loose ends of my soul. At the time, I had planned to have an easy summer and had been considering various recreational activities. Yet, I was aware that the vision — although inconvenient — needed to be taken seriously if I was going to find my way back to my old self. Upon receiving the vision, I knew I would be returning to Peru.

As I told friends and colleagues of my plans, they asked to me to consider whether I was sabotaging myself in the last stage of analytic training — given all that I still needed to accomplish in order to graduate. I acknowledged that maybe I was but I felt that ultimately I did not have a choice. Like Peter Pan who had to return to Wendy's nursery to retrieve his shadow, I had to return to Peru to retrieve a part of my soul.

In my younger years making the major decision to go to Peru so quickly — based upon a vision — would have felt hasty and impulsive. Most likely, I would have begun to "second guess" myself and doubt the authenticity of the experience. Throughout my life, people have told me that I should strive to slow down in order to become more grounded — maybe I should. These days, I worry less about these kinds of things. Learning to have faith and to trust my intuitive sense has been a lifelong process of discovery for me, fortified by personal experience. For me, deciding to return to Peru to reclaim parts of my soul was grounded. I was listening to my own intuition, what I knew and felt in my body rather than using the beliefs of others as guiding principles. Returning to Peru became imperative.

As the date to leave for Peru for the third time grew closer, I made all the necessary travel arrangements. This time Perry was finally planning to come with me. We were both determined that we would take this journey together. I was eager to share the shamanic experience of Peru with him, for him to meet the Q'ero shamans, climb mountains, and be together in fire ceremony.

Perry was excited about the upcoming trip as well and had renewed his passport in anticipation — well in advance. Perry had been working with a *mesa* for as long as I had, but in prior years some unforeseen life event had always prevented him from joining me. We had been looking forward to this trip together for months, had booked flights, and arranged accommodations. Yet even with all the planning, we would be reminded that fate is often beyond our control.

In the past, a couple of weeks prior to leaving on such a journey, I usually start to feel connection with the *Apus* I would be working with, and would often meet with them during dreamtime. This year while preparing for the upcoming trip to Peru, I had no memories in waking life of receiving visits from the *Apu* spirits in my dreams.

The night before departing, just before falling asleep, I closed my eyes and felt myself moving into an altered trance-like state that I associate with entering into sacred space. Shifting my awareness deeper into this perceptual state, I became flooded with a sense of well-being and began to feel the loving presence of a masculine mountain spirit, who I sensed I would be visiting shortly.

May 29, 2010

Using words to describe energetic body experience is difficult because it frequently occurs in the absence of thoughts or images. I could not exactly explain how I knew the presence was masculine — but I did. Perhaps it was sensing the deeper voice, or experiencing being held by what felt like a loving father energy. When I mentally asked my spirit visitor his name, the comforting voice replied, "Ausangate," and I became aware of a powerful warm and nurturing presence surrounding me. As I quietly sat with my eyes closed, I felt myself being carried into the future realm of the vision of what was yet to come. I experienced physical pangs in my heart as I felt it expanding and opening energetically. I noticed that a warm, tingling sensation was running through my body. While in an expanded Heart state, I continued feeling that I was being held by the comforting presence throughout the night as I slept. I was conscious of experiencing this strong presence when I awoke yesterday morning. I continued "tuning into" and maintaining my connection with this energy while preparing to leave for the airport.

Everything seemed to be as it should be — until we were driving to the airport. On the trip to the airport, I decided to double-check our travel documents, which I had packed in my money belt days before. When I unzipped the compartment and looked at the opened passports, it took me a second to comprehend what I read. My stomach suddenly sank. I was carrying Perry's passport that had expired the year before. Somehow, the old document had mistakenly been placed in with the travel documents instead of his new one.

Because we had left for the airport early, we had extra time. When Perry's current passport was discovered missing we quickly turned the car around and sped home to find the correct one. Hoping we would make the flight, we raced down the empty Saturday morning freeway at speeds exceeding 90 miles per hour. We were a prime target for a major speeding ticket. Perry reassured me that he had asked the spirits for help and that we were being protected. Even still, I covered my eyes, braced myself, and hoped for the best. True to his word, we arrived home safe — although scattered.

After the car had come to a stop, we leaped out and dashed into the house. We frantically looked anywhere the missing passport could possibly be. We tore through bookshelves and the remaining unpacked boxes from our move. It was nowhere. It seemed to have vanished. Days later after looking everywhere — behind bookshelves, under the computer, through drawers, boxes, and bags — repeatedly — the passport had not turned up. I was reminded once again that the fate of our lives is often in the hands of something much greater than our egos.

The emotional part of me was definitely in denial. I grasped at straws, trying to avoid the harsh reality that was becoming more apparent to me by the minute. I still hoped I would be able to change the trajectory of unpleasant events taking place within the next two hours. After searching everywhere — multiple times — I suggested to Perry that we go to the airport and see if anyone at the airlines could help us find a solution. The more rational part of me that I was trying to keep walled off from my conscious awareness knew that after 9-11 there would be no way any responsible airline official would consider allowing Perry to board a plane without current travel documents — yet I still could not believe this was actually happening.

I continued the futile struggle against the thoughts I was having. My mind kept racing to conjure up solutions, trying to think of anything to make the cruel reality of the situation not so. The stubborn, ego-driven part of me was still in shock, fighting a losing game against fate. I continued to wrestle with trying to figure out ways that I could somehow make this work. We had recently bought a house and moved. Financially, we were still extended. I had stretched our cash flow and resources as far as I could to cover monthly bills, our recent move, and the cost of the trip. I knew that at the time I did not have any extra cash or assets that I could responsibly pull more money from.

Forty-five minutes later, I sat and waited in the terminal for Perry to return from talking with the airline officials about what could be done. Time was drawing near to board the plane, and I realized that I would be forced to make a decision whether or not to go. If I went, I would leave Perry behind. I felt myself starting to panic as the conscious reality began to sink in. I began to feel more fully what Perry's not having his passport meant. Perry most likely would not be able to board the plane. The unwelcome realization was sinking like a lead weight into my psyche. I was once again returning to Peru alone — if I was going. I digested the unpleasant fact that in less than two hours, I would most likely have to leave for Peru without Perry.

As I started crying harder in a state of despair, I suddenly began to feel a calmness washing over me, coming from a source outside of me. In that moment, in the midst of my mental churning and emotional upheaval, I heard the kind voice of the presence that had been with me over the last twelve hours saying, "*Mijo*, it's okay. You must go — you need to return to Peru."[46]

The reassuring strength of the voice began to permeate my body. I sensed the part of me that had been resisting and fighting the painful truth of the current circumstances gradually begin to soften and surrender to a deeper part of me that knew I was going

---

[46] Why the voice called me *mijo*, which means "my son" (in Spanish it is a contracted form of *mi hijo*) instead of *mija*, which means daughter, I would discover in Peru.

to Peru alone. I had the sensation of being lifted and carried into a conclusion that was no longer a decision. A couple minutes later, Perry returned from the ticket counter. He sat down next to me, took my hand, and I saw that he had also been crying. I looked into his warm, dark brown eyes. He quietly told me that he was not meant to go to Peru with me this time, and he knew it.

Through his own inner connection, Perry had asked his guides what he should do and was told he was being blocked. Instead of leaving for Peru, he needed to stay behind to work on the invention he had been developing — and he needed to till the soil of the land at our new home. We both cried, knowing what was right and hating the impossibility of what felt to be another harsh set of circumstances. Enough had happened in our lives over the last seven years since we began practicing shamanism to accept that forces of nature that significantly affect our lives exist beyond our control. A week after arriving in Peru, the inevitable conclusion Perry and I were reaching would be confirmed in a coca leaf reading given by the shaman Adriel.

The flight was leaving. We had run out of time and were being forced to say good-bye. I boarded the plane and my solo journey back to Peru began.

After the plane had taken off, a documentary about lightning was playing on the overhead screen and caught my eye. A couple of people who had been struck by lightning — who had survived — were being interviewed. In Peru, being struck by lightning frequently occurs during the initiation of the *altomesayoqs* — the most powerful group of Peruvian shamans. The documentary also described the phenomenon of "positive streamers," which are clouds of charged ions emerging from the earth. When the ions meet the negative particles from the sky, there are eruptions of lightening. This seemed a bit synchronistic to me, given that my husband's recent experiences involved working with electrical atmospheric energy.

May 30, 2010

Sitting in the Lima airport coffee shop at one o'clock in the morning has become an annual ritual for me in recent years. I plan to spend the next five hours drinking Peruvian coffee, while I am waiting for my 6 AM connecting flight to Cusco. It is May 30, 2010, another year has passed, and I am returning to the Sacred Valley for the third time, to climb mountains and dialogue with the Q'ero shamans of Peru. In my upcoming journey, I will reconnect with my *ayllu*, a small community of Western *mesa* carriers who have worked together for the last couple of years to learn from the *pampamesayoqs* and *altomesayoqs*, the shamans who are the medicine people that are the direct descendents of the Incas. The members of the *ayllu* are healers, medical doctors, scientists, and psychologists who practice shamanism as part of daily living. For most of us, this practice involves attempting to find equilibrium between both worlds — or as Jung described, a psychological balance of adaptation between inner and outer conditions.[47] During this time of global transition, our collective purpose as a group is to bring the wisdom of the mountain spirits back to our Western world, with the intention of aiding the planet. As individuals making this expedition, many of us have found ourselves in transition, as we try to hold balanced footing in the ordinary reality of our professional lives in our modern world and the nonordinary realm of shamanism. Toggling back and forth between two worlds has proved to be challenging to say the least.

Last summer, the reentry process of returning home to everyday life (after receiving a series of initiations that deepened our connections with the mountain spirits) was painful for many of us. I have learned part of the difficulty reacclimating back into the modern world after a deep initiatory experience is because the aftermath of the actual experience is intangible and impossible to

---

[47] C. G. Jung, CW 18, p. 449.

describe in words. Shamanic experience occurs energetically in the luminous and somatic bodies as a feeling. A numinous experience can be experienced as well-being, feeling energized, a sense of expanding beyond one's physical body, a vibration, a buzzing or tingling, and/or an altered state in which everything is more vivid. I have heard Q'ero shamans describe this state as a process of rewiring of the energy residing in the luminous body. Although a literal and accurate statement, it is a concept that is foreign to most Westerners and not easy to explain. In the past, when I have feebly tried to offer up theoretical explanations, I have found that the explanation rarely makes sense to anyone who has not shared a similar experience. This is because shamanism is felt and experienced directly through the body, and understanding occurs through opening the Heart. Making meaning and integrating any shamanic experience ultimately must come through connection with the energy centers in the body.

Last year after returning home, for months the only dreams I could remember were recapitulating the vision I had experienced in waking life on the sacred mountain of Waquay Wilka in the Andes. This year, in a vision given to me by the mountain Ausangate, I was shown that this is because when one moves farther into the energetic realm and comes back, there are layers or a temporary split that occurs between the world of ordinary and nonordinary reality. These splits act as veils or boundaries that keep the worlds separate except when in a deep dream state. During the period of integration, it is nearly impossible to access this information in a conscious waking state. Reflecting on this now, I am not exactly sure why this split occurs, but my hunch is that it has something to do with the ego's need for structured boundaries in order to process and assimilate information.[48]

In my trip to Peru last year, although I had welcomed the exhilarating state of ecstasy connecting with the spirit of the mountain, the process had been intense and exhausting for me. While in the experience of sitting on the mountaintop of Waquay Wilka, I had gazed out across the mountain range of the sacred mountains and had felt a powerful light energy vibrating and radiating through my body. In the midst of the experience, as I attempted to hold and ground the forceful energy permeating me, the intensity was painful and cognitively disorienting. After returning from Peru, as the year progressed, I became acutely aware that I had left part of myself behind during my light encounter on the mountain. I felt scattered, yet at the same time was overcome with an incredible sense of longing to return to the place where I had sat on the mountain.

In becoming split off from sensing a greater connection to the energetic experience of the land in my body, I felt incomplete and terribly lonely at the same time. I found myself wanting to be alone. I spent a significant amount of time struggling to ground myself back in my outer modern world. Other than feeling a connection with the clients I saw in my psychotherapy practice, I stayed primarily solitary, spending hours painting and writing pages and pages about what I had witnessed in an attempt to understand what had happened to me. I heard myself telling people that I felt like Richard Dreyfus in the movie *Close Encounters of the Third Kind* when he obsessively attempts to recreate the encounter he had with aliens by building mounds and generating tones. My companions, who had been with me on the

---

[48] These splits also occur in reaction to trauma as dissociation or soul loss, an ego defense against becoming overwhelmed and flooded by powerful psychic energy.

journey to Waquay Wilka, described having similar experiences. They told me they had noticed feeling extremely fatigued for months after returning home to their lives, with a need to "burrow" into nature and the recesses of their inner world. Sitting outside in nature, experiencing the life force of the land, made it easier to integrate the energetic experience in the subtle body.

June 11, 2010

As Adriel and I sat cross-legged, facing each other in a tent on the mountain, I watched him carefully select ten individual coca leaves from the small plastic bag of leaves he carried with him. As he had done in the past, Adriel blew on the leaves offering a prayer and asking Pachamama and the mountain spirits for guidance. With a quick snap of his wrist, he threw the leaves down on top of the notebook that I had offered him to use as a flat surface. Adriel sat quietly for a moment with his hand on his chin. His piercing dark brown eyes narrowed as he looked intently at the configuration the leaves had landed in. As Adriel studied the pattern formed by the leaves, he began to chew on the coca leaves that had been tucked in the side of his cheek. Finally, he looked up at me and said in his pleasing Spanish singsong lilt that I could now recognize anywhere, "Seeester, your husband's trip was interrupted because he wasn't meant to come this time. Climbing this mountain and being in the cold would have caused problems for his feet. He will return with you next year."

Although Adriel knew nothing about Perry, other than that he was my husband, his statements corresponded to information I remembered about Perry's history. Nearly four decades ago, while in his early twenties, Perry had spent four long months in a hospital after his feet had been badly frozen. He received experimental medical care at Ohio State University Hospital and was forced to cut the skin off his own feet to prevent gangrene from entering his blood stream. Even though Perry had been fortunate enough to save his feet, he has continued to struggle with circulation problems throughout his adult life, and has often complained about his feet being cold. I pondered Ariel's statement that the cold nights camping on the mountain in temperatures below freezing would have been problematic for him, even with the appropriate gear that he had planned to bring with him. As a rule, Perry often has sought out activities that involve dealing with the challenges of nature because he enjoys them. I, on the other hand, am clear that the reason I choose sleeping on the ground in freezing temperatures over sleeping in a comfortable bed is to be on the mountain.

A couple of hours after the coca leaf reading with Adriel, while contemplating the unexpected twist of fate in regard to Perry's missing passport, I reflected on the fact that his trip being interrupted by outside forces did not seem particularly unusual to me. Years earlier, I would have assumed the misfortune was due solely to poor organization on our parts. There were, of course, rational ways to explain what had happened with Perry's missing document. We had not checked closely enough — we had misplaced it and had forgotten where we put it. Yet this did not seem to me to be the case. In preparation, I had set our passports in front of the computer weeks before, to prevent such an event from happening. I felt that Perry's staying behind had been our destiny. His path was to stay at home and tend the visions he had already received by becoming a steward of the land, while mine was to return to Peru to reclaim parts of my soul that had been left behind and to commune with my beloved mountains.

27. Sacred Pilgrimage

You must tap into and shapeshift into the aspect in you that knows other states and other universes.

— *Apu* Huascaran,
ceremony with Dona Alahandrina's *mesa*, 2011

The following pages were taken from the daily journal I kept during my third visit to Peru in June 2010. The entries have been arranged chronologically to provide some sense of continuity. I was frequently in an altered state when I made the journal entries. To make the material less confusing I have described the events as they occurred.

June 2, 2010

After returning to the Sacred Valley yesterday, I have felt myself entering an altered state. My hearing is more acute and the colors around me are brighter. I am feeling a bit spacey as I adjust to the sensation of being in a zone approaching the outer limits of ordinary time and space. I feel energized and light. My sense of myself feels expansive, larger than my actual physical body. I find this experience pleasant — both in the physical sensations and in the emotional experience of returning home. I am anticipating being in the mountains with the shamans I have come to know and love. In some ways, I feel as though I never left. I remember being on the mountaintop being blasted by light as if it were only yesterday — rather than as occurring almost a year ago. Yet I can feel the subtle but profound changes in myself that have occurred. During the last year, I have attempted to integrate the energy that was downloaded into my luminous body on the mountain.

I see old friends and I note changes in them as well. Perhaps they are wiser and a bit more settled. Many have told me that reentry for them was also a difficult process. I notice that the experience remains difficult for me to put into words. I suspect they may have also been fundamentally changed. I hope that this year I will be more prepared for what is to come. Tomorrow will be our first meeting with the *Apus*.

The energetic, intersubjective field created between the members of a group of people entering into dialogue with the *Apus* will directly affect an *altomesayoq's* ability to open the gateway between worlds. In my very first trip to Peru, I was part of a group of people who had been invited to receive *altomesayoq* initiation rites. For several days prior to entering into the ceremony, time was spent developing the energetic *ceke* lines between the members of the group, to create an energetic field that would support the shift into collective transformation. A couple years prior, I had been with a group of visitors in which factions and negative undercurrents had developed between members and, as a result, a ceremony with the *Apus* abruptly ended. What I noticed between the groups were differences among members in their ability to work with their own personal shadows.

In the *ayllu* last year, we received advanced initiation rites. The personal narrative was understood to exist, but the focus had shifted. Rather than staying caught up in the distraction of attending to superfluous details pertaining to personal life, the group's focus shifted into one of openness and availability. Holding space energetically in service of Pachamama and the *Apus* became the spotlight.

June 6, 2010

Yesterday, we had our first meeting with the *Apus* in a ceremony conducted by the young *altomesayoq* Juanito and were visited by the benefactor spirits of his *mesa*. As in the past, the ceremony was held in Moray, the small village in the Sacred Valley located about an hour away by car from Urubamba. We are staying on the outskirts of the village of Urubamba before we begin our mountain journey.

Juanito is a thirty-year-old man about 5'4" weighing approximately 120 pounds. As is common among *altomesayoqs*, Juanito was struck by lightning during his initiation ceremony with his benefactor, and the left side of his body is slightly paralyzed as result. He is humble. Quiet and soft spoken, Juanito has a gentle gaze and rarely makes eye contact, preferring to look down at the ground during conversation. Here is my memory of the ceremony:

We enter the small, rectangular, windowless, stucco room off the courtyard. After entering the room, Juanito carefully tends to the table altar located in the front of the room in order to prepare for the upcoming ceremony. One of Juanito's benefactors is *Apu* Chauipicaro, a spirit from the mountains of Bolivia. During the ceremony, the presence of *Apu* Chauipicaro will provide the portal that allows other spirits to enter and create the opportunity for other winged beings to manifest into physical reality. The table is covered by a brightly colored Peruvian textile. It holds flowers and soft drinks in honor of the *Apus* who will be visiting Juanito's *mesa* during the ceremony. Juanito's *mesa* lies open at the front of the table. It is a simple *mesa*, consisting of a few *kuya* stones and large crystals, arranged in a familiar configuration established over time during the course of working with the *kuyas*. Juanito places each of our closed, bundled *mesas* on the table to receive blessing from the *Apus* during the ceremony.

When the altar is finally prepared, Juanito is seated on a wooden bench in the corner at the front of the room. This is the customary location for the *altomesayoq* to sit during the ceremony. The eleven or so members of my *ayllu*, including myself, are seated on rows of wooden benches, facing toward the front of the room. As usual, the room is cold, and we have all put on layers of clothing with hats and ponchos to prepare for the hours that lie ahead, through which we will remain seated.

Before meeting with the *Apus* all electronic and metal objects have been removed. After we have found a seat, blankets are placed around the doors to block any light from entering the room. Light is disruptive to the spirits' passage through the space between worlds.

Sitting in the pitch-black room, we are all silent, listening to Juanito's quiet prayer, calling his benefactor by name. His soft words are followed by a couple of long whistles before he falls silent. Suddenly, a couple of moments later, we hear a loud flapping of wings emanating from the wall on our right, indicating Señor Chauipicaro's arrival. Next, there are heavy thumping noises that seem to be moving across the table, and I can hear the sounds of crystals rubbing together. I see flickers of light about three feet above where I imagine the table to be, which appear connected to the clicking crystals.

In a warm, soft-spoken masculine voice, Señor Chauipicaro greets us in Quechua. We respond by answering, "Ave Maria Purisima," the customary ceremonial salutation to the arrival of an *Apu*. This introduction is followed with the sounds of more wings flapping and thudding noises. *Apus* continue to arrive. The *Apus* are collective entities that are composite spirits of the sacred mountains surrounding us.

The *Apu* Señor Ausangate arrives, followed by others whose names I am unfamiliar with. The Mountain of Ausangate is considered one of the holiest mountains in Peru and one of the more evolved of the collective mountain *Apu* spirits. When Señor Ausangate comes in ceremony, an aspect of the mountain collective is visiting us. This is similar to the relationship of God and Christ in Christianity, Christ is not God but an aspect of God.

I am pleased to hear the reassuring sound of Señor Ausangate's voice. In response, I feel my Heart again opening and expanding in the connection we have formed, which started only the night before my journey back to Peru began. I listen to Ausangate's soothing voice, and then the meaning of his words being translated from Quechua into English.

Ausangate tells us that to increase our capacity we must remember through our bodies using our intent. The message is familiar and I let the *Apu's* voice begin to settle in on many levels as I feel the harmonic resonance of his voice entering my body. I am beginning to rock back and forth as I feel the vibration of his energy beginning to pulse more intensely through my body. I allow myself to further sink into the deepening trance state I am experiencing.[49] I continue rocking back and forth and side to side, as I sit on the wooden bench next to my companions.

The members of the *ayllu* are asking the *Apus* questions. When there is a space of silence in the room, I ask Ausangate about a scientific invention that Perry has been working on. I am aware that part of my motivation in asking this question is to bring connection with Perry into the room. I want Perry and Ausangate to experience each other. Ausangate politely responds to my question by asking for more information about what it is that I

---

[49] Eliade (1964) characterized shamanism as a "technique of ecstasy." Webster's dictionary has defined it as "excessive joy," and a "kind of cataleptic trance (1939)." Michael Harner (1980) described shamanism as "a great mental and emotional adventure" and wrote, "Ultimately shamanic knowledge can only be acquired through individual experience (pp. xiv-xv)." These definitions reflect that understanding energetically beyond words does not occur in the Mind, it can only occur in a state experienced through the body, primarily the Heart and the Belly.

would like to know. I realize that I do not have a strong enough grasp to articulate what it is that Perry is trying to create. I struggle to find words. Part of me is attempting to communicate using words, while the rest of me continues to experience the deep-centered energetic state that I am feeling in my body in my connection with Ausangate.

Ausangate tells me he will need to communicate with Perry directly. He instructs me to tell Perry to light a candle before going to sleep and entering dreamtime and to call his name, and that Ausangate will then be able to locate Perry. The *Apu* says it is easiest to communicate during dreamtime. As he is telling me this, I remember this practice of lighting a candle and calling the *Apus* from what feels like some other time before.

After I have thanked Ausangate for answering my question, I feel myself sinking deeper into the altered state. I notice myself becoming more fully centered in my body. I hear and understand the words being spoken. As the dialogue continues, the sensation of energy running through my body becomes the central focus of my attention, rather than any specific thoughts that happen to running through my brain. I feel as though I am in the ocean, deep underwater, with the words being spoken far above on the surface. I feel very safe.

Sometime later, as the ceremony is ending, I feel the cool spray of rose water landing on my body as we receive the *Apu's* blessing. The *Apu* sanctifies each of our *mesas,* which have remained on the altar through the ceremony. I hear the tops of the soda bottles that had been placed on the shaman's altar as offerings popping off, followed by sounds of liquid from the bottles spraying in the front of the room. Señor Ausangate jokingly complains that there are no beverages with sugar cane. There is more stomping across the tabletop. I hear sets of wings flapping, followed by more sets of other wings flapping, and the *Apus* are gone.

We are alone again. When we emerge from the dark room, several hours have passed, nightfall has come, and the outside temperature has dropped significantly. We quietly return to where we are staying, eat a light dinner, and retire for the evening. I sleep heavily and do not remember any of my dreams.

June 9, 2010

Dona Alahandrina is one of the few female *altomesayoqs* living in Peru today whom I have had the opportunity to work with. Although warm and engaging, her appearance is very different from Juanito's demeanor. Dona Alahandrina is a large woman with a commanding presence. I liked her from the moment I first met her a couple of years ago. She was trained as a nurse, and has continued to aid local doctors in diagnosing physical ailments in hospitals near Cusco. Her shoulder-length, thick, black hair is curled and neatly styled, pulled back from her face that is framed in bangs. Today she is wearing a bright red sweater with black pants. I notice that she is wearing modest gold jewelry and lipstick. As she greets each of us as we arrive back in Moray, she looks us in the eyes and hugs us, bringing us into her big embrace. I can tell that Dona Alahandrina is no-nonsense. She wants us to get down to work. We settle in a circle on the ground around her and she begins to speak to us in her clear and direct manner, looking intently in each of our eyes as she tries to convey to us the importance of what is at hand.

Dona Alahandrina begins to talk about the *Mosoq Karpay* and *Hatun Karpay* initiation rites that we will soon be receiving during our sacred pilgrimage in honor of the mountain. As Dona Alahandrina is speaking about the *Mosoq Karpay* rites with knowledgeable authority, she reminds us that time is running out and that we are entering a new *pacha*. For the first time in their history, the Q'ero shamans are sharing their lineage outside of their villages to aid in helping our planet move into the new stage.

These sacred rites are being given to Western apprentices so that the information being given will be brought back and passed on to our families and communities, to serve in healing the collective. I become aware of the responsibility associated with receiving the sacred initiation rites.

Dona Alahandrina tells us that according to the Q'ero cosmology, we are living in a transitional time of opportunity, when the veil between worlds is shifting and loosening. Because we are now living in an age of technology, a bridge between the old and new culture is needed to bring the ancient teaching of the Incas forward into the emerging world. She tells us that *Mosoq Karpay* refers to the inscription of code from sacred crystals given by the *Apus* into the luminous body. *Hatun Karpay* is the collective sacred lineage of the Q'ero shamans being passed down to us, as *mesa*-carrying apprentices, simultaneously by four shamans.

June 10 – 16, 2010

Today, the group of *mesa* carriers I am traveling with have begun our journey — in elevations reaching 14,000 feet and sleeping on the ground in tents in 20 degree Fahrenheit weather — to receive the sacred *Mosoq Karpay* and *Hatun Karpay* rites. I am aware that personally I would not undertake this kind of journey — unless it was a sacred pilgrimage. Over the course of our entire journey we will cover about fifty miles on foot — up and down the Inca trails, which lie on the great sacred mountain of Ausangate — as well as on each of the neighboring mountains surrounding the Sacred Valley. I feel my connection with Ausangate growing stronger. I am happy I will have the opportunity to immerse myself more fully in his powerful energetic presence.

As our walking journey began, I became mesmerized. I looked up toward the magnificent mountain that lay only miles ahead of me and saw the sunlight radiating off the snow-covered peaks. I took in the splendor of the vision that stretched beyond the range of my normal sense, attempting to mentally inscribe the jagged outline of the rugged crests into my Mind's eye — to never fail to remember the appearance of this majestic mountain in my mind. I feel that Ausangate's presence has already been etched in my Heart. I want his image to be imprinted in my brain, as well, so that I will continue to carry it with me — like a lover's face one does not want to forget. I felt as if I am Dorothy seeing Oz for the first time. Even though I had seen Ausangate years before from a distance, I felt myself falling more deeply in love with the great collective mountain spirit.

Hiking up and down mountains to reach the base of the glacier of Ausangate is an act of love, a sacred pilgrimage. As the hours of silent walking passed on, I dropped into a state of allowing the energy of the mountain — and Pachamama — to carry me up and down the steep terrain as we moved forward and onward. While sliding down narrow dirt paths of loose gravel, I shifted my awareness deep into the earth in order to become one with Pachamama and maintain my balance. While going up the mountain, I continued blowing prayers into *k'intu* leaves, asking the mountain for strength that I could source from. As I continued walking, I maintained a quiet meditative state that fell into a rhythmic breathing as I put one foot in front of the other.

On a couple of occasions when I lost my footing and slid on the rocks and pebbles underneath my feet, Don Francisco, one of the Q'ero shamans who was traveling with us, would suddenly appear out of nowhere. During a particularly precarious stretch, he smiled and gently offered me a firm hand, helping me to my feet or down a steep slope. I was given the option of riding one of the steadfast horses that were accompanying us on our journey. I declined. I needed to trust the mountain — and my commitment to learning to source more deeply from Pachamama.

Occasionally I would stop and look at the peak of Ausangate that was always visible — continually radiating and pulsing with energy and light. The days were warm — reaching 70 degrees in the intense sunlight; the nights were cold — dropping to as low as 20 degrees. We were in the dry season and there were rarely any clouds in the sky. We continued a routine of adding and subtracting multiple layers of clothing throughout the day — adjusting our body heat to the current temperature conditions.

At times, I could see a faint image in the sky of a mountain range behind the great mountain peaks of Ausangate. I knew that the range I was looking at did not exist in physical reality. Perhaps what I was seeing was a perceptual afterimage created by the receptors in my eyes in reaction to the vibrancy of the peaks — or perhaps I was sensing something else that existed in the veil between worlds. Through this process, I was learning to accept that I do not always understand what I am sensing and experiencing — and that I really do not need to.

The day we received the *karpay* rite, we underwent a process of purification to prepare for the evening ceremony. The men and the women split off into two different groups. Each group underwent cleansing rituals separately, by bathing and immersing our *mesas* in the ice-cold waters of the lagoon that lay at the foot of the glacier. We emerged from the freezing waters, feeling alive and refreshed. It had been our first opportunity to bathe in nearly three days. We silently dressed, opened our *mesas*, and returned to our individual dialogue and communion with the great mountain.

After a period of quiet reflection and recapitulation, we prepared a large *despacho* of many *k'intus*. The leaves were downloaded with the energy of our direct intent for deeper communion with the mountain. These celestial *despachos* were being created in service of the *Apus* — in preparation for the upcoming initiation. I included the stray condor feathers that had been lying on the ground, which I had gathered along the way.

As I blew into the *k'intus*, I fell into a familiar energetic, hypnagogic state. The words of the prayers I was saying in my mind gradually dropped away. I deepened the energetic communion with the glowing light — in my mind and in my body. The purifying heat was soothing. It felt like rays of sunlight on a comfortably warm, summer day. It felt peaceful and relaxing. I felt myself dipping deeper into the fluid state of relaxation. My thoughts continued to fall away and I became more acutely aware of the radiant energy that was now pulsing through my entire body.

A couple of hours later it was time to reconvene as a group and continue preparation for the initiation ceremony that was to take place later that evening. After the men and women of our *ayllu* rejoined the *pampamesayoqs*, together Jose Luis, Don Sebastian, Don Francisco, Don Alarijo, and Adriel created a large celestial *despacho* on a piece of plywood they had brought from the Sacred Valley. The sheet was approximately four feet by five feet. Wood and kindling materials for the evening fire offering were placed underneath the platform that would hold the *despacho*. The creation of the ceremonial gift of the *despacho* was conducted at a great rock that Incas had used for centuries, where the ancestors had arranged ceremonial offerings for the sacred mountain.

In prayer, each *ayllu* member silently prepared 32 *k'intus*, which in total consisted of 108 leaves from each member, for the *despacho* offering being created in tribute to the great mountain spirit. When we had each finished assembling our *k'intus*, we divided them into three sections, giving one to each of the *pampamesayoqs* individually. The shamans blessed the individual offerings and added them to the collective *despacho* under creation.

Mandalas were adeptly formed as the *k'intus* were arranged by each of the shamans in circular configurations. The leaves were adorned with colorful flowers, candy, grains, and small symbolic icons. As the *despacho* ceremony continued, we sat with our *mesas* open, in a state of prayer. This *despacho* was the largest I had seen to date. Assembling the elaborate and massively crafted work of art took a couple of hours. In the late afternoon, after hours of prayer and preparation, the *despacho* was lit on fire. As is customary in fire ceremonies, we turned our backs to the fire and walked away — not looking back.

It was time for dinner. As usual, chicken and quinoa stew was our common meal. Quinoa is a plant native to the Andes Mountains, cultivated for its seeds, which are then ground and eaten. Quinoa stew is nutritious and hydrating — and great for preventing altitude sickness. That evening after supper, the initiation ceremony for the *Mosoq Karpay* and *Hatun Karpay* rites began.

Evening of June 16, 2010

I sat around a fire with the other members of the *ayllu*, looking up into the vast evening sky that lay beyond the great snowy peaks of Ausangate. The moon appeared as a glowing crescent on the edge of a luminous sphere. I saw stars I had not seen since being on the island of Maui over three decades ago. Venus, the Southern Cross, the Milky Way were each clearly visible.

Sitting in silent darkness, as we waited to be taken to the mountain by the shamans, I found myself slipping into a trance state and entered a series of visions. While in this state, I recalled two dreams I had during one night over a year ago, which had been forgotten. The memory of the dreams was sparked by the realization of the parallel between what had occurred in the dreams and what was now reoccurring in my present vision state. According to Jungian dream theory, dreams that occur the same night usually are interpreted as pertaining to similar themes. I understood the meaning of both of the dreams within this context.

In the first of the dreams, I had left the earth and was being beamed up by a brilliant light emanating from a UFO. In the second dream, I was moving toward a radiant white light, while darkness whisked past me at increasingly rapid speeds. In the dream, I heard a voice telling me to keep looking at the light.

Sitting cross-legged in the moonlight at the base of the great mountain of Ausangate in my state of vision, I saw a wormhole of light and sensed the presence of the Birdman, who instructed me to stay focused on the light. As had occurred in my dream a year before, indiscernible dark objects were flying past me at rapid speeds. I focused my intent toward staying connected with the light. Staying focused on the light required concentrated intention to avoid becoming distracted by what was quickly moving by me. I sensed that I was being given some kind of test.

As this vision process continued, I felt myself merging with the Birdman. Then I became a bird. As I soared effortlessly high in the sky, I became aware of extending talons where hands had been. I felt an incredible freedom of movement in stretching them. Almost automatically, I experienced swooping down and grabbing a small animal that I carried off with me. With my prey in my grasp, I aggressively flapped my wings, rising higher and higher into the moonlit sky.

Being someone who shies away from eating meat, the small part of me that was still human felt a bit horror-struck at what I sensed was to become the fate of this small, innocent creature. Suddenly I found myself swiftly pulling the animal close to me, ripping into its flesh with my beak. I began to eat and devour it. I was surprised to discover that what I had previously considered an aggressive instinctual act actually had an element of tenderness that felt extremely intimate. I felt deep affection toward the prey I was eating — sensing we were one in the same — an integral part of nature.

Figure 7: Experiencing the Great Condor

Then out of nowhere from the dark sky above, a great Condor appeared abruptly. It dipped down, swiftly snatched me up, and began devouring me. The great bird consumed my heart and then my intestines. Strangely, this act also felt very loving to me. I experienced being held and cared for. A moment before I was being eaten, I had been eating — and loving my prey, holding it close to what had been my heart. I heard the soothing voice of the Birdman telling me that I had entered his realm and that my heart and stomach, as they had existed, were gone. The Condor started packing these areas of my body with light. I felt the presence of the light living inside of me.

Then the vision shifted. I heard Ausangate's commanding voice calling me "mijo," as I had heard in the past. I looked down and saw that I had the arms of a young adult or adolescent male. My upper torso was bare except for decorated armbands. A neck ornament and a headdress I was wearing were made up with feathers. My skin was dark. I looked up and saw a great, intimidating, and magnificent figure standing in front of me. He was also wearing an ornamental headdress made of brightly colored feathers and gold, on a scale much grander than the one I was wearing. I was humbled and awed in his presence. He was so tall that I could barely see his face, which was both the face of a bird and the face of a man. The figure instructed me to continue to reach and direct my gaze higher. I attempted to stretch my vision to meet his eyes, which was at a height far beyond what I could see.

In that moment, I realized that I was in the midst of a ceremony — and in the process of being sacrificed. I was not afraid. Somehow, I knew that this was a great honor and an act of divine love. I fell into a state of ecstasy, surrendering into a sacred communion. At some point, I became aware that I was standing on a raised platform, in midday sunlight, in front of a mass of hundreds of people. My hands were extended out to them and I was speaking. I knew intuitively that these were my people, and that I was in some leadership role of knowing and trying to convey a message. I did not understand the words I was speaking.

The vision shifted and my body became altered again to what felt to me to be the image a wise old woman. I was experiencing myself as her, within her body. Then the vision changed again and I was walking up stairs made of light. I knew that I needed to trust that somehow I would be held — even though I appeared to be literally walking on air. I agreed that I would sacrifice everything to the light. Then I was walking through fire. I kept looking up — higher and higher and I felt my personal self dropping away. Staying in open relationship with the light required concentrated intent on my part. I felt myself continually stretching, constantly reaching for and moving toward the light. As I moved higher, I was aware that I was losing my identity and sense of self, yet somehow I maintained my focus — I became the focus.

In the real time of ordinary reality, I was gathered by one of the shamans from my place near the fire. He held my arm and guided me into the *Mosoq Karpay* ceremony, toward the shaman who Dona Alahandrina had lent the crystals, to perform the sacred initiation rites. Under the guidance of the great mountain *Apu* Ausangate, these encoded crystals, had been borrowed from Dona Alahandrina's *mesa* for inscribing the celestial code onto the luminous bodies of those of us receiving the rites. I saw the great mountain of Ausangate in front of me. One of the shamans instructed me to open my eyes so that I could receive the sacred knowledge being transferred into my body and *mesa*. The crystals that the shaman was holding in his hand became illuminated as they were rubbed together. I felt energy pulsing through my body as it was being transmitted through the *Mosoq Karpay* rites. My body bent and arched backward, stiffening somewhat spasmodically. I was aware of trying to hold the energy that I was being given, that was downloaded into my luminous body.

One of the shamans helped me walk back to the fire. I sat down and fell back into a deeper state of trance. I felt my body starting to convulse, similarly to the way it had the year before. The convulsions started deep in my Belly. I allowed myself to surrender, collapsing and giving way into the movement of what was taking place. A series of waves of energy rippled through me. I found myself again reaching for the light.

After a period, someone came and guided me by the light of the stars and the moonlight to another circle of four shamans for the *Hatun Karpay* rites. One of the shamans held me steady, keeping me on my feet. The three other shamans together rhythmically pounded me gently all over my head and body with their *mesas* to reinforce the lineage that had been newly wired through the *Mosoq Karpay* rites. During the initiation ceremony, one of the shamans placed a *kuya* in my hand. This was to bring the presence of Ausangate into my *mesa* and strengthen the energetic tie between my medicine body and the great mountain spirit.

After the second set of initiation rites, I sat down again next to the fire and fell back into another a vision state. I found myself climbing a staircase of light, reaching for the light source that lay directly in front of me. In that moment, I perceived that another energetic shift was occurring. I was aware that the great mountain of Ausangate had begun downloading light into the medicine body of my *mesa*. I held my intention on maintaining the connection to the golden thread between us, trying to remain an open vessel.

Then, unexpectedly, the person who I had come to find particularly disruptive and bothersome over the course of the last several days plopped down inches away from me and abruptly knocked into me. In an automatic startled response, I was immediately jolted out of my vision state. This was the same person whose heavy ornamental wooden plaque had fallen on my head three days before — she had carelessly left it unsecured in an overhead shelf during a particularly bumpy bus ride. I reacted to the intrusion internally by feeling angry and annoyed.

I tried to move back into and recapture the blissful vision state where I had been only seconds before, but I could not find my way back. My vision had evaporated and was gone.

An overwhelming sense of loss passed over me as I realized I had failed an important test being given to me by the mountain. Although I had sacrificed myself to the mountain and trusted the mountain enough to walk on air and through fire, I had allowed myself to become distracted by simple personal irritation — and I had failed.

The intrusive experience with my shadow woman had been given to me by the mountain, another trial in my commitment to serve the experience rather than to fall under the influence of my own personal shadow. I remember reading Carlos Castaneda's own account of these kinds of interactions as encounters with "petty tyrants,"[50] individuals who have been put in our path to challenge our self-importance. I heard myself try to reassure myself that it was okay — that I would be able to reopen myself to the download I had been receiving — but the deeper, wiser part of me was aware that this was as far as I would go for this year. The Birdman concurred. The person that I then became angry with was myself, but I knew anger toward anyone would not ultimately help either. I was stuck in personal experience. I had fallen out of *ayni* — right relationship with the universe. Rather than being negotiable in my position, I had been claimed by a personal ego state rather than remaining in a state of connected collectivity. I realized that I would return the following year or however many years it took to repeat the process of surrendering to the mountain.

After the evening initiation ceremony was complete, the festivities began. A hot beverage of tea and *pisco* (grape brandy) was passed around the campfire as the shamans played their flutes and sang. Still finding myself in somewhat of an altered state, I was appreciative of the dark. I burrowed deeper into the heavy mantel I was wearing to shield me from the freezing cold as we sat across from each other, gazing into the fire. Eventually we made our way back to our tents in the dark and retired for the evening. I continued to find myself in a hypnagogic state. I was aware of energy continuing to move through my body, but the dream images for the evening had ceased.

---

[50] C. Castaneda, *The Power of Silence.*

June 17, 2010

The next day, trudging silently up a face of the great mountain in a meditative state, the voice of the mountain spirit told me that the person that I had been upset with was a mirror reflection of my own combustible, sulphuric nature. Last night's ceremony had brought me face to face with an aspect of my own shadow. I reflected upon how many times in the past I might have had a similar effect on the quiet contemplative state of another human being. I wondered if I might also have unconsciously interrupted someone else's peaceful state with a burst of my own uncontained enthusiasm. I became aware that I had allowed these bursts of distraction to hijack my own process of moving into a deeper energetic connection. I heard the voice Ausangate firmly reminding me of this aspect of my own nature, and my spiritual homework over the course of the next year would be to work on becoming more conscious of my own bull-in-a-china-shop tendencies. This continues to be my Achilles heel — and perhaps my life's lesson in this incarnation.

After hours of walking in a silent, contemplative state in an ongoing direct dialogue with the mountain, I found myself listening less with my ears and more with body. My mind had quieted down and I felt a sense of gratitude welling up inside of me. At times, when I encountered other Westerners along the mountain path who were maintaining ongoing conversations with each other, rather than listening to the verbal content in their words, I became aware of an underlying anxiety permeating the continual stream of chatter.

What I heard in their voices I had heard before in myself. Was this an indicator of misalignment from staying plugged in too long to the matrix of Western culture, in a state disconnected from nature? As I thought about the pages I had written the previous year, I recognized that what seemed to be the most difficult for me was the trap of falling into describing the experience and losing the sense of living the experience. Jarring sounds and loud noises, bright lights, constant stimulation, and external factors in the outer environment were elements that eroded the lifeline to the energetic collective that I had experienced through the mountain — and that my sulphuric nature of fire and air could easily attach to. I considered how feeding and maintaining a relationship with the mountain — and all living things — was an active process that must be tended to daily. After returning to a modern world of industry, the mountain becomes a memory that must be kept alive by active remembering, to prevent it from becoming intellectualized into a metaphor.

June 19, 2010

Shamans from the Andes have prophesized that the next group of shamans will come from the West — and will need to be able to bridge both worlds. Days later, in conversation with Señor Chauipicaro, the director of the *altomesayoq* Juanito's *mesa,* I was told that while in my vision state, I had been met by the great mountain, Ausangate, and that through my sacrifice of dying and being reborn, I had surrendered to something bigger. Señor Chauipicaro informed me that I was walking along my path in this process of death and rebirth, and that for a *karpay* to occur, the death of an old cycle is followed by emerging into the phase of a new cycle, that both a negative and positive aspect were needed — death and rebirth. My job was to continue to work on learning to silence my Heart and Mind in the midst of my busy world.

June 20, 2010

Today, our *ayllu* entered into another dialogue with *Apu* Señor Chauipicaro through Juanito's *mesa*. The sound of the *Apu's* fatherly voice is reassuring. I sense I am in the presence of a being that is very old and very wise. Señor Chauipicaro offered several stories that served as metaphors to describe the transitional process we were undergoing. He started by telling a story about a man who rode into town on his burro, and desperately went from person to person asking if they had seen his burro, only to learn that he had been riding on it all along.

Señor Chauipicaro then recounted the tale of a young man who told his stern and controlling father the following narrative. According to the story, there once was a hen living in a cage that came across an egg. The hen did not care whose egg it was but wanted to nest and nurture it into life by sitting on it. Eventually, the egg matured and hatched, and a duck emerged out of the egg and immediately began swimming in the water of a nearby pond. The hen cried to the duck, "You can't swim in water — come back!" The duck replied to the hen, "This is who I am — I swim in water."

Next, Señor Chauipicaro told an anecdotal tale about a priest who was trying to teach an altar boy the difference between what was right and wrong concerning the "evils" of alcohol. In a lesson designed to illustrate the point he was trying to make, the priest placed a worm in a carafe — and the worm drowned. The priest then told the altar boy, "See, these are the effects of alcohol." The altar boy struggling to understand the lesson the priest was trying to teach him thought to himself, "Then I must drink a lot of wine to kill the worms living inside of me."

In conveying these stories, Señor Chauipicaro was illustrating how things are often not what they seem. Human perception is often an illusion created by our unwillingness to move out of our head and to experience what is actually occurring in the world around us. This is caused by our inability to move beyond our own complexes or self-absorbed mental and emotional states into beginner's mind. In the story Señor Chauipicaro told about the burro, the answer was right under the man's nose. If he had only looked around and had paid attention, he would have been able to stop searching for something he already had. The story of the hen and the duck seemed to me to be a lesson in the futility of the ego trying to control what the psyche has in store for us — and the natural order of that which is beyond its control. The tale about the priest and the boy demonstrates that there are different ways of making meaning, depending on one's subjective understanding, and that there is no one way to understand anything.

As the dialogue with Señor Chauipicaro continued, the *Apu* encouraged each of us to become negotiable, and not attached to assumptions created by our minds. As I sat in the room, I felt myself fluctuating from a deep trance state of being in my body, to hearing the words of Señor Chauipicaro's stories in my mind. I felt myself shifting back and forth between mind and body. He said that if we were able to maintain a connection as clear channels, there would be nothing more we would need to do. The psyche heals by being in the *Apus'* field, in a state of being.

Ayllu members began asking questions about sacred lineage. In response, Señor Chauipicaro described how initially forty-two *ceke* lines were connected to forty-two *wakas* or places of power that contained twelve different ancestral lineages of medicine people. Over time, the lineage of the sacred ancestry has slowly died out and there are only three lines of lineage remaining in Peru today. The Q'ero shamans are also in the process of losing their connection to their sacred lineage and soon there will only be two — located in the sacred areas of Vilcabamba and Salkantay. There are only two celestial *mesas* left which are buried somewhere in the mountains. Señor Chauipicaro stated that the collectives of these sacred mountains are deciding what to do with these *mesas*. The concerns of modern man — and many of the *altomesayoqs* who are now living in the modern world — have shifted from serving the collective toward personal need. Señor Chauipicaro encouraged us to take personal responsibility and to deal with the personal so that we could listen to and hear the collective — not through our minds, but through a state of being.

Señor Chauipicaro said after the *karpays* we received we are now vessels, capable of holding the energy of the *Apus*. As our availability in serving the collective increases and we are claimed less by our personal shadows, our capacity to hold power will increase. We need to take the light into the darkness of our unconscious to increase the capacity of maintaining this state of being. As I listened to Señor Chauipicaro's words, I remembered Jung's famous quote about taking the light into darkness as the path of individuation. The *Apu* used the metaphor of the temple of the moon, which remains in darkness until a certain time of night when the moon becomes aligned with the structure — and the light shines through, exposing the darkness. Our session with the *Apus* lasted for a couple of hours, and I noticed — as is usually the case for me after *Apu* sessions — feeling relaxed and tired.

After the session ended, Jose Luis described his experience of translating Señor Chauipicaro's words into the English language. He said that the metaphors are more difficult to make into sentences than translating the *Apus'* actual words. He also said that it is easier to translate the words of the *Apu* than the questions of humans.

June 20, 2010

During a session with the *Apus* through Dona Alahandrina's *mesa* a day later, each member of our group was given an *Apu* benefactor. The benefactors are mountain spirits that wanted to work with us and become directors of our *mesas*. Sitting again in the pitch-black room, we heard the familiar flurry of flapping wings, followed by a series of loud thumping noises across the table. As an assorted sound of booming masculine voices with different pitches and tenors began emerging in the dark, I reflected to myself that, oddly enough, these activities had become regular daily occurrences. I no longer questioned the authenticity of what I was experiencing or tried to understand intellectually what was taking place — I had learned that it was futile anyhow.

I waited in the dark with anticipation and curiosity. *Apus* were linked with initiates — by either party's request. Eventually, a voice who identified himself as *Apu* Kilke, announced that he would become the benefactor of my *mesa*. *Apu* Kilke is the guardian spirit of the west gate of the city of Cusco. He deals with a main *ceke* line in the direction of the holy mountain Salkantay. I saw and experienced the presence of a golden light but struggled to remember the *Apu's* name — repeating it repeatedly in my head. I wrote it down quickly in my notepad immediately after emerging from the darkened room into the sunlight.

We prepared to leave for home the next day. Before leaving Cusco, I had hoped to journey to the mountain to pay homage and begin forming a relationship, but time ran out as my journey ended — and once again, my return home began.

28. The Third Reentry: Returning Home

And a cosmic vision, a cosmology, is nothing more than the processes that lead life into fulfillment.

— Don Alarijo, *pampamesayoq*, 2011

A month before leaving for Peru for the third time, Perry and I had moved to a house situated on three acres of land with two very large willow trees in the yard. Perry and I found the house one day while driving around looking for a new place to live. As we were driving down the street, Perry announced that the horse standing in a pasture directly across the street from the house had told him to stop. We did and loved the house in front of us immediately. Although there were no for sale signs posted, we searched through public records and found the registered owners of the house, who agreed to sell it to us. We finally had a home again. The land we are now living on has become a sanctuary.[51]

July 15, 2010

Returning to a piece of land I can work with has made my transition back from Peru easier this year. As I have continued to

---

[51] In the last two years, we have planted hundreds of plants and trees that have taken root over the course of the last two years.

recapitulate my experience in Peru this summer, I am gardening for long stretches of time — planting trees — sometimes late into the evening. The trees, particularly the willows, seem to be the governing bodies or directors of our property. They serve as portals connecting us to the spirit of the land. I find myself building altars around them with rocks and plants. Establishing a relationship with Pachamama through the presence of the trees has sustained me, allowing me to continue an ongoing dialogue with nature. I have trimmed bushes, moved rocks, and continued to plant. Perry has helped me move large boulders and has cut dead limbs from the branches that are too high for me to reach.

As the summer months have passed, Perry has continued to work on installing an elaborate sprinkler system. Each day he has tended to the baby willow trees he is growing from the tree cuttings he collected from the ground after a particularly intense thunderstorm while I was away in Peru. It has been exceptionally hot during the last weeks of August and the recently transplanted trees and flowers have required constant care and attention. Yesterday, Perry watered each of them three times.

Friends and family have laughed and commented about our eccentricity — planting a garden and installing a watering system was taking priority over creating a working kitchen with a stove. It makes perfect sense to both Perry and me. I have noticed that, in addition to connecting with Pachamama in the process of daily gardening, Perry and I are also deepening and reestablishing our connection with each other. We are finally both feeling at home, in a deeper spiritual sense.

Last year, looking back, I realize that the reentry process was agony. Living in a house that I was renting by myself — without a garden — left me nowhere to grow and lay down roots. Instead, I turned to writing pages and pages in a stream of consciousness — quoting other authors who may have had their own experiences with the unknown. I had hoped they might help me understand. I intuitively attempted to make connections between paradigms, trying desperately to find some way of connecting the dots into something that would somehow be meaningful. I floundered. Last year's writing was a testament that if I cannot connect with the earth and drop roots, I struggle to stay connected. I hear Don Sebastian's words, "Shamans serve the experience." For me, this is the heart of shamanism. I am like the flowers I recently planted, trying to establish a root system connected in the land. In coming home, I continue to search and feel for connections between my daily life and my experience with the shamans on the holy mountain of Ausangate. This is what I need to continue feeling alive.

August 7, 2010

About a week ago, I came across the alchemical text of the Mutus Liber, or "mute book," a series of fifteen images depicting the spiritual transformation of movement between heaven and earth through working with the ethers or energy field that connects all living things. In the first plate there are two angels climbing, which, according to scholars, represents Jacob's ladder. As I reflected on the meaning of the image, I became struck between the similarity of this plate and my own vision experience of climbing up the staircase of light to meet the *Apu* spirit of the mountain Ausangate, which Peruvian shamans describe as one of the winged beings. What I saw in the illustration was close to what I had actually experienced!

As I read my words from last year, I am hit with an interpretive understanding of the process described in the sequence of images of the Mutus Liber. Each of the images in the mid-section are illustrations of a man and woman working together in a process involving a substance that they are heating and cooling, pouring it back and forth between containing vessels. Their activities are being performed in areas defined by boundaries created by walls,

Figure 8: Mutus Liber

windows, tables, flasks, etc. These images of the Mutus Liber are describing the need for containment, which alchemists have referred to as *separatio*. As alchemists have written, some aspect of *separatio* is necessary — to separate to avoid being overtaken by the energy of the experience.

I notice as I seek to gain understanding, like the alchemists, I also am resorting to use of symbols. I consider that the hard geometric lines seen in this section of plates in the text reflects the need for boundaries in order to contain the energy in order to

Figure 9: *Mutus Liber* **Image of Working with** *Prima Materia*

integrate it. Maybe this year's reentry process has been easier than the last because I have developed a better capacity to hold the energy within myself — and because, in the process of gardening and working in the land, I have intuitively discovered a way of containing the energy that I am bringing back.

August 23, 2010

This year, the process of reentry has been much gentler — perhaps because I have continued to engage with the land and Pachamama has become a safe *temenos* for my work in progress.

Yet as I reflect upon my activities in the weeks after I returned —
frequently gardening on the weekends until 1 AM in the morning,
and working thirteen-hour days during the week without difficulty.
Gradually, I am regaining a normal sleep schedule, striving for
eight hours. Perhaps, the fact that I am forcing myself to limit my
activities — and sleep even when I do not want to — shows insight.

Perhaps the capacity for insight and responsible behavior,
rather than energy level, should be the criteria to evaluate
inflation. Yet still, I find myself attempting to manage my psyche's
split between Western practices and shamanism. For months,
prior to going to Peru, a radiologist wanting me to come in for a
follow-up on a mammogram had contacted me repeatedly. I
ignored the letters and calls but eventually acquiesced and
reluctantly agreed to go in for a follow-up exam. After examining
the X-rays, the radiologist "strongly recommended" that I obtain a
breast biopsy, on the same breast and in the same location that
was biopsied twenty years ago. After spending time with the
shamans, excellent trackers for illness, who had not mentioned
anything about anything growing that shouldn't be, and
considering my light initiation on the mountain top, I was strongly
opposed to any invasive medical procedure — and told her so. I
also complained to the nurses in her office that being self-
employed in this country with a high deductible in my insurance
plan made the procedure very expensive.

I journeyed to the mountain and to my inner guide, the
Birdman, who told me I was "fine." Perry also told me that I was
fine but commented that I would probably need to go through the
medical procedure anyway because I would be anxious not
knowing. I scheduled the procedure and canceled — and
rescheduled and cancelled again. I was ambivalent. I complained
— and ranted — about the health care system in this country
comparing it to countries with socialized medicine. I felt somehow
that I was being given a test. Did I trust Western medicine or

shamanism? I resented that I was in the position of having to make a choice. I was a difficult and unreasonable patient to say the least and I did not care. Now, I understand that my ranting was an expression of my irritation toward myself for not believing and I was projecting it onto the health care system.

Eventually, something inside of me quieted down and I decided to go ahead and have the biopsy. Perry went with me to the appointment. When I arrived, I decided that the medical technologist was human, so I decided to curb my feistiness and to become agreeable. It was not her fault I was contending with ambivalence toward Western medicine once again.

Lying on the table during the procedure, I fell (and willed myself) out of my body and I returned to the mountain in a vision. The Birdman cloaked me protectively in his wings and I knew the procedure would be fine — oddly enough, this vision state was the deepest I had experienced since returning from Peru. I heard Ausangate's sweet voice calling me "mijo" again. The sound of his voice warmed my heart and I felt like crying. I asked him why it had been so difficult to feel him after I returned home. He showed me energetically that a split had occurred between upper and lower — spirit and matter — ordinary and nonordinary reality. He told me that I was not remembering where I was going in dreamtime. In that moment I remembered that the night before I had woken myself up, talking in my sleep, telling the Birdman I loved him. I could not remember where I had been. I felt my heart opening and I wondered if I had begun to shut down to avoid feeling the pain of separation from my beloved mountains without realizing it.

A day later, I reflected that this scenario symbolized the evolution of in my belief system that continues between integrating my shamanic experience with living in this culture. Is this why I have been so invested in fighting the good fight in the name of shamanism? Perhaps.

Many people would tell me that it would have been irresponsible not to have gotten the biopsy, and my friends have told me that I "did the right thing," but I wonder — did I sell out? Did I not trust what I already knew? Is it okay to get validation just in case? The wiser part of me tells me, I am still not quite there yet, that I have not reached the level of trust I experienced in my dream and in vision states, trusting that I will be able to fly if I jump into the void. I suppose maybe I would have felt worse if I had allowed breast cancer to go undetected than challenging the information I had been given from the spirit world. Yet somehow, my decision feels like it lacked integrity on a deeper level. I knew what I had experienced in Peru was authentic, and that to have breast cancer would have been incongruent with what I experienced. I know I am going to bump up against another situation — or be given an option — that will again challenge what I believe.

29. Conclusion

Walk in beauty, walk with strength, and walk with clarity
— Don Alarijo, *pampamesayoq*, 2011

The essential energetic level is always present in each of our lives. For shamans, it is not a state of *becoming* — it is a state of *being* — and for a shaman this always occurs in right relationship with the land. I am aware that wandering or sitting quietly in nature in a receptive state brings us closer to the land. When we experience the living world around us — and Pachamama — with all of our senses, we are able to remember. Feeling the earth with our hands and the bottoms of our bare feet, smelling the moist earth, hearing the wind, seeing the energy surrounding plants and trees when we relax and soften our eyes bring us into a deeper connection. This is what shamans refer to as sourcing.

The beloved mountain Ausangate is a collective ego or soul that I have learned to source from. I am one among many that hold this connection dear and close to my heart. Ausangate is the collective inter-psychic experience of many souls that become one in *munay* — that has force through love combined with will. We lack the equivalent of the Q'ero word *munay* in this culture.

Figure 10: Sourcing

Perhaps this is because in our culture we tend to understand love as an individual rather than collective experience. I have fallen in love with Ausangate — but this feeling is not limited to me and does not belong to me. I am a part of this state of connection that exists between all living things.

Our capacity to hold power depends on our willingness and ability to commune with the land. When we see the particles of light dancing around us that extend out into the vast sky beyond us, we transcend our personal selves and become negotiable. If we can give up our definition of our self — even for a minute — we have the opportunity to become fluid and connected with what is around us. We start to feel our place, where we belong.

Attachment psychologists[52] recognize that humans are preadapted for relatedness. They propose that an innate understanding and desire for connectivity exists in each of us in order to make meaning. Through our relationships with others, we understand ourselves. At the beginning of my writing, I quoted the shaman Don Sebastian as saying, "The shaman serves experience," and would now add, "by keeping it alive through the process of remembering." These pages have been my process of remembering and recapitulating what has happened to me — my own attempt to serve the experience by describing it through my personal narrative.

Perhaps personal experience itself becomes the veil — the transitional state between existing and non-existing — the way the energetic experience is manifested into physical reality. I am not the first to describe moving beyond symbols into the void. I imagine that if my cultural orientation had been different, my conceptualization may also have changed.

Perhaps I would have less of a need to understand — and less of a need to explain. In writing these words, I am describing my personal journey. The writing I have done about my experience of piercing the veil has been an effort of reasoning — an attempt to try to organize my experience in an effort to make meaning. Similar to my writing process two years ago, after I finished the first draft of this writing, caught in a pattern of repetitive compulsion, I found myself painting the blast of light I had witnessed on the mountain — over and over — to digest what felt overwhelmingly enormous.

---

[52] Wallin (2007) and Fonagy (2001).

In entering the shaman's world, my life changed drastically and what has felt to me to be a force of nature has taken over. Being an intuitive, my way of connecting with something greater must come somatically through my body.[53] This is necessary for me to anchor my experience. For me, shamanism is the glue that keeps me connected in a deeper relationship with the living world around me, which begins and ends with Pachamama.

Part of my motivation in writing has been to describe and illustrate the potential pain associated with shamanic experience, as one faces aspects of their shadow at deeper, more intense levels. My path has toggled between becoming a shaman and becoming a Jungian analyst. I have loved Jung's spirit. Jung has been a role model for me and I am grateful. Jung himself experienced this in his own descent into the unconscious, and at one time also wondered if he might be losing his mind. Like Jung, I have also found the dismemberment and reentry processes to be extremely painful at times. Companions I have met along my journey have agreed that reentry is often a painfully intense experience that is difficult to explain using words.

Jung wrote,

> It is dawning on us to what extent our whole experience of so-called reality is psychic: as a matter of fact, everything thought felt or perceived is a psychic image, and the world itself exists only so far as we are able to produce an image of it. We are so deeply impressed with the truth of our imprisonment in, and limitation by, the psyche that we are ready to admit the existence in it

---

[53] Borrowing from the Jungian analyst, Marie Luis Von Franz and using terminology of the Myers Briggs personality test, my sensate function is my inferior function, my weakest, least developed function. For most people this is their religious function — or means of accessing numinous experience.

even of things we do not know: we call them the unconscious. (C W Jung, Psychological Commentary on the Tibetan Book of the Great Liberation," in *Psychology and the East*, p. 107, par 766).

Shamanic experience is a way of the Heart and individuation is a search for one's soul. In the process of writing, I am using my Mind to understand. I believe I have developed greater conscious awareness of my soul in this process. I have come full circle — and the uroboric snake eating its tail — or tale — comes to mind. This leads me back to Jung and the words I wrote over two years ago, describing how Jung understood the energetic collective:

September 20, 2009

Understanding the veil both as the essence of the archetype and as an archetypal symbol is analogous to the performance artist's premise that art is both the process of creating art and the outcome or product of the experience. Archetypes are the link between the physical and the psychic world. If there is deeper movement into the archetypal psyche — away from subjective experience, the psyche becomes increasingly objective and universal. As progression continues along this continuum, archetypes of the objective psyche, or the collective unconscious, eventually cross over into the realm of matter referred to as the psychoidal realm. Jung understood the psychoidal realm to be the central ground of empirical being, existing beyond time and space.

Both Jung and Von Franz have written about the existence of an *anthropos*, "the ancient idea of an all-extensive world-soul, a kind of cosmic subtle body" (Von Franz, 1985 p. 85). Jung refers to this as the *unus mundus*, or "one world," which is a "composite universal Self" that exists in the psychoidal realm. According to Von Franz, matter and psyche merge into one — the *unus mundus*, at the deepest level of the collective unconscious. When the *unus mundus* is activated energetically, the latent energy is expressed

Figure 11: World Soul

in a double manifestation. Using this framework, the archetypal veil becomes both the gateway to conscious understanding and the bridge between spirit and matter.

In her description of the objective psyche, Von Franz (1985) stated, "As this central unified area of the unconscious is approached, time and space are increasingly revitalized. That deepest area of the unconscious that is simply a unit or the center... without extension" (p. 84). Like the "home tree" in the film Avatar, at this deep level of the psyche the *unus mundus* is not divided in individuals, but is connected with all living things.

Jung considered the *unus mundus* to be an ultimate unity of physical and psychic energy. This concept of the *unus mundus* is a way of understanding the collective consistent with shamanic cosmology. Emphasis is on the functional relationship between things rather than on the things themselves, and on the relationship of the relationship. In a shamanic context, this occurs in the energetic collective, where everything is fluid and connected energetically.

Both Jungian depth psychology and shamanism are paths toward the numinous — one individual and the other collective. I can hear Ausangate's loving voice saying to me, "Mijo, ultimately they are both pathways to the divine."

Appendix. List of Despacho *Ingredients*

alabaster man and woman figurines — duality, serving in reciprocal unison

alphabet noodles — communication and the ability to use language

anise seeds — sweet fragrance attracts spirits

bread — in this tradition binds the family together. It is commonly used in soul retrievals.

candles — used for light and illumination

candy — represents harmony and attraction. Harmony in an environment occurs through sweetness, especially flower shaped candies. The candy represents germination, fulfillment, and fruition. Every *pacha* brings fruition.

candy house or car — the metaphor is for success, as you define it

candy man and woman — symbolizes harmony in the couple. The element of two is very important because it not only symbolizes right relationship among humans, but also between humans and the collective.

chocolate frog — harmony and the cycles of water

coca leaves — primary ingredient of *despachos* that prayers are blown into. Coca leaves are frequently replaced with bay leaves in the West.

cotton — symbolizes purity on which you lay all the gifts by placing it on the top of the other ingredients. Symbolizing clouds, it can also be cycles of water and rain. In a *despacho* for Pachamama, it represents water. In an *Apu despacho* it represents heaven and purity.

corn (*maize*, or *sara* in Quechua) — production and abundance

crackers / wafers — flour products represent your *anima* (spirit)

dough wafers — with a picture of St. Nicholas it is given to the *Apu* spirits who bring good news; with a picture of a cross it symbolizes health and is used in health *despachos*

incense — attracts Spirit

llama fat — (*untu* in Quechua) the act of bringing forth through vision. Coca leaves and llama fat are combined. They are basic to calling the *Apus* and bringing them.

llama fetus — to give birth and bring potential into manifestation, to get rid of sadness

lima beans —because of the color, they harmonize the *despacho*. Sometimes we give a positive and a negative ability in different *despachos*.

loadstone / magnetite — brings attraction. It is a favored item when doing business *despachos*.

metal frog — attraction. The frog is the one that calls. The messenger.

metal hand — friendship. The hand is flanked by symbols of winged beings, and is the dynamic nature of all relations that must be served.

metal moon (*luna*) — symbolizes the agricultural calendar. The spirit of the moon is feminine and referred to as Mama Killa.

metal sun (*sol*) — symbolizes the social calendar, social interaction. The spirit of the sun is masculine and referred to as Inti.

metal star (*ch'aska*) — protection

mica — represents silver, and maintaining the integrity of the soul as it grows stronger

molasses candy — harmony

papel de regalo — decorated wrapping paper used for *despachos*

pewter horseshoes — fluidity in business and good fortune through "right relationship" and reciprocity

pewter left hand — receive, you must give and receive — a circular process

pewter right hand — positive, giving, welcoming

qolqi — silver, symbolizing spiritual wealth and lunar energy

qori — gold, symbolizing spiritual wealth and solar energy

rods — amplify sound

sequins — ornamental décor to provide decoration

shell — the womb of the heavens and the container in which creation sits. Sometimes you pour some wine inside. It is also the spirit of the waters. This is a metaphor for creation. We are creating a venue. *Despachos* are traditionally mediums to propitiate right relationship. If you put items into the *despacho* that you are missing, you will propitiate lack. It needs to be an open and active dialog of creation.

seeds —the basic complement that the land needs so the land can bring abundance back to you

sugar — sweet to attract spirits

tacu (red clay) — can bring positive or negative outcomes and is often used in *kuti despachos*. It can wash off negativity or repel what is sent to you, depending on affinities.

thread — white and yellow, gold and silver thread binds and brings wholeness

tobacco — attracts spirits of North America. Tobacco is also used to attract the spirit of the plant in *ayahuasca* ceremonies.

wayruro — a small red and black seed representing the masculine and feminine principles that brings protection. Two of these seeds are often placed in the center shell for good luck.

wine — red wine for Pachamama, the earth, and/or white wine for Wirachocha, the heavens.

winkiki seeds — a seed that grows underground and has a
supernatural presence. Used to attract. It also has the ability to
bring together polarizing energies, such as man and woman.

Glossary

ally — the intermediary or necessary conduit between the ego and otherworld experience

altomesayoqs — the most highly respected group of Q'ero shamans, with the capacity to serve as gateways between ordinary and nonordinary. They each have membership with a particular mountain and speak directly to spirits of that location. These shamans source (derive) energy from the directors of the holy mountains, the *Apu* spirits, by engaging in an active exchange with the energetic collective.

anima mundi — Stanislav Grof's term that describes the universe created and permeated by a superior creative intelligence

anthropos — the ancient idea of an all-extensive world soul, a kind of cosmic subtle body

Apu Chauipicaro — a collective mountain spirit from the mountains of Bolivia, the director of the *altomesayoq* Juanito's *mesa*.

Apu Kilke — an *Apu* benefactor of my *mesa* from the city of Cusco, close to the sacred mountain Pacha Tucson

Apus — referred to as the winged beings, the great collective mountain spirits. The *Apus* of a mountain are an expression of the collective composite of Pachamama or Mother Earth. The collective has different creative expressions that mirror people through the land.

archetypal or mythic realm — the third level existing outside of linear time, where synchronistic events are connected

assemblage point — a point of perception in the subtle body responsible for shifts into different states of heightened awareness

Ausangate — the mountain considered one of the holiest mountains in Peru, and most evolved of the collective mountain *Apu* spirits

Ave Maria Purisima — the ceremonial salutation to the *Apu* during ceremony

ayllu — a small community of *mesa* carriers practicing shamanism

ayni — the balanced state of reciprocity between all living things

brujo (feminine is *bruja*) — Carlos Castaneda's term for a medicine man that follows the path of sorcery to gain personal power and knowledge

ceke lines — existing energy lines that connect the energy meridians in the earth. These *ceke* lines intersect at *wakas*, places that are power spots infused with energy. By activating *ceke* lines in areas such as Peru, the veil becomes more transparent, allowing for a greater flow of energy and communication with the collective. Being in these power spots heightens a person's perception, and it becomes easier to achieve expanded states of awareness. The Peruvian *altomesayoqs* enter into dialogues with the *Apus* and work to open *ceke* lines in the mountains to promote healing in the earth.

celestial *mesas* — *mesas* bestowed directly by the *Apus* upon the highest *altomesayoqs* with the greatest capacity to hold the power

collari — the feminine principle governing the left side of the body associated with formlessness

despacho — an offering to Pachamama or Mother Earth, given through the fire or buried in the earth. It is a circular arrangement of coca leaves (bay leaves are used in the United States), resembling a mandala — embellished with grains, candy, and other colorful objects that symbolize gifts to the upper, lower, and middle worlds. After carefully separating the coca leaves or *k'intus* into groups in three, the shaman transfers intent into the leaves using breath, and each group of leaves takes on a specific prayer or pattern to be let go of and given to the fire. The leaves surround a central symbolic object that is determined by the type and purpose of the *despacho*. Most *despachos* are gifts to Pachamama, although some are for releasing *hucha* or negativity, and some are visionary *despachos*, requesting blessings from the *Apus* before initiation ceremonies.

energetic collective — the fourth level, the *essential* or *energetic* level of spirit or collectivity, corresponding to the *unus mundi*

hampuy — the Quechua verb "to come" used by shamans when calling sacred space

Hanaq Pacha — the upper world.

Hatun Karpay — the Great Initiation — collective sacred lineage of the Q'ero shamans passed down is the fourth level of initiation, which comes with the understanding of numinous experience and the energetic collective

Huascaran — the tallest mountain in Peru in the Vilcabamba region, and the director of the *altomesayoq* Dona Alahandrina's *mesa*

hucha — negative energy

ikaro — words spoken by shamans during ceremony and ritual

illa — creation

inkari — the right side of the body governed by the masculine principle of linearity

Inti — the sun

journey — shifting into an otherworld state of consciousness to retrieve information *k'intus* — a group of three coca leaves carrying the energy of direct intent

karpay — the shamanic initiation rites given when the shaman's body of knowledge and the power of the shaman's ancient lineage pass to the apprentice through the *mesa*. The *karpay* is integrated by the *p'aqo* into conscious awareness through a process of recapitulating and remembering through the body by working with the *mesa*.

kausay — the energy of creation that is often experienced in the body as a vibration or in the heart as a feeling of universal love towards everyone and everything, not attached to any person or outcome

Kausay Pacha — collective energetic realm

Kay Pacha — the middle world, the world of consensual reality

kuya — a rock, crystal, or stone that is part of a shaman's *mesa* that energetically carries the shaman's medicine body or capacity to hold power

the land — what the Q'ero shamans refer to as the collective expression of the numinous in nature

literal level — the first level, normal awareness and existing in the concrete world of every day, out-in-the-world experience

llank'ay — will or intention

luminous body — the energetic container that holds the totality of psychic experience, between consciousness and the collective unconscious that extend beyond the physical body

luminous energy field — a record of personal and ancestral memories that surrounding the physical body. It is an archive of past life events, including former lifetimes.

Mama Killa — the moon

mesa — a collection of individual stones (*kuyas*) assembled over time, a living representation of the shaman's medicine body. A full *mesa* is usually comprised of about twelve stones, wrapped in a *mestana* cloth, which is a square piece of material that carries the stones. The *mesa* is the carrier's connection to the collective *energetic* realm and the world of consensual reality. It serves as a bridge or gateway, linking the shaman to lineage of ancestors from the past and children of the future.

mesa carrier — a person who works with a ceremonial medicine bundle consisting of sacred objects that are usually stones or crystals that have been collected and worked with over time; the objects that hold energy for that particular individual in Q'ero shamanism

Mosoq Karpay — the inscription of code from sacred crystals given by the *Apus* into the luminous body, creating a shift from physical to energetic expression at the fifth level of sacred work

munay — the universal feeling state of love connecting us to the land and every living thing around us

numinous experience — an energetic state of ecstasy and connection to all living things

oferendas — present for fire ceremony

p'aqo — a Q'ero medicine person

pacha — an intersection of time and space, an Inca map of consciousness referring to the structure that contains *kausay* in Andean cosmology. In every person's life there are significant events occurring at specific times and places that shape personal fate and destiny. These pivotal points on one's life journey are considered to possess greater amounts of *kausay*.

pachakuti — a time of upheaval and transformation, such as we are living in now

Pachamama — Mother Earth

paqarina — feminine places of emergence associated with water and caves

phikhuy — the ritual act of blowing an intention three times into the leaves of a *k'intu* in order to establish an energetic connection linking the three worlds

Q'ero shamans — one of the sacred lineages of Inca ancestry living in the Andes mountains

Quechua — the native language of the Q'ero people

Salkantay — one of the two sacred mountain areas where a celestial *mesa* is buried

sami — the refined light energy of plant spirits

saminchasqa — the act of blowing prayers in order to establish an energetic connection linking the three worlds

Santa Tierras — the feminine spirits that come up from the earth through the floor during ceremonies with *altomesayoqs*

shamanism — Eliade described shamanism as a "technique of ecstasy." Webster's dictionary has defined it as "excessive joy" and a "kind of cataleptic trance." Michael Harner described shamanism as "a great mental and emotional adventure" and wrote, "Ultimately shamanic knowledge can only be acquired through individual experience (pp. xiv-xv)." These definitions reflect that understanding energetically beyond words does not occur in the Mind, it can only occur in a state experienced through the body, primarily the Heart and the Belly.

sonqo — Heart center

symbolic level — second level experienced through dreams, metaphors, and images. Winnicott described this as the transitional space of the imaginal realm between fantasy and reality. Jungians have described this as the imaginal realm where inner dialogue using the technique of active imagination can occur.

tupay — a warrior's way to resolve conflict through working with the *mesa*, the one who challenges and is willing to meet one's Self

Uhu Pacha — the underworld

unus mundus — the deepest level of the collective unconscious and the place or state in which matter and psyche merge into one world; a composite universal Self that exists beyond time and space

urpicheeyas — "sweet dove of my heart"

Vilcabamba — one of the two sacred mountain areas where a celestial *mesa* is buried

waka — a power spot in nature.

Waquay Wilka — one of the seven sacred mountains in the Andes

wilka — sacred

Wirachocha — the heavens

yachai — the energy center in the Belly

yanai — clear vision

yuya — the organizing principle of wisdom

References

Altered States. (1980).

Avatar. (2009).

Bache, C. (2000) *Dark Night, Early Dawn: Steps to a Deep Ecology of Mind*. Albany, NY: State University of New York Press.

Bion, W. R. (1950). The Imaginary Twin. In *Second Thoughts*. London: Maresfield Library.

Blavatsky, H. (1999). *The Secret Doctrine*, Vol. I. Pasadena, CA: Theosophical University Press.

Bollas, C. (1987). *The Shadow of the Object: Psychoanalysis of the Unthought Known*.

Casper the Friendly Ghost. (1995).

Castaneda, C. (1971). *A Separate Reality: Further conversations with Don Juan*. New York: Simon and Schuster.

Castaneda, C. (1972). *Journey to Ixtlan*. New York: Simon and Schuster.

Castaneda, C. (1981). *The Eagle's Gift*. New York: Simon and Schuster.

Castaneda, C. (1984). *The Fire from Within*. New York: Pocket Books.

Castaneda, C. (1987). *The Power of Silence*. New York: Washington Square Press.

Castaneda, C. (1998). *Wheel of Time*. New York: Pocket Books.

Close Encounters of the Third Kind. (1977).

Delgado, J. L. (2006). *Andean Awakening*. Canada: Council Oaks Books.

Edinger, E. (1985). *The Anatomy of the Psyche: Alchemical Symbolism in Psychotherapy*. Chicago: Open Court Publishing Company.

Eliade, M. (1964). *Shamanism: Archaic Techniques of Ecstasy.* Bollingen Series LXXVI. Princeton, NJ: Princeton University Press.

The Fly. (1986).

Fonagy. P. (2001). *Attachment Theory and Psychoanalysis.* New York: Other Press.

Fordham, M. (1961), Neumann and Childhood. *Journal of Analytical Psychology, 26:99-122.*

Hague, K & M. (1980). *East of the Sun and West of the Moon.* Orlando, FL: Harcourt Brace Jovanovich Publishers.

Hall, M. P. (2003). *The Secret Teachings of All Ages*. New York: Penguin Group.

Harner, M. (1980). *The Way of the Shaman*. New York, NY: HarperCollins Publishers.

Jung, C. G. (1969). "Psychology and Religion: West and East." *Collected Works,* Vol. XI. Princeton, NJ: Princeton University Press.

Jung, C. (1970). "Mysterium Coniunctionis," *Collected Works,* Vol. XIV. Princeton, NJ: Princeton University Press.

Jung, C. G. (1977). "The Symbolic Life: Miscellaneous Writings." *Collected Works,* Vol. XVIII. Princeton, NJ: Princeton University Press.

Jung, C. G. (1978). "Psychological Commentary on the Tibetan Book of the Great Liberation." In *Psychology and the East* (p. 112). Princeton, NJ: Princeton University Press.

Jung, C. G. (1989). "The Symbolic Life." *Collected Works,* Vol. XI. Princeton, NJ: Princeton University Press.

Jung, C. G. (1989). *Memories, Dreams and Reflections*. A. Jaffe (Ed.), R. Winston & C. Winston (Trans.). New York, NY: Pantheon Books.

King Kong. (2005).

Knight, G. (1978). A Practical Guide to Qabbalistic Symbolism. Boston: Weiser Books.

Lewis, C. S. (1950). *The Lion, the Witch, and the Wardrobe.* New York: HarperCollins Publishers.

Lord of the Rings. (2001).

The Matrix. (1999).

Mindell, A. (1985). *Working with the Dream Body.* London: Routledge & Kegan Paul.

Ogden, T. H. (1989), On the Concept of an Autistic-Contiguous Position. *International Journal of Psycho-Analysis, 70*:127-40.

Perera, S. (1981). *Descent to the Goddess: A Way of Initiation for Women.* Toronto, Canada: Inner City Books.

Rilke, R. M. (2002). *Letters to a Young Poet.* London: Dover.

Star Trek. (1966).

Star Wars. (1977).

Summers, F. (1994). *Object Relations Theories and Pathology: A Comprehensive Text.* Hillsdale, NJ: The Analytic Press, Inc.

Von Franz, M. L. (1972). *Creation Myths.* Boston: Shambhala Publications.

Von Franz, M. L. (1972). *The Feminine in Fairy Tales.* Boston: Shambhala Publications.

Von Franz, M. L. (1985). *Projection and Re-Collection in Fairy Tales.* Peru, IL: Open Court Publishing.

Wallin, D. (2007). *Attachment in Psychotherapy.* New York: Guilford Press.

Wilcox, J. P. (1999). *Masters of the Living Energy.* Rochester, VT: Inner Traditions.

The Wizard of Oz. (1939).

About the Author

 ***Deborah Bryon, PhD,*** is a licensed psychologist and diplomate Jungian analyst in private practice in Denver, Colorado. She completed a BA in psychology at UCLA, a BFA in drawing at Metropolitan State College of Denver, and a PhD in Counseling Psychology at the University of Denver. Deborah obtained her analytic training with the Inter-Regional Society of Jungian Analysts and is a psychoanalyst through the National Association for the Advancement of Psychoanalysis.

Since 2005, Deborah has received in-depth training with Q'ero shamans in Peru and has undergone a series of sacred initiations with the shamans she has worked with. Deborah is writing, teaching classes, and leading groups combining Jungian depth psychology, psychoanalysis, and shamanism. She is the author of several articles on shamanism and psychoanalysis.

Deborah spends her free time gardening, traveling, and is an artist and member of Spark Gallery. She has taught in the psychology departments of the University of Colorado and Metropolitan State College of Denver. Deborah has two adult sons, Devin and Colin. She lives with her husband Perry, two dogs, cat, and a macaw.

For Further Studies of Shamanism

Please visit PineWindsPress.com for more information about shamanism and the latest information about classes, seminars, and travel opportunities.

CHAPTER 13

Sample Ministry Strategy

Below is one example for creating a ministry strategy. It is called the "Full Scope Ministry Model," and it may be beneficial.

Full-Scope Ministry Part 1: Scripture and Worship

One of the great cries of the 16th-century Protestant Reformation was *sola scriptura*, or "Scripture alone." What does this mean? It means that the starting point of understanding Christ and his church as well as the foundation for all that is necessary to one's spiritual walk is found in the Word of God alone. If anything is taken as an authority over it or as a necessary addition to the Word, it is not the Gospel. This understanding is fundamental to any ministry, and it is on this rock that we must build our ministry framework.

This may seem like an obvious starting place, but statistics suggest that this is not as clear as one would suspect. In a 2017 Gallup study, their survey found that only 24% of Americans believe the Bible to be the literal Word of God. Most Christians feel it is inspired but not inerrant, and 26% of Americans believe it only to be a collection of secular stories. The first number (24%) is the lowest in a descending trend that goes back over forty years. What do these statistics tell us? I believe it points to years of failure on the part of the church in stressing the infallibility of the Bible. It shows that the church leaders have failed to give the Bible the weight it deserves when it is taught. It also reveals that we are often willing to compromise the integrity of the Scriptures for cultural relevance. If you are to have a fruitful ministry, you must anchor it in the truths of the Word; otherwise, you are merely teaching from the viewpoint of morality and humanitarianism. These points of view can be found outside the Church, but neither of these save nor transform hearts for Christ.

The Word gives us an unmatched standard. It gives us a guide and a framework for how to do ministry. Rather than allowing culture to set our ministry's content, we should allow it to inform the dissemination of the context. If we get this backward, we lose sight of the goal of ministry. Fortunately, the Scriptures reveal the key ingredients necessary for the growing and shepherding of Christ's flock.

Every teacher needs a textbook, and the Bible is God's manual for us. It teaches us:

- Who God is,
- How He loves,
- How we have failed,
- What He did to save us,
- How we can be saved, and
- How we are to honor and be transformed by him.

We are to meditate on his Word day and night, teach our children about Him, keep His Word in our heart, and make disciples of all nations in his name, teaching them to observe all that He commanded. Instruction is one of the primary uses of the Scriptures commanded in the Bible.

Full-Scope Ministry Part 2: Fellowship and Outreach

Fellowship and outreach are lumped together because there should never be a fellowship event that is not an outreach event in disguise. Everything we do should have an eye toward the Gospel. We need not forget this.

Often, we have a hard time justifying why we need outreach and fellowship as a key pillar to our youth ministry strategy. I want to offer some opinions on the argument. There are typically one of two sides taken in this debate. The first is as follows: "My calling is to disciple the students that want to be here and teach them to go out and make disciples." This is a theologically sound philosophy in and of itself, but I believe it neglects a directly missional component. The other side of the discussion is this: "My job is to reach as many students for Christ as possible." This is also a theologically sound approach. However, holding strictly to either of these positions fails to FULLY embrace our calling as youth directors. Both positions omit something precious that the other holds.

The main argument that I have for fellowship and outreach comes from the examples laid out by Jesus. We see Jesus repeatedly going out to the masses, feeding them and sending them home. We see his first miracle being one of providing wine for the enjoyment of a wedding party. In Jesus, we see a genuine humanity in his emotions. We see him weep (John 11:35), we witness his sinless anger (Mark 3:5), and we see him (almost) distraught (Matthew 17:17). Though there were deeper reasons for his actions, I think it is safe to look toward Jesus as one who spent time in fellowship but was always looking for a teaching opportunity.

A second biblical argument for fellowship and outreach can be seen in the example of Paul. Paul went to the Gentiles. He would walk around the city, finding events and locations that he could use to his advantage to teach the Gospel (Lydia in Acts, the acropolis). He shared the Gospel outside of the temple or synagogue.

The thrust of these examples is this: Be intentional about committing time to disciple the students who desire to be there, but do not neglect those outside the church walls. We are called to make disciples of all the nations, not just the nations that attend our church.

I would argue that neither of these approaches mentioned above is incorrect; rather, they are incomplete. As a youth director, you must be willing to go out of your way to interact with the lost in their contexts but be prepared to disciple them on your terms. Both are equally needed and, unfortunately, society often demands one or the other.

Full-Scope Ministry Part 3: Discipleship

Author Jared Wilson makes three points as to why discipleship matters:

1. Discipleship matters because fidelity to Christ matters.
2. Discipleship matters because the integrity of the church matters.
3. Discipleship matters because the expansion of God's glory matters.

Wilson is drawing out something valuable from Matthew 28:19–20a, "Go therefore and make disciples of all nations, baptizing them in the name of the Father and of the Son and of the Holy Spirit, teaching them to observe all that I have commanded you."

Discipleship should matter to us because it mattered to Jesus. Samuel Chadwick once said, "No man is uneducated who knows the Bible, and no one is wise who is ignorant of its teachings." We should desire to be a church that goes beyond just proclaiming the Word to our students. We should be taking their hands and walking them through the Word. This is what it involves to disciple students. It means that we are committing our time and energy to be sure that our students are grounded in the Scriptures, which will allow us to help guide them in their sanctification and encourage and equip them to do the same for others.

The Great Commission does not simply command us to preach the Gospel, although that is certainly central to it, but we are also called to make disciples, a process that takes an enormous amount of time and energy as well as prayer and guidance from the Holy Spirit. Discipleship is key. One way to evaluate whether or not you have invested enough time in student discipleship is to consider your students' spiritual maturity. How many would you consider disciples of the Word? How do you predict they will respond when confronted with secular worldviews in college and beyond? Disciples of the Lord will know His voice. Are your students able to distinguish His voice from others?

We must recognize that discipleship is not a solo endeavor. It has been said that a human being can only emotionally invest themselves in twelve to fifteen people at a time. This means that if you have a youth group of more than five students, you probably cannot effectively disciple the youth group of your own accord. Therefore, you are going to need help. Most of us do not have the luxury of hiring one intern for every five students in our youth group. Where do you turn? First, you encourage and assist the students' parents. They are called to be primary discipleship authority in their children's lives (Deuteronomy 6).

Next, find volunteers who desire to invest in the lives of your students. The rule of thumb, if possible, is "not a parent, not a peer." Students need someone older than themselves who has the life experience they do not. However, this may not be a luxury that you have. The needed volunteer base might be lacking in your church community. This is why the family discipleship dynamic is so indispensable to the lives of our students. In a healthy family unit, students will talk to their parents and discover a natural avenue for discipleship. And more than likely, the things they do not feel comfortable talking with them about will be the things the students will discuss with you. This empowers the youth ministry to function in the healthiest way possible: as a ministry that is an extension of the church to partner with families throughout their interactions with students.

Full-Scope Ministry Part 4: Missions

This may be the most straightforward element of Full Scope Ministry for which to argue for many reasons:

- I do not know anyone who can rationally argue against the biblical directive to participate in missions.
- I imagine that many youth leaders have a member of their church that believes that youth missions involve raking leaves for an elderly member in your congregation (who may or may not be able to afford to pay for the service).
- I have never heard anyone claim "Missions are not my spiritual gift" because, deep down, everyone knows that it does not hold water in light of biblical teaching.

Instead, I believe that most youth directors run into this subtle but substantial disconnect in their approach to missions: the theology in which their missional endeavors are grounded in is lacking. Solid theology is needed in youth ministry, and there are two components to every aspect of "missions": spiritual and physical. Let's address the Spiritual first.

Spiritual Missions

Spiritual missions are the proclamation of Christ to the end that men believe and are converted. What does the spiritual aspect of missions look like? Generally, we would define this as being a witness for Christ. Spiritual missions tell others about who Jesus is, why he came, what he did, and what he expects from us now. It is about helping the world acknowledge the glory and majesty of our Lord and Savior. It is about letting others know that we are fallen and in desperate need of being saved. Spiritual missions entail proclaiming to the world the message of John 3:16. This aspect of missions is the most significant because it has eternal ramifications on the souls of those around us. When we neglect the world's need for Jesus, we deny the world the truth of their eternal destination. Everything we do must be done with this in mind.

Physical Missions

Physical missions relate to activities of service, compassion, and charity. This would include assisting the elderly, helping the homeless, building wells in other countries, and tutoring those struggling in school. These are all excellent and worthwhile ventures. In fact, oftentimes, if you are routinely involved in physical missions, then most people would assume you were religious and, more than likely, a Christian. But there is a subtle danger of being involved heavily in physical missions that may dilute our students' understanding of why we do physical missions. This is where solid theology can be of help.

Is the Church's calling to be people who do "good," or is it to be people who make disciples of all nations? Mere good deeds do not inform people of the saving name of Jesus. They may lead to questions about why you perform the good deeds, but the action in itself does nothing. Martin Luther once wrote, "Works, since they are irrational things, cannot glorify God, although they may be done to the glory of God, if faith be present." And here is our question: Are your mission efforts humanitarian or Christian? Are you taking part in missions for the physical relief that it brings others, or are you doing missions for the eternal ramifications that the Gospel has on the souls of those who hear it? Because missions must include both. Missions, from a biblical perspective, are actions done with the intent of witnessing to who Christ is. If we take the spiritual element out of missions, we risk confusing our students. From there, they may be unable to discern why the Christian church is truly any different than the Mormon church, the Buddhists, or the Red Cross.

Why is the church different from everyone else? Because our missions are always influenced by the commission of our Lord Jesus Christ: to make disciples of all nations. If your church and student body cannot qualify this distinction, too little focus on the theology of missions has occurred.

As a closing point of clarification, I do not condemn humanitarian aid. It is a great honor and privilege to be able to assist those in need. It is a necessary component of loving your neighbor. But as the church sends our youth to do missions, they should have a higher calling in mind. Once we boil down the Christian idea of missions to simple acts of charity, we will have turned the Gospel of Jesus into a message of good works, resulting in our faith's core beliefs dissolving.

Full-Scope Ministry Part 5: Apologetics

This is possibly the most objected element of Full Scope Ministry. There is an invading movement among Evangelical Christianity to focus on "deeds not creeds." This is a massive shift from what the church has been for the greater part of 2,000 years. There is also a greater tolerance of plurality in the church. Christianity in the West has made a shift from objective truth to experiential Christianity. Because of this trend, there has been a great loss of appreciation for the role that *apologetics* (defending the faith) should play in the lives of our students and adults.

We are given this command in 1 Peter 3:15, "But in your hearts honor Christ the Lord as holy, always being prepared to make a defense to anyone who asks you for a reason for the hope that is in you; yet do it with gentleness and respect." This verse, along with many more, gives us a clear statement of expectation for Christians in every circumstance: be prepared to defend your faith. It is important to note here that this does not necessarily point towards a roundtable debate with Stephen Hawking. Rather, this is a command to be able to convey the reason for our joy. If our students are unable to articulate why they have joy and faith in Christ, we have not only failed to equip them, but we have sent them forward as adults filled with vague concepts of morality that likely will be attacked with precision and challenge their worldview.

I find immense value in helping our students prepare for the attacks thrown upon their beliefs. They are already taught in public schools that science and faith are at odds and that you cannot have faith and still think rationally about science. I highly encourage this "next level" of apologetics in your ministry strategy. Our students need to be able to process through the difficult questions while they have the benefit of a supportive environment.

CHAPTER 14

Making This More than a Quick Read

A book like this can seem overwhelming if you are brand new to youth ministry. The reality is that there will never be a perfect ministry run by the perfect youth director. However, we should be able to avoid poorly run ministries led by ill-equipped ministers. It is the ill-equipped leaders who earn the "big kid" label. And that is the perception that I hope this book alters. Instead of "big kids," I long to see a generation of youth ministers cultivate the disciplines necessary for long and fruitful ministry.

Recommendations on How to Use This Book

It is always helpful to utilize what we read and learn. Here are a few pointers for using this book:

Use it as a starting point.
Once the whole book has been read, go back and highlight the chapters that particularly resonated with you. With one color, identify the areas in which you currently excel. With another color, mark the disciplines in which you need strengthening

and resolve. Use this system to begin shoring up your ministry weaknesses.

Map it out.

Take out a sheet of paper and write down all the areas in which you excel in one column and all the areas you believe you do not in another. Make the small adjustments necessary in the areas in which you excel and create a plan for strengthening your weaknesses.

Ask for help.

I am not naturally a detail person, and I've found that many youth ministers fall into this same camp. For the first three years at my current employment, I asked certain youth committee members with a detailed personality-type to edit my emails and other communications. They helped with this until I acquired enough proficiency to take this routine task upon myself. Find trusted people who can help you grow in areas where it is needed.

Take baby steps.

Seeds take time to mature. You cannot expect bad habits to disappear overnight. Be patient! One way to measure your growth is to chart your progress via a personal journal.

Use it as a litmus test.

A Gut-Check

The process of writing this book was a stark reminder: I can always do better. Everyone needs periodic evaluation to keep them optimized, efficient, and effective. As we get comfortable, we sometimes fail to do the little things that make a big difference.

Use it as a reference/datum.

Know where to find this book.

There are certain books on my shelves that I turn to when I feel lost. Perhaps this book can become a reference when transitioning to a new church or discerning why things have become messy. If you feel so moved, keep it in sight, and refer to it when needed.

Use it for training yourself and others.

Interns and Assistants

I try to impart practical wisdom and advice to all of my staff to help them as they mature and grow in their ministry roles. One purpose for writing this book was as a training manual for my interns and assistant youth directors. May it be of similar assistance to you.

Use it for new youth leader training.

Pastors and Churches

This book would be an excellent tool for a weekly training session. By providing your new youth leader with this book and mapping out a weekly reading plan, the new leader would be systematically trained regarding healthy habits and disciplines that promote successful ministry.

Appendix: Resources

Defeating Laziness Idea Prompts
1. Send an encouraging text to a student you haven't seen in a couple weeks.
2. Post one of your favorite youth ministry memories on social media.
3. Write down one way you believe you can make a difference in the life of one student this week, then follow through.
4. Ask a student how you can pray specifically for them.
5. Ask a parent how you can pray specifically for them.
6. Spend one hour improving some part of your physical meeting place.
7. Respond to emails that you have failed to find time to respond to.
8. Ask a youth ministry volunteer how you can help them this week.
9. Find and take an honest critique of one facet of the youth ministry. Take it to heart.
10. Take a parent to lunch or coffee.
11. Review your budget. How can you optimize it?
12. Spend one hour researching other church youth facilities. What looks good? What areas of your space seem dated?
13. Have you had your quiet time today?
14. Call your mom, she misses you.
15. Create a weekly to-do list. Complete priority items first each Monday.
16. Text/post a verse of the day for your students.

17. Hold a student accountable for their quiet time.
18. Choose a devotion book to gift your volunteers.
19. Identify one area that you need to do better, and lay out a plan to do that.
20. Clean your office.
21. Put a creative twist on a classic kids game (duck, duck goose with a twist, etc).
22. Find a guest speaker for youth one night this month. As a result, spend that time investing in relationships with your students by participating as a youth, not as a leader.
23. Pray specifically for five students today.
24. Hand write a "Thank you" note to your volunteers.
25. Find a way to make the youth group visible in church this week: sit together, take up the offering, do the announcements, etc.
26. Memorize a Bible verse.
27. Connect with that one parent that drives you crazy.
28. Connect with a student that you haven't seen in over a month.
29. Review the youth page on your church's website. Update and declutter the page.
30. Create a plan to be consistent on your youth group social media pages. Create content ahead of time.
31. Find a creative and crazy way to advertise your next youth meeting.
32. Find a "loner" student and plug them into an area serving the ministry that can give them ownership and purpose in the group.
33. Check on the other ministries. See if you can help them with anything.
34. Visit with another local youth leader. Pick their brain.
35. Add a new tool to your toolbox (graphic design, video editing, presentation tools, etc.).

8 Things Successful People Do That Lazy People Do Not

1. https://www.inc.com/nicolas-cole/8-things-successful
   -people-do-that-lazy-people-do-not.html

Resources for Fighting Pornography

1. Accountability VPN: www.Covenanteyes.com
2. The Samson Society: www.samsonsociety.com, *Samson and the Pirate Monks: Calling Men to Authentic Brotherhood,* by Nate Larkin
3. *Finally Free: Fighting for Purity with the Power of Grace* by Heath Lambert
4. *Every Man's Battle: Every Man's Guide to Winning the War on Sexual Temptation One Victory at a Time* by Stephen Arterburn and Fred Stoeker

Resources for Engaging Parents

1. https://fulleryouthinstitute.org/blog/engage-families
   -ministry
2. https://childrensministry.com/parent-connections/
3. *7 Family Ministry Essentials: A Strategy for Culture Change in Children's and Student Ministries* by Michelle Anthony and Megan Marshman
4. https://orangeblogs.org
5. *Family Ministry Field Guide: How Your Church Can Equip Parents to Make Disciples* by Timothy Paul Jones

About the Author

Weston Blaha has been working in student ministry for over 15 years. He is currently the Director of Youth and Family Ministries at Lakeside Presbyterian Church EPC. He is married to his wonderful wife, Candace, and has two children: Eva and Judah. In addition to his normal work at Lakeside, Weston speaks at youth conferences, leads student ministry training events, and runs Student Ministry Field Guide, a Facebook page in which he offers advice, tips, and resources for student ministry leaders.